COMMENTS ON...

EXPERIENCING WORSHIP AND WORSHIPING EXPERIENCE

Sally Morgenthaler, author of *Worship Evangelism*

"I really appreciate your well-grounded, historical and biblical perspective. It's one of the clearest, most user-friendly pieces of writing on the subject that I've seen. And that particular issue is pivotal to what we're doing with contemporary worship…Thanks for being a voice of sanity and wisdom!"

Greg English, church planter

"The whole subject of worship has been redefined for me as a result of reading this. If the world is to be reached effectively for Christ the method must be culturally relevant, while remaining solidly committed to absolute truth—allowing for both the "modernist" and "postmodernist" to worship in spirit and truth. Thank you! This truly is one of the most balanced (and timely) treatises on worship I have read."

Loren Fischer, pastor and professor

"This is exciting and so very informative to me. All of my life I have valued and emphasized the wedding of truth and experience. Never truth to the neglect of experience and never experience to the neglect of truth."

EXPERIENCING WORSHIP AND WORSHIPING EXPERIENCE

THE CHANGING FACE OF EVANGELICAL WORSHIP
IN POSTMODERN CULTURE

DANIEL RADMACHER

MODROCKER MUSIC

Experiencing Worship and Worshiping Experience: The Changing Face of Evangelical Worship in Postmodern Culture

Published by Lulu.com

© 2004, 2008 Daniel Radmacher. All rights reserved.

ISBN 978-1-4357-0650-7

No part of this publication may be reproduced, stored in a retrieval system, or transmitted in any form or by any means—electronic, mechanical, photocopy, recording, or any other—except for brief quotations in printed reviews, without the prior permission of the publisher.

Additional information may be obtained through www.danradmacher.com.

All Scripture quotations, unless otherwise indicated, are taken from the Holy Bible, New King James Version. NKJV. Copyright © 1979, 1980, 1982, 1997 by Thomas Nelson, Inc. Used by permission of Thomas Nelson. All rights reserved.

Printed in the United States of America.

Cover photo: Anja Hild

For my Super B

CONTENTS

Chapter	Page

1. THE PROBLEM AND THE PARADIGM-SHIFT 13

    The Stirrings of Experience

    A Paradigm-Shift in Worship

    The Impact of Culture on Worship

    A Few Definitions

2. FROM MODERN TO POSTMODERN (PART I) 27

    The Pendulum Swing of Postmodernism

    When Knowledge Was Power

    Enlightenment Modernism

    When Reason No Longer Persuaded

    19th Century Romanticism

        The Epistemology of the "Deep Interior"

        The Unassailable Quality of Mystical Experience

        The Interplay of Imagination and Knowledge

        The Reawakening of Supernaturalism

    Experience as Knowledge

3. FROM MODERN TO POSTMODERN (PART II) 47

    Behind the Curtain

    The Puzzle of Postmodernism

        The Proliferation of Perspectives

        The Curious Authority of the Splinter Narrative

Chapter	Page

      A "Pastiche" Approach to Reality

      Imagination and Meaning

      The Source of Authoritative Knowledge

   Experience as Power

   Is Postmodernism a Neo-Romanticism?

4. THE POSTMODERN WORSHIPER 63

   Modernism Demythologized

   The Rise of Experience

   The Jesus movement

   Pentecostalism

   The Postmodern Worshiper

5. TWO WORSHIP PARADIGMS (PART I) 79

   "I wasn't able to worship"

   The Difficulty of Definitions

   The Modern Paradigm: Worship as Edification

      An Intellectual Enactment of Praise

      Music as Teaching

      The Path of Spiritual Growth

      The Sermon as the Goal of the Service

      A One-Way Interaction

      A Lifestyle of Worship

6. TWO WORSHIP PARADIGMS (PART II) 97

   The Neo-Romantic Paradigm: Worship as an Experience

      A Supernatural Conversation of Praise

      "Manifest Presence"

Chapter	Page

        "Numinous"

        Emotions and Pleasure in Worship

        Music and Experience

        The Quest for Intimacy with God

        The "Spirit and Truth" Question

        Aesthetics as a Cultural Language

        Individualism in Worship

    Two Cultural Paradigms

7. THE GOD WHO IS THERE 121

    Bridging the Distance

    God's Presence in Ancient, Near Eastern Culture

    Tabernacle and Temple Worship

    The End of an Era

    Immanuel

    The Manifest Presence of God Takes on Flesh

    Christ's Presence Manifested through the Spirit

    Spiritual Gifts as an Experience of God's Presence

    A Final Question

8. THE DRAWBACKS OF EXPERIENCE (PART I) 147

    The Attraction of Experience

    Characterological Dangers of Experience

        The Danger of Experience Becoming the Purpose of Worship

        The Danger of Misunderstanding the Spirit's Work

        The Danger of Trying to Generate a Worship Experience

Chapter	Page

       The Danger of Experience Sidetracking Spiritual Growth

       The Danger of Individualism

       The Danger of Losing Worship as a Lifestyle

9. THE DRAWBACKS OF EXPERIENCE (PART II) 167

    Epistemological/Other Dangers of Experience

       The Danger of an Experience Under-balanced With Truth

       The Danger of the Similarity of Religious Experiences

       The Danger of Losing Our Critical Thinking Ability

10. THE STRENGTHS OF EXPERIENCE 177

    The Delight of Worship

    The Wholistic Nature of Experience-Open Worship

    Delighting in God as the Heart of Worship

    Spiritual Growth through Experience-Open Worship

    The Value of the "Numinous" Experience

    Experiencing God in Worship

11. REVEALED AND EXPERIENCED TRUTH 197

    The Critical Complement of Experience

    The Importance of Narrative in Worship

    Worship as a Tripartite Concept

    Worship as a Countercultural Activity

BIBLIOGRAPHY 213

ABOUT THE AUTHOR

Dan Radmacher is a singer, songwriter and worship leader in Southern California, and currently leads worship at Christ Church of Pasadena. He received his degree in classical voice performance from Biola University in 1990, and then embarked on a career in the record industry. Sensing a call to ministry, he began as a worship leader at Lake Avenue Church in Pasadena, first in the college ministry, and then as part of a team that started an alternative service called the Warehouse.

In 2004, he completed his M.Div at Talbot Seminary, having left his career at Virgin Records to pursue more theological training. While at Talbot, he became involved as a worship leader in the Intentional Character Development program. His seminary thesis on worship garnered the Zondervan Outstanding Thesis Award, and he also won the Louis T. Talbot Memorial Scholarship, an award that is presented in recognition of academic excellence, exceptional Christian commitment, and zeal for practical ministry.

Since then, he has led worship in a variety of venues around the country, including the 2004 Spiritual Formation Forum at the Los Angeles Hilton. He continues to lead worship in chapel at Talbot Seminary, and is involved as a worship leader with the Spiritual Formation Institute at Biola University. In 2006, he released his second worship recording entitled *In the Space Between*, and is now in the final stages of completing a third worship project with the worship team at Christ Church Pasadena. More information is available at www.danradmacher.com

CHAPTER 1

THE PROBLEM AND THE PARADIGM-SHIFT

The Stirrings of Experience

Growing up Evangelical in the 1970s was an interesting challenge. At that time, the word "Evangelical" was less a politically-correct term for a fundamentalist, and more a loose grouping of those Protestant churches who wanted to be considered separate from the mainline denominations. "Separate" is perhaps the key word in this description. As a Baptist, I think that I probably spent the majority of my adolescence wondering who was "in" and who was "out," who was "one of us" and who was religiously deluded. What is a Presbyterian? What is an Episcopalian? At a young age, those words sounded just as foreign as Buddhist or Muslim, and so must certainly fall outside the camp of those who were truly "saved." The divisions and boundaries between denominations, let alone religions, were as foundational as those between truth and error, as real as the difference between black and white. My concentric circles of orthodoxy seemed to get smaller and smaller until they just barely encircled our family. One might say that my worldview was singular to the extreme, with very clear-cut definitions of truth.

While truth was unquestionable, my faith practice was confused and fragmented. As I reflect on the genesis of my spirituality, I find an odd conglomeration of faith experiences that were strangely dissimilar. The main event of our religious life was a "worship service" on Sunday morning, a stand-up/sit-down routine that featured a choir anthem and a few hymns which sandwiched a lengthy sermon. We always sat in the second row while my mother played the organ, and the hymns became very familiar. My entire family is musical, and made such fun out of singing parts that I never found the hymns to be dirge-like, boring or inscrutable, as others have confessed to me. I am a little ashamed to admit that I enjoyed singing with people all around me, particularly when they noticed the quality of my voice. There was something of a performance element to worship even at that young age, at least as I understood and practiced it. I knew what to do with my voice, but was not sure how my heart was supposed to be involved.

At any rate, the basic experience of the worship service was largely found in the theological content that we ingested together, both in the hymns and the sermon, and although the message may at times have been convicting, I would certainly never have said that I "experienced the presence of God" there. There was theologically accurate truth about God throughout the music, but rarely a sense of joy, excitement or delight in the service. On occasion, the choir would present special cantatas, and I remember brief flashes of wonder, moments of awe or transcendence that I could not explain. During one such cantata at Christmas, an especially good tenor sang about "when the fullness of time had come, God sent His Son to redeem those under the law." Although I was not sure what it meant to be "under the law," my heart thrilled at the words "the fullness of time." The phrase was so poignant and powerful, cutting right to my heart, and I never understood why the simple words brought tears to my eyes. The inner sensations that it invoked were unlike anything I had ever known in worship. During the rest of the year, however, the worship service seemed primarily content-driven, generally devoid of any inner experience for me. My deeper self was uninvolved, and I began to get the notion that the worship service was largely planned to engage my intellect. My mind and heart began to learn that in worship, they were not only separate, they were also unequal.

The church we attended also had a vital youth group. During Sunday school and after the evening service, we would meet and sing songs together. These were different kinds of songs, songs that were simpler and more fun, but repertoire that we would never have thought to sing in church. Interestingly, I never asked why we sang songs together; it was just what we did before whatever teacher got up to speak to us. I never asked what I was supposed to think or feel. I never realized that this activity might catalyze deeper

CHAPTER 1: THE PROBLEM AND THE PARADIGM SHIFT

stirrings in my heart, or that I might manifest some kind of emotional response to what I was singing. Did anyone even call this time "worship"? I had no thought that God might be listening to the words of my heart more closely than the words of my lips. Rather, my experience of worship in the youth group was an activity, in much the same way that we would play games, and so I focused on the best performance of that activity.

The other piece of the Evangelical pie was summer camp. Before girls entered the picture, we loved summer camp for the sense of adventure and the wild counselors. Everything at camp was high-energy, but every evening we would settle in for a time of singing around the fire. The singing would start with songs like "I like bananas, coconuts and grapes," in the usual high-energy fashion, but would finish by quietly singing songs like "Seek Ye First"[1] and "Pass It On."[2] Along the way, I began to feel stirrings in my heart of a deeper desire. As the quietness ensued, surrounded by nature and the crickets chirping, something vast and momentous seemed to be happening. There was a longing in my soul that seemed to be aroused by those times, as if I were taking a deep drink of water and discovering an unquenchable thirst. The words of that campfire song would resound in my mind: "That's how it is with God's love, once you've experienced it. You want to sing, it's fresh like spring; you want to pass it on."[3] Though I understood God's love from the words in my Bible, I had no idea what it felt like to "experience" it. I held God's truth in my hand, but was unsure what it felt like to be held in His.

I found myself wanting more and more, and so I would take long walks in the woods at camp, pen, notebook and Bible in hand. I was drawn to the woods like a moth to a flame, drawn to the solitude and to the majesty, as if I were expecting to stumble upon the hidden throne room of a secret king. I recognized that these longings were somehow connected with God, but did not know how. I had no idea what I was looking for or how I would know when I found it. But I knew that when I walked through the woods, there was an awareness of a kind of presence, and if I listened, a sort of inner voice that would sometimes speak to me. I would open the Bible and read the words of truth printed on the black and white page, but could not determine how that holy book connected with the sensations I *felt* in this holy place. My senses had discovered an entire world of truth and my heart had responded, but was it God that had called?

I experienced a longing to keep coming back to that place, drawn to the solitude, thirsty to drink in the reverence of the scene, but unsure exactly what I was consuming. There was something there in the woods, a presence that I could not put my finger on, but I knew that it awakened the deepest desires in my soul. I knew that God was everywhere, and especially present on the pages of the Bible open before me, so why was this place special? Was God more present here? How did the truth of what I was reading connect with the truth of what I was feeling? I did not know how to locate and worship God in the real world, for I did not feel Him at church in the way that I felt Him here. Church was about the words of the Bible and God's commands to live my life in obedience to it. God's voice was always printed in black and white in my Baptist church, and so what I experienced of Him was only through what I read. So I would inevitably fall back upon this cognitive approach to God, and would make pledges to read my Bible and pray more. I thought it was the only way to locate Him. I knew I was a Christian and that Jesus lived in my heart, but did my heart detect His voice or my own?

Looking back, I realize now that I have wanted God my entire life. I have been searching for Him, and have never trusted that what I was experiencing could be truth, just as surely as those words on the page. Certainly every word was "true," and the same could not be said of every experience. But the lack of trust, the lack of belief that God could and would speak to me caused me to stop listening. It caused me to reach for the Bible instead of prayer when I wanted to hear from God, with the result that I would flip through pages in times of crisis, searching for words of consolation, not listening for the words that God might have desired to speak into my life at that moment.

I had no conception how to bring the blessing of "revealed truth" together with "experienced truth," how to connect the details of my sensations together with the words that God had spoken into history. I thought that I heard a voice inside me, thought that I sensed a presence, but could not trust that it might actually be Him. What should God's voice sound like? How would I experience it? How could I know that it was truly His voice, and not mine? I never knew how to answer those questions, and no one ever told me. Moreover, there was no way to guarantee the validity of this experienced truth in the same way that the Scriptures had been guaranteed by our doctrinal statement. We could not control experience in the same manner that we circumscribed revealed truth. No one had taught me how to bridge the gap between the Scriptures and my spiritual experiences, and nothing other than the experiences themselves validated their authenticity. Hence, my separate worlds began to drift further apart, and my spiritual life became fragmented between cognition and sensation, intellect and emotion, reason and intuition.

What was stirring within me was a deeper experience of God, a spirituality that had been purposefully brushed against by something divine. My spirit was awakened from slumber, and was longing to be nursed. The strange and mysterious experience was as attractive to me as the idea of God, not realizing that the two might be connected, and so I suppose I lingered longer in the woods because I wanted that experience more and more. It was the first time that my soul had been touched by the finger of God, and so I welcomed the emotions that rose within me. That sense of awe, wonder and delight was wonderful and addictive, and I began to look and listen for it throughout my life. But my practical theology did not really allow that this experience could actually be God's voice or touch, and so my faith practice became disconnected from experience. Religion was something that I thought about, but this aesthetic experience was something that I deeply felt. Worship involved my mind, but my inner life involved my entire being.

I began to seek these sensations in the experiences that seemed to invoke them, and found something of the awe, wonder and delight in romantic love, in music and the arts, and in poetry and prose. It was certainly thrilling and invigorating when girls began to notice me, and the sensations attached with sexuality and romantic attachment were a little similar to the joy I had once experienced. I became very involved with the fine arts, and the kind of acclaim that performance brought inspired feelings that were momentary, yet grandiose and exciting. Moreover, I began writing poetry and prose in the quiet of my room at night, and I began to experience peace and tranquility as I would pour out my inner life upon the blank page in front of me. God was somehow involved in all of these experiences, yet somehow divorced from them. My inner life could not reveal God, for I believed that His truth could only legitimately emanate from the pages of Scripture. So I pursued other avenues in which to find joy and meaning in my life, but they never really seemed to deliver. There was occasional happiness, but never joy in them. There was excitement, but not awe or wonder. There was enjoyment, but never delight.

These were basically my experiences of worship, and they remained essentially disconnected from one another. Everything I knew of "heart worship," that is, worship that penetrated deeper than the intellect alone, seemed separated from the formal worship activities that I encountered. "Worship" became a cognitive exercise of praise, at least as I understood it, in which my inner experiences of God were uninvolved. It described the activities we did on Sunday, and although I mildly enjoyed those things, I certainly did not experience them on a visceral level. They were as divorced from my summer-camp conception of God as they could be. Rather, the worship service seemed something like the school play in which God was the collective audience of parents. We all dressed up in our costumes, learned our lines, and assumed that He was pleased by our performance. Whereas, my experience of God in the woods was like plunging into a deep pool and finding that I could breathe underwater. That is how diverse the two activities were in my understanding. I had learned to disconnect mind from "heart," if you will, in the experience of worship.

A Paradigm-Shift in Worship

I have begun to notice that over the last twenty to thirty years, there has been a paradigm-shift occurring in the practice of worship across the world of Evangelicalism. While I do not desire to generalize from my experiences, I have noticed that the changes which were drastic in my experience have begun organically to surface throughout a wide cross-section of worship culture. There is a rebirthing of worship philosophy in practical garb that is permeating our entire approach to worship, cutting a swath across a variety of denominations. It is an elemental shift that is motivated by the forces of culture, a change that responds to the fragmentation of the mind and heart in worship, a transition towards an experience of worship that invigorates more of the human constitution. The change is so obvious, it is easily noticed, and many have remarked upon it. Yet it is manifested in such a mosaic of smaller modifications—like repertoire, style or flow—that it is easy to miss the fundamental character and paradigmatic nature of the shift.

Whereas worship once consisted of an exercise or an enactment of praise, it is now being practiced as an "encounter" with God, an immediate experience of His presence. Whereas worship represented a one-way conversation in which worshipers extolled God, it is now being pursued as more of a spiritual "exchange" in which both parties are given the opportunity to speak and to listen. Whereas worship featured a sacrifice of praise in which truths of God were spoken *about* Him, worshipers now long to speak truth *to* Him. In essence, worship is pursued less and less as a spiritual activity that one *enacts* for God, but more as an encounter and experience in which the worshiper *interacts* with God.

The key to understanding this paradigm-shift is grasping what is meant by the concept of "experience." Experience is a very flexible word, as it can denote all sorts of interactions. One might talk about his or her "experience" at the carwash, and would likely be referring to what happened—the external sequence of events that occurred. In this usage, experiences are personal stories or narratives that place a series of happenings within a personal, cognitive, interpretational structure. Along these lines, one might also say that he or she experienced God in worship on a Sunday morning, and be referring to the fact that the Scripture passage was instructive or intellectually applicable to his or her personal narrative. The data found within God's word produced a cognitive revelation that related to his or her life in a significant manner, perhaps even inducing an emotional response. While these scenarios are indeed experiences, they basically miss the mark of what is intended by "experiencing God in worship." In this understanding, experience denotes an interaction that is far more internal and mystical, in which the rational receptors are augmented, and perhaps even superseded, by the sensations.

Experiencing God's presence in worship means that one *senses* His presence on an internal level, through one's emotions, intuition, or some kind of spiritual perception. By definition, this is the essence of a mystical interaction, which depends upon internal perception or sensations to recognize a spiritual presence. Webster describes a mystic as someone who "believes in the possibility of attaining insight into mysteries transcending ordinary human knowledge, as by immediate intuition in a state of spiritual ecstasy."[4] This is a kind of knowledge that is non-rational, that is, that accesses one's belief system through a different door than the cognitive processes of logic or reason.

Sensation is the central feature of this experience, but in this context, it does not solely denote the eyes, mouth, ears, nose, or skin, but rather refers to an inner, spiritual perception or receptor of knowledge. Thus, one's "sensual" experience—including emotions and intuition as well as external sensations—becomes a yardstick of a real metaphysical force, an immaterial or incorporeal presence. In other words, one *feels* God's presence in worship. One well-known worship leader reveals this presupposition during the worship time. He regularly will remark to his congregation that what they are "sensing is the presence of God."[5] In this mindset, experiencing God's presence means picking up on His immediate and immanent activity with both rational and non-rational receptors.

While this inner sensation is in theory a kind of spiritual perception, in practice it is almost exclusively the invigoration of one's emotions. While "Dave" might feel that he deeply sensed God's presence in the worship service, what he is often describing by way of sensations is the variation that he experienced in his emotions. This statement is not meant to suggest that Dave did not actually sense God's presence, but simply that the inner manifestation of this presence is often an emotional response. Texts that catalogue religious and mystical experiences almost categorically describe them in the language of the emotions that the subjects related. Indeed, emotions are so intertwined with mystical experience that they are basically inseparable. Therefore, "experiencing God in worship" usually signifies that one's emotions were affected in a particular manner, and that this variation was interpreted to be a visceral response to the Spirit's activity. Like it or not, emotions have become the sensual barometer of spiritual experience.

Experiencing God's presence in worship also suggests that the worshiper was deeply ministered to and affected in the region that we would call the heart, meaning the nexus of the affections, thoughts, and volition.[6] Experiencing God in worship means that the worshiper did not simply enact an offering of praise, speaking or singing accurate and wonderful statements about God's works and character. Instead, "Mary" experienced a mystical connection with God in her "deep interior,"[7] [†] facilitated by her emotions as well as her cognition, and that a profound, supernatural interaction happened that was deeply transformational. Worship is not simply a one-way offering of praise, but a reciprocal relationship in which the worshipers are deeply and thoroughly affected by God as they praise Him. Experiencing God in worship invites the invigoration of one's entire being—intellect, emotions and will—by the object of one's reflection, God Himself.

As a worship leader, I can witness this shift first-hand through the manner in which Christian leaders and writers talk or write about the experience of worship, as well as in the grass-roots practice of worship across a variety of denominations. There is an increased preoccupation with the presence of God, particularly entering into His presence in the act of worship, without a lot of explanation regarding what that phrase means. Experiencing God's presence has become a popular concept, but few texts or individuals can articulate the exact nature of that interaction. Rather, it has become common language for invoking a worship experience. Second, there is a much more exalted emphasis on the experience of the individual worshiper, particularly in the new worship repertoire, which has seen radical changes throughout this period of history. The worshiper's experience of God, including his or her emotional response to Him, has often replaced theology as the

---

[†] Kenneth Gergen relies heavily upon the term "deep interior" in order to describe the inner self, particularly as surfaced in the romantic movement. He may or may not have coined the phrase, as it does appear in other literature on romanticism. Gergen does not, however, use the phrase in the context of worship.

central element of the worship song. Third, the experience of worship has become much more individual in nature, focusing on the personal experience of the worshiper with God. Rather than worship functioning primarily as a community activity, it has become a time of private devotion with God, more like a personal spiritual discipline, with songs representing extended prayers or meditations. These are some of the changes that flow from this paradigm-shift, changes that will be addressed in the second half of this work.

The Impact of Culture on Worship

While there is a lot of discussion about these individual changes in the literature of the "worship wars," they are rarely discussed in conjunction with the broader changes inherent in the fabric of culture itself. Culture has more to do with this paradigm-shift in worship than anyone might have realized. Conflict over musical styles or repertoire has largely dominated the literary field, undermining or sidelining a more serious discussion. Yet, it is more than coincidental how this transition in worship philosophy and practice is highly consonant with changes in popular culture that have been occurring over the last twenty to thirty years. The label "postmodern" has become something of a buzzword in many Christian circles, with the result that it has lost some of its epistemological force. And yet, the changes in worship practice have a great deal more to do with epistemology than any kind of musical or stylistic changes. Epistemology—how one approaches and appropriates truth and knowledge—is central to these changes, and a critical analysis of how postmodernism has affected society and popular culture in general will expose the roots of this paradigm-shift. While there are plenty of fruitful worship discussions to be had about hymns and praise songs, the deepest and most profound shift involves how the individual pursues knowledge and truth. This is the playground of postmodernism.

Just as I experienced a fragmentation of mind and heart in my approach to God, many others—particularly of recent generations—have experienced the same. We are "postmodern worshipers." People of this worldview are reaching for ways of knowing that transcend the highly cognitive form of the "modern" worldview. Postmoderns ask that all of their receptors, both rational and sensual, be incorporated into their approach to knowledge. This pursuit is especially true for those who accept a supernatural universe, and desire to discover more than what can be proven by scientific data alone. Moreover, their approach to knowledge has become far more experience-oriented and individualistic in nature. Even the concept of truth has been shattered into perspectives, formed around the particular context of each person. Indeed, accepting this epistemology of experience requires that one become comfortable with the fact that others' experiences might yield truths different from one's own. The approach to knowledge through experience has produced an attitude of radical inclusion regarding the very definition of truth.

With this emphasis on experience as a belief-forming structure, it makes sense that the postmodern worshiper desires to do more than recite someone else's truths about God in worship. The postmodern worshiper desires and expects to experience the truth of God, particularly His immanence, for himself or herself. The worship service becomes the primary venue in which this belief-forming and maintaining activity takes place, as the postmodern worshiper expects to "meet" God there. Even the phrase "meeting God" suggests a very different perspective, and represents a supernatural encounter that will manifest itself in the entire array of human receptors, from cognition to sensation. The postmodern worshiper is no longer content simply to rehearse truth about who God is and what He has done in history. He or she desires to experience God in the here and now, in the reality of his or her own narrative, in order to know Him and thereby affirm His reality. In the transition to postmodern culture, the concept of worship has shifted in a similar direction, to worship as an experience of God's presence.

The cultural changes associated with postmodernism have contributed to a paradigm-shift in the Evangelical approach to worship, in which the concept of worship is now increasingly being understood as an experience of the presence of God. In order to demonstrate this thesis, it will be necessary to examine the currents of postmodernism, along with the precursors of modernism and romanticism. Along the way, it will also be necessary to discover how postmodernism has impacted popular culture in general, and how that cultural shift has prefigured and predisposed the change in Evangelical worship. Chapters two, three and four will critically examine these issues. Then, chapters five and six will compare two resulting paradigms of worship, the "modern" paradigm and the "neo-romantic" paradigm (as they will be labeled), in order to lay the groundwork for a more thoroughgoing analysis in chapters eight, nine and ten of the drawbacks and strengths of an "experience-oriented" and an "experience-open" approach. In the middle of this discussion, chapter seven will exegetically undress some basic misconceptions regarding the presence of God. Finally, chapter eleven will ask how these two forces of experienced truth and revealed truth should ideally come together in the worship activity.

A Few Definitions

Before this study commences, it will be necessary for clarity's sake to introduce a few preliminary definitions. Given that this work focuses exclusively on the changes that are occurring across the landscape of Evangelical worship, it will be necessary to define exactly what is intended by the word "Evangelical." The term is going the way of most labels, becoming less specific as its usage widens. While its form goes back to the Greek word for "good news," the word has been variously conscripted over the course of modern history to describe both the Protestant movement coming out of the Reformation, and the various evangelical revivals of the eighteenth and nineteenth centuries.[8] In the twentieth century, the word has become linked with "fundamentalism," although most Evangelicals are trying to distance themselves from that increasingly pejorative term. While the word "fundamentalism" has become something of a frightening label in this post Nine-Eleven world, in an academic context it simply specifies those Protestant churches that profess the "fundamentals" of Scripture.

When at the beginning of the twentieth century the mainline denominations were becoming more and more liberal in their professions, fundamentalists asserted what they saw as the basic biblical beliefs that were necessary in order to be considered orthodox. In general, Evangelicals believe in the actual, historical events of the Bible, particularly the virgin birth, the miracles of Christ, and His death and bodily resurrection. They also stress Christ's atoning work on the cross as the only means of salvation, the sole authority of Scripture for faith and practice, and some, the inerrancy of Scripture in the original manuscripts.[9] Others have identified additional elements of Evangelicalism as an inner experience at conversion—being "born again"—and a passion for evangelism.[10] There is certainly a degree of flexibility in the boundaries of Evangelicalism, which is why only a few years ago the Evangelical Theological Society was reconsidering what constituted an Evangelical. However, that discussion is outside the scope of this work. While the many changes in worship that will be described herein are certainly reaching a broader cross-section of churches than those that are Evangelical, the focus of this work will only deal with this particular movement.

Within this movement, there are of course a variety of approaches to worship, with the most obvious being that of the charismatic churches. Charismatic churches have long been an inherently experiential arm of the Evangelical movement, dissimilar in this respect from the rest of the movement. Therefore, many of the broad characterizations regarding Evangelical worship are intended as an evaluation of the movement as a whole, and assume that the charismatic movement is only one slice of a much larger Evangelical pie. Certainly the exponential growth of the charismatic denominations has significantly contributed to a more experiential approach across the entire spectrum of Evangelical worship. As this work will suggest, however, the growth of these denominations is as much a result of this broader cultural shift as the changes in worship philosophy and practice throughout Evangelical worship as a whole.

Second, an extensive description of "experience" as a mystical interaction has already been given. However, I will use the term in a more flexible manner, sometimes referring to the events and happenings of one's life, and sometimes referring to the senses and sensual occasions that one uses to accumulate knowledge. I will regularly specify which meaning I intend, referring to either external and life experiences, or internal, mystical and sensual experiences. The category of sensual experiences will include emotions and intuition, given that these are intricately tied to inner experience. In the final analysis, however, both types of experiences contribute to the way in which one approaches knowledge, in that both possess an epistemological authority and influence how individuals think about truth. Furthermore, these avenues constitute a category of knowing that is distinctly different from the knowledge one gains from "propositional truth," or stated principles of reality. This division will be the fertile ground of our discussion about modernism and postmodernism, to which we now turn.

---

[1] Karen Lafferty, Seek Ye First 1972 Maranatha! Music (admin. by The Copyright Company) & CCCM (admin. by Maranatha! Music)

[2] Kurt Kaiser, Pass It On 1969 Bud John Songs, Inc. (admin. by EMI Christian Music Publishing)

[3] Ibid.

[4] Webster's Encyclopedic Unabridged Dictionary of the English Language (1989), s.v. "mystic."

[5] Sally Morgenthaler, Worship Evangelism (Grand Rapids: Zondervan Publishing House, 1995), 277.

[6] John Coe, "Healing the Heart's Deep Beliefs in the Spirit: Intentionalizing Spiritual Formation through Soul Work" (lecture presented at the Talbot One-Day Spiritual Retreat, La Mirada, California, 26 September 2003).

[7] Kenneth J. Gergen, The Saturated Self, 2d ed. (New York: Basic Books, 2000), 20.

[8] Dave Tomlinson, The Post-Evangelical (El Cajon, CA: emergentYS Books and Grand Rapids: Zondervan, 2003), 26.

[9] Ibid., 27.

[10] Mark A. Noll, The Scandal of the Evangelical Mind (Grand Rapids: William B. Eerdmans Publishing Company, 1994), 8.

CHAPTER 2

FROM MODERN TO POSTMODERN (PART I)

The Pendulum Swing of Postmodernism

In life, actions beget reactions. Nowhere is this principle more predictable than in the movements of culture, which spawn wholly different trends simply from the energy of their demise. There is an inevitable swing of the pendulum that produces an inverse reaction, usually in direct proportion to the energy of the first enthusiasm. Perhaps this is based upon human temperament and the facets of identity formation, or perhaps it is just a principle of physics that works its way throughout the fabric of existence. As a student of music history, I find these trends to be relatively easy to trace. When in the mid 1970s disco music swept the nation, the late 70s featured the angry and belligerent response of punk music, captured by bands like the Sex Pistols, among others. When the antics of Jerry Lee Lewis, Little Richard and Chuck Berry pushed the envelope of rock and roll in the 50s, culture responded by producing the sanitized sounds of groups like the Everly Brothers. When late romantic composers like Mahler and Richard Strauss pushed lush orchestration and chromaticism to the limit, composers like Schoenberg and Webern responded by creating twelve-tone and aleatoric music, in which tones outside of the diatonic scales landed in random juxtaposition to one another. Culture creates extremes.

Unfortunately, when one movement reacts to another, it can often tend to become "reactionary," that is, the energy of the first movement pushes the second to excess, and a good deal that was valuable and positive is discarded for no apparent reason. The rush of energy towards the new fascination eliminates any vestige of the first, and so balance gets incredibly misplaced in this frantic transition of energy. Because this process of cultural displacement is greatly heightened by the degree of energy in the preceding movement, cultural realizations that are based in particularly enthusiastic ideologies, like Christianity or communism, tend to produce counter reactions that are equally polarizing. The shift can be dizzying, especially when one is caught in the nexus of the change. The world long sought the existence of Anastasia, the daughter of Czar Nicholas, not because her presence would restore any semblance of old Russian values, but because many pined for some residue of what was lost in the rush to the new communist paradigm. Responses to the new paradigms are often exaggerated, one group becoming drastically opposed to the change, while the other group becomes wholeheartedly committed to it without counting the cost or considering what is lost. Valuable resources frequently are trampled in revolutionary transitions from one cultural movement to another.

Postmodernism has been one such revolution. Although the changes of this philosophical shift have been greatly feared within the circles of Evangelicalism, some have felt that liberation from the modern "tower of Babel" has been a long time coming.[1] Quite a bit of literature has been generated on the subject, and quite a lot of attention focused on a shift in philosophy that actually has been much more gradual than the corresponding conservative reaction. People have positioned themselves on either side, clinging feverishly to the old paradigm, or grabbing eagerly onto the lingo of the new. Even the word "postmodern" has become something of a label that many use to classify people and ideas for their own purposes. A friend mentioned a church where the pastor claims to be called to minister to "postmoderns," as if they lived in a certain section of town or came from a certain region of the country. How does one identify these postmoderns? Do they wear a label on the back of their shirts, an armband of a particular type, or is their hair combed in a special way? Would you know a postmodern if you saw him or her walking down the street? Of course not. And yet, the concept is present in a great deal of Christian discourse because it is a convenient way of describing current philosophical trends and tendencies in thought and culture.

Indeed, what has happened is that the pendulum has swung from something that preceded postmodernism, modernism, which might never have been as good as it now seems in one's reminiscences. As the phrase implies, postmodernism is not modernism, although describing it as such is probably a misnomer. Rather, postmodernism exists because it was catalyzed by the currents of modernism, that is, the central principles of modernism served as an "incubator" for the prevailing attitudes of postmodernism.[2] The pendulum has swung again, and it would seem wise to consider what is being discarded, but more importantly, to analyze what is being uncritically accepted and adapted into the current cultural forms. Yet, understanding postmodernism requires that one grapple with the vacuum of modernism that sucked it into being. Furthermore, since this is essentially a transitional period, many aspects of modernism are still in full force, being played out alongside the growth of postmodernism.[3] Therefore, it is doubly important to have an adequate grasp on the currents of modernism, before an adequate understanding of postmodernism can be explored.

When Knowledge Was Power

During my undergraduate days, I took a series of acting classes with an acting coach who was—as many artists are inclined to be—both extreme and brilliant. He was convinced that interpersonal relations—and by extension, acting—could be boiled down to a power struggle between characters. Human beings seek to gain and maintain power over one another, in an attempt to guarantee control over their own lives. Underneath all of the striving that humanity rehearses, the deepest desire is not for money or sex, but for power, and thereby, control, so that they might satisfy at will their secondary needs and desires. Power turns the universe, and it is power that we bitterly struggle to achieve. With this mantra as our guiding principle, we would engage in acting as aggressively as the World Wrestling Federation. I remember one occasion when our teacher observed a particularly lethal, verbal chokehold that one student perpetrated on her acting partner. He exclaimed,

"Did you see that? She just cut your legs off!" Power was the Midas' touch of culture, in his estimation, allowing one to transform glitter into gold.

In truth, much of life is a struggle to gain power—sometimes over other individuals, but primarily over one's own life. The Enlightenment, and the modern period that it introduced, was the dawn of a day in which power could be taken and held by the common man, and later the common woman. This power would enable man to lift himself up out of the rigid hierarchy of feudalism, and create a better life for himself and his family. The weapons of his warfare were not sword or mace, however, but intellect and reason, and when combined with his senses and observation, these weapons would lead to knowledge and truth. The darkness of the Middle Ages was quenched by the light of reason, and with the ascendancy of man over his surroundings rose a new dawn of the "modern" era.

The genesis of any superimposed, historical category is difficult to trace, because it is just that, a categorizing label. Few in the field of music history can give a definitive moment, for example, when the baroque period shifted into the classical period, though most can look back over the stretch of history and describe the differing compositional preferences of Bach in comparison to Haydn. In like manner, many of those who analyze modernism will broadly identify the Enlightenment period as the centrifuge in which the prevailing attitudes of modernism were formed.

There were a number of identifiable, concrete changes from medievalism that could be analyzed in much the same way that one would contrast the music of Haydn and Bach, and these changes all dealt with the decentralization of power. For example, the development of the movable-type printing press, with the first printing of the Gutenberg Bible, marked a significant technological turn that eventually brought literacy and "knowledge" to the masses. Moreover, the Protestant Reformation marked liberation from the sweeping, spiritual authority of the Roman Catholic church, taking control of people's eternal salvation away from their spiritual fathers, and leaving it to their own individual consciences.[4] These are well-documented, quintessential elements of change that could be fully analyzed in order to pinpoint the shift, if this work was meant to deal comprehensively with the subject. Suffice it to say that the changes that occurred during the Enlightenment, changes that facilitated the empowerment of the individual, created a "zeitgeist" (spirit of the age) that can be characterized with the following descriptions.

Enlightenment Modernism

The Enlightenment was the grand period of human achievement, motivated by a prevailing "belief of progress,"[5] and characterized by the indomitable will, determination and potency of the individual human to better his or her condition. Progress meant that individuals could lift themselves up out of the malaise of the Middle Ages, in which their existence was once so vulnerable to the vacillations of nature, and fashion better lives for themselves. It signified that the societal structures could be challenged by the individual, and that a person's place in the world should be based upon innate ability, rather than the fortune or misfortune of family or position. Power could be taken up like a scepter, for the authority and capacity to wield it would no longer be external to the commoner. The Enlightenment, due to some of the philosophical and technological changes it entailed, brought a conviction that power and control over one's environment could be attained through human ability, and this conviction was built upon several factors.

First, reason and logic—rational thought—were identified as the critical tools by which people could observe nature and obtain knowledge, and thereby be empowered to assert mastery over their environment.[6] This was the essence of the scientific method, which was introduced by Francis Bacon.[7] Knowledge and objective truth was accessible to the human mind by utilizing one's senses in conjunction with one's rationality to make observations about how nature operated. Understanding how nature worked was the first step towards controlling it, thereby yielding it a tool in the arsenal of human achievement. No longer was humankind marked as a victim in the hands of capricious natural forces. Rather, reason and cognition were invigorated as the supreme tools through which knowledge could be obtained, nature controlled, and human progress facilitated.[8]

The primary significance of this change was both epistemological and practical: the individual could know truth objectively by utilizing his or her reason and senses, the intimate and integral cooperation of intellect and observation. The so-called scientific method made it possible for the majority of humans through observation to accumulate true beliefs, data that was confirmed by the careful coordination of their innate faculties. Truth was knowable, usable and profitable. Knowledge became a valuable commodity, and rational thought was the avenue to that treasure hoard. In a sense, "man" learned to measure all things, and thus became the measure of all things.

Second, this scientific approach radically empowered humans, making them the masters of their environment by virtue of their reason, and thus putting them in control of their own destiny. All creatures had sensation and some degree of cognition, but only humans had the capacity for rational thought and reason. They could rise above the rest of the natural order by virtue of these functions, granting them sovereignty in Darwin's scheme of natural selection, which appeared in a later era.[9] The vision of human progress and the notion of a better tomorrow was the natural result of humanity so empowered by knowledge. As the old Schoolhouse Rock programs used to proclaim (as Francis Bacon before them), "knowledge is power." Reason, in conjunction with observation was the primary tool by which humankind could lift itself up by its bootstraps, and orchestrate the rest of the natural order. The Industrial Revolution, which came at a much later stage, was the result of this critical shift in the approach to knowledge.[10]

Third, the result of this empowerment was a radical autonomy and individualism that humankind had never really known. In time past, men and women had to scratch their living from the earth in much the same manner as their ancestors had ages earlier. The medieval serf was not so different from a post-Edenic Adam and Eve in this respect. Due to the vicissitudes of an agrarian and barter-driven economy, people were largely dependent upon nature, their scant resources and the community in which they operated. Autonomy was not a consideration. There was little chance for accumulation of wealth, and the tiny equity they possessed was in the sweat of their brow. As long as one's health held out, working harder was the only means of im-

CHAPTER 2: FROM MODERN TO POSTMODERN (PART I)

proving one's position. In addition, many were bound to the traditional structures of authority and power—the feudal landlord and the church—and as such, were enslaved to the unrelenting cycles of subsistence farming.

Although these conditions did not change overnight with the Enlightenment, the scientific approach to knowledge basically opened the door to self-advancement. It was like the great American dream, but for the pre-modern, feudal society, radically altering the destinies of many. It opened possibilities for the common person by capitalizing on a commodity they did possess—reason—and eventually broke down what had before been a stratified hierarchical web. Intelligence and education now would become the arbiter of one's place in society, and so knowledge became a primary means of advancing oneself, beyond its previous capacity to empower. The significance of this point is that the power of the individual mind held the potential for advancement, and as a result, a radical individualism and autonomy ensued. Indeed, the foundations of capitalism, described by Adam Smith during this time period, resulted from the scientific and philosophical endeavors of the Enlightenment period.

Because of the radical autonomy that was blossoming, a fourth shift happened as well: the nature of authoritarian structures changed. There was a strong conception that authority rested in divine right, especially the authority to govern, and so one's position in life had an almost caste-like quality. These basic beliefs are found throughout works like *The Canterbury Tales* of Geoffrey Chaucer or Boccacio's *The Decameron*. Whether a governmental or ecclesiastical official, authority was clearly related to one's lineage, gender and position in society, and the tiers of the ensuing hierarchy were essentially inflexible and non-negotiable. With the advent of the Enlightenment, however, these attitudes began to change. "Authority by 'divine right' or 'divine inspiration' could most effectively be challenged through reason and observation. These ingredients of human nature ennobled the individual, and gave him (and more questionably her) the capacity for discerning truth and choosing appropriate action."[11] The combined powers of reason and observation composed the force that gradually undermined the prevailing attitudes towards authority, and shifted the power base.

While this change would seem to shift authority into the individual, that was not exclusively or inevitably the case. As a result of the exaltation of the scientific method, authority actually came to be grounded in the intellectual elite, particularly in the expert or the professional. Although there is a certain degree of authority that is released by the invigoration of one's own reason and reflection, this authority is undeniably trumped by those with greater knowledge. Authority is often naturally deferred to an external source. Gergen remarks:

> Those groups to whom knowledge is attributed are generally granted the privilege of making decisions. We want knowledgeable people, rather than the ignorant and uninformed, to decide on matters of importance. Thus the power of decision making is often granted to scientists, experienced politicians, learned judges, medical doctors, and so on. Their words reflect the realities of accumulated experience.[12]

Humans found authority and power in their capacity for rational thought, but the same capacity caused them to gravitate towards those with a knowledge base—including many scholars and ministers—for critical decisions. The end result is that while the individual may have inherited the prerogative of choice from the Enlightenment, in modernism, the expert became king. Because of reason, authority was no longer arbitrarily endowed to another, but it still was given to an external executor.

As might be suspected, the fifth change is that the scientific approach cast doubt upon all supernatural explanations, creating an inherent anti-supernatural bias that began slowly to permeate society.[13] The genesis of this development is not difficult to follow. If truth and the approach to knowledge are based solely upon what can be observed by the senses and correctly evaluated by the intellect, then supernatural explanations of any kind would be seriously undermined.[14] Religious experience itself is cognitively sketchy, and connecting the dots of religious experience or supernatural manifestations with what can be "scientifically" observed in the natural world became questionable in that era.

Furthermore, the whole approach of the scientific method, although not hostile to the supernatural, is not essentially geared to deal with supernatural phenomenon; rather, the scientific method is specifically intended to observe truth in the natural world. If the scientific method is idolized, however, then one can see how any explanation from the supernatural world would quickly lose favor, and eventually be ignored. This process was already gathering steam at the time of the American Revolution, when Thomas Jefferson conveniently snipped out portions of the Bible that did not suit his notions of truth.[15] It is interesting to note that these attitudes did not eliminate church or religion, because the social and communal aspects of those institutions were at that time too fundamental to the fabric of society. However, this philosophical shift did create a struggle with whatever aspects of religion did not fit in with the prevailing worldview, and the exaltation of reason and the scientific method tended to exclude any approach to knowledge that relied upon an experience of supernatural origin.

When Reason No Longer Persuaded

A remarkable change has been afoot in the field of advertising, an industry that is often quick to seize upon subtle cultural trends. In past generations, the Madison Avenue executives would rely heavily upon the opinions of experts to sell their products, because the advice of professionals was considered thoroughly persuasive. When nine out of ten dentists recommended chewing a particular gum, it was especially convincing and many parents received their admonitions nearly as objective fact. In recent years, however, the marketing platform of the television appeals has subtly shifted. Whereas knowledge and the accumulation of knowledge found in the opinions of experts used to be power, it has become clear that something else has now overturned its reign with a higher authority—the life experience and inner conviction of the common person.

This shift is demonstrated in a recent advertising campaign for Excedrin. The pharmaceutical companies that compete for the pain-reliever market used to sell their wares by quoting percentages and statistics, and relying upon their persuasive capacity. Recently, Excedrin took a different tack. A winsome spokesperson, dressed not in hospital attire but regular street clothes, confides to the camera his personal experience. He asserts that he could quote the statistics about Excedrin, but instead claims that he uses the product because he just knows that it works. The advertisement relies not upon the empirical data that the modernist would acclaim, but upon the individual's personal experience with the pain reliever and his inner conviction regarding its effectiveness. He appeals in part to his observations, but more deeply to his intuition and a deeper way of "knowing." If empirical knowledge was once the highest power, this trend shows that experiential knowledge, both internal and external, is rapidly replacing it.

This was the same sort of value shift that brought down the curtain on the era of Enlightenment modernism, and ushered in the era of romanticism. Most writers on the subject of modernism and postmodernism will trace the principles of the Enlightenment throughout the course of modern history in unbroken lineage, commenting how various developments pushed Western culture further along in the pursuit of knowledge, power and progress. However, psychologist Kenneth Gergen, in his text on postmodernism *The Saturated Self*, includes an interesting excursus on romanticism, the literary and artistic movement of the 19th century, as a break in the playing out of Enlightenment ideals.[16] He actually divides modernism into Enlightenment and 20th century instantiations, and investigates at length the trends of the romantic period, trends that preached surprisingly antithetical values. The point is that the sweep of modernism and its ideals has not been unhindered or unbroken, as movements with opposite values have regularly inserted themselves into the tapestry of culture.

When analyzing these cultural movements over the course of history, it is typical for experts in the field of art, music or literature to identify the pendulum swing between romantic and classical tendencies,[17] which are often somewhat simplistically described as the emphasis towards structure and order and the reverse emphasis towards passion and expansion. For example, the music of Haydn or Mozart features a tighter structure and form, more stately and elegant melody lines and in general, slightly understated passion. Although Haydn did experience what is known as a "storm and stress" period,

CHAPTER 2: FROM MODERN TO POSTMODERN (PART I)

he never ultimately converted from the compositional principles coherent with classical ideals.

By contrast, his pupil Beethoven made a career of emotional contrasts in his work. Dramatically expanding the range of dynamics, he created unbridled highs and desperate lows that were drastic and sudden, while experimenting with precipices of major to minor tonality, and color shifts that pulled the rug out from under the listener. In a sense, he captured the inner, emotional life of the romantic listener. Some would say that his revolutionary Third Symphony at the turn of the 19th century was itself the genesis or turning point of the romantic period, and so Beethoven, at least as far as music history is concerned, became the father of romanticism.[18] A clearer understanding of the basic values and ideals of romanticism is essential to this study, as it will create a critical window with which to view postmodernism.

19th Century Romanticism

The Epistemology of the "Deep Interior"

Romanticism primarily focused on the "deep interior" of the self, which lay hidden underneath the "conscious reason" that modernism highlighted.[19] If the domain of the Enlightenment was reason and the intellect, then the domain of romanticism was the deep emotions and inner passions—particularly the longing and desire often associated with romantic love—a fascination with the transcendent and the mysterious, and a deeply spiritual communion with nature. Romanticism was reacting against the seemingly dry and soul-less approach of rationalism,[20] affirming that a much more profound vision of reality resided deep within the individual. "It is a perspective that lays central stress on unseen, even sacred forces that dwell deep within the person, forces that give life and relationships their significance."[21] Mining the deep interior was the fascination.

For some, the ambiguous deep interior was conceived of as the soul, while for others, it was simply a "passionate force" of nature.[22] It was something that transcended the material world, a reality that was greater than what lay on the surface, and whether the soul or some mystical connection with nature, it seemed to contain a special kind of knowledge. This inner sanctum of the individual was the residence of the passions and emotions, and so the exaltation of this deep interior meant that the passions, which were viewed as an expression of the soul, received a sacred and significantly more exalted emphasis than they had in the modern conception.[23] Whereas the emotions were fickle, inconstant, unpredictable and often prone to error in the modern mindset, the romantic viewed the passions as more fecund and fundamental to the true self than the superficial reason that modernism had so highly touted.[24]

Thus, the inner self became a more authoritative path to knowledge than reason and cognition. In a sense, the experiences of the inner self inherently possessed a greater profundity, as they emanated from a deeper level in the self than the workings of rational thought. By "experience," I am basically referring to the knowledge that arises from the processes of the inner self, like emotion, intuition, inner sensation, or any kind of special or non-rational perception. The deep interior was thought to possess higher methods of knowing than the "cool logic of the Enlightenment thinkers," which was viewed as a thin "veneer" on the surface of the self,[25] and so the passions and processes of the inner self were exalted above reason. William James reflects this understanding when he writes, "The unreasoned and immediate assurance is the deep thing in us, the reasoned argument is but a surface exhibition."[26] The heart was conceived as an "organ of knowledge," and so "the mind was demoted from its controlling position and replaced by the heart as the means of perception."[27] To that end, Lillian Furst quotes David Hume in his landmark *Treatise of Human Nature* of 1739, who remarks "reason is, and ought only to be the slave of the passions."[28] It wasn't that the cognitive processes were inherently flawed, but simply that they were "inadequate,"[29] and so the romantic insisted upon trusting heart over head in the pursuit of knowledge.

The Unassailable Quality of Mystical Experience

If observation was the avenue to truth and knowledge in the modern paradigm, then inspiration was that pathway in the romantic mindset. By inspiration, I am referring to the inner, mystical connection with the divine or with the forces of nature that yields a particular type of knowledge. Whereas one pathway relied upon the "external" senses in cooperation with reason, the other highlighted a spiritual perception or "inner" sensation that dove deep into the human being for knowledge. Gergen comments "many romantics considered the central inhabitant of the deep interior to be the soul. This view linked the individual both to God and to the natural world of God's design, making the individual both divine and natural in aspect."[30] The deep interior allowed a connection with God or nature on a more fundamental level—inspiration—yielding knowledge that was higher than that which reason could provide. Furst, commenting on this period, asserts "the heart must be believed before the reason because here lies that essential part of man wherein he is linked to the universal spirit."[31] Whereas modernism simply observed nature, romanticism communed with the divine.

A key epistemological aspect of this perspective is that the locus of truth and knowledge moved from a partially external process—the scientific method—to a wholly internal reality, the deep interior. Observing and evaluating nature involved the intellect, but the knowledge itself was accessed outside of the individual. The knowledge that the romantic desired, the knowledge that was connected with spiritual and mystical forces, was accessed through an internal process. While reason and cognition provided a certain kind of knowledge, it was knowledge that was external to the self. The pathway to truth was now found within, and so the challenge of the romantic became accessing those catacombs of truth. The arts—particularly music, painting and poetry—became one vehicle through which the deep interior could be sounded.[32] Another vehicle was mystical experience, meaning the inner perception of a transcendent reality.

Mystical encounters and experiences, as a direct route to inner knowledge, were empowered with an authority that was accordingly higher than rational thought. William James agrees that there is a "curious authority" in the mystical experience.[33] James was an eminent psychologist and author, and his landmark text *The Varieties of Religious Experience* was published in 1901, during the late romantic era. In this sweeping work, he catalogues an incredible variety of religious and mystical experiences, investigating the nature of the mystical episode in general and assessing its comparative value. The thrust of his text, which came to be a foundational work in the field of psychology, was that religious experience precedes dogma or theology in the development of religion.[34] According to James, the doctrinal truth that is expounded by religious institutions has been preceded by religious experience, and therefore builds its propositional truth upon experiential foundations.[35] Hence, religious experience has a kind of special authority that supersedes the later systematizations of doctrinal truth.[36]

In analyzing such a wide cross-section of religious experiences, James contended that mystical experiences contain a perceived authority for those who report them that significantly outweighs any rational argumentation. He claimed that these experiences possess a certain "noetic quality" which makes the experience itself appear to be a special, somewhat exalted form of knowledge.[37] "Although so similar to states of feeling, mystical states seem to those who experience them to be also states of knowledge. They are states of insight into depths of truth unplumbed by the discursive intellect."[38] He goes on to describe mystical experiences as "direct perceptions of fact for those who have them" and "absolutely sensational in their epistemological quality."[39] For their subjects, mystical experiences are instances of knowledge that are absolutely incontrovertible by logic or rational argumentation.

> If you do have them, and have them at all strongly, the probability is that you cannot help regarding them as genuine perceptions of truth, as revelations of a kind of reality which no adverse argument, however unanswerable by you in words, can expel from your belief....
> ...If a person feels the presence of a living God after the fashion shown by my quotations, your critical arguments, be they never so superior, will vainly set themselves to change his faith.[40]

Although James did not necessarily agree that mystical experiences are instances of knowledge, or that they warrant the level of authority produced in their devotees, he convincingly demonstrated these undeniable facts through his extensive research.

The Interplay of Imagination and Knowledge

In keeping with these trends, imagination was exalted over reason as a critical conveyer of knowledge,[41] in that the creative mind possessed a unique perception into supreme reality unlike anything that reason could approximate. Imagination can best be described as the inner creativity of a person to recombine or fashion features of reality into a possible world. In doing so, the mind makes a picture of the world, imbuing this secondary creation with its own interpretation of reality, hoping to apprehend a deeper truth than is visible or accessible on the surface.[42] "The mind imposes itself on reality, shaping it. Imagination has a central role, therefore, in knowledge."[43] One can see how this fascination would be particularly strong for poets and artists, whose approach to knowledge involves rearranging and highlighting aspects of the world they see around them. Coleridge wrote "the primary imagination I hold to be the living Power and the prime Agent of all human perception."[44] Hence, Coleridge and many romantic poets viewed imagination as critical to knowledge. In a letter to a friend, the poet John Keats exclaimed "I am certain of nothing but of the holiness of the heart's affections and the truth of imagination. What the imagination seizes as beauty must be truth."[45] Imagination became an exalted way of knowing.

The key to this elevation of imagination was primarily its connection with inspiration, or that divine source of knowledge—however one conceived it—that was accessed through the deep interior. In essence, the creative process draws upon various sources of knowledge within the individual in order to recombine them in "non-actual" realizations. Imagination is able to tap into a higher revelation of truth, by envisioning or imagining possible truth that is beyond the visible or material world. Thus, it contains a kind of interlocking relationship with inspiration, and becomes a sort of knowledge, or an expressway to that divine commodity. "The metaphorical structure of Romantic poetry tends to move inside and downward instead of outside and upward, hence the creative world is deep within, and so is heaven or the place of the presence of God."[46] It was the tool of this more profound way of knowing—the experience of the inner self—as it was thought to access hidden, divine knowledge.

Although different in certain aspects, this was basically the conviction of the Christian novelist George MacDonald.[47] MacDonald believed that the imagination created new revelations or embodiments of God's original creation, the ground of all truth, and felt that it was central to knowledge in both the arts and sciences. "We dare to claim for the true, childlike, humble imagination, such an inward oneness with the laws of the universe that it possesses in itself an insight into the very nature of things."[48] Imagination rearranges knowledge in order to touch transcendent truth.

In keeping with this assertion, the imaginative genius was exalted, not the genius of the cool logician, but of the creative neurotic.[49] This was the era of the mad artist, tormented by the creative visions of his or her inner self, nearly insane with the demands of inspiration and creation. This was the era of Vincent Van Gogh, who engaged in self-mutilation, or Peter Ilyich Tchaikovsky, who drank water contaminated with diptheria (and died), most likely a result of depression over a lack of popular response to his Sixth Symphony. In his or her imagination and creativity, the genius creator/artist was thought to drink deeply from the well of inspiration, and therefore, tapped into some truth much deeper in the inner self than could be accessed by cognition. In essence, the creator/artist became god-like in the romantic period due to his or her ability to access more profound truth. This development is in keeping with the current generation, in which the MTV "artist" has achieved a certain god-like status.

Many of the creative geniuses of this romantic era found another avenue into the experiences of their deep interior, through the growing allure of opium. The burgeoning opium trade of the period allowed this experimentation to occur. In the early eighteenth century, opium was like a household drug that doctors would prescribe for a variety of ailments, an "analgesic and tranquillizer" called upon to treat everything from hysteria to cholera.[50] Because opium produced "dreams" or hallucinogenic effects, however, it was particularly attractive to those artists who placed so much emphasis on imagination as a component of literary creation. Although Coleridge and De Quincey are the most well-known opium devotees, all of the romantic poets (except Wordsworth) are known to have experimented with it.[51]

CHAPTER 2: FROM MODERN TO POSTMODERN (PART I)   43

Furthermore, nearly all of the romantic poets recorded their dreams, whether or not they were opium-induced, for the romantic artists became obsessed with dreams.[52] Dreams were thought to access the most fundamental and enlightened picture of reality, another route into the profundity of the deep interior. Hayter writes: "There one's eyes, clouded by the mists of ordinary waking life, might be purified by the light from beyond, from the innermost source of essential reality…"[53] Therefore, a transcendental trip into the inner recesses would tap into that sublimated truth, allowing the imagination to compose a broader revelation of knowledge.

The Reawakening of Supernaturalism

Finally, as might be expected, a preoccupation with the deep interior exalted a sense of reality beyond what is seen—the immediate—and resulted in a renewed interest in spirituality. Just as modernism downplayed the supernatural, the romantic period was obsessed with spirituality, especially with the idea of the unseen, the mysterious, the sacred and the transcendent. The romantic affirmed that there is much more to reality than what can be observed in nature with the reason and the senses, and so scorned the capacity of the scientific method to get at the deepest stuff of life. In this respect, the reaffirmation of the supernatural was "in part a reaction from the arid rationalism of the Enlightenment."[54] As a result, religion in general saw a revival throughout the romantic period.[55] A preoccupation with spiritualism, particularly the practice of séances, became very popular as well, a result of this fascination with the supernatural world.[56] Whereas the Enlightenment spawned distrust of supernatural explanations, the romantics found spirituality to be its true life force.

Experience as Knowledge

The importance of these observations, at least in part, is to confirm three notions. First, in the romantic period, power shifted. If knowledge was power in modernism, then experience—particularly an experience that drew upon the inner self—became power in the romantic period. The Enlightenment exaltation of reason was viewed as shallow and superficial by the romantic, as a more significant vision existed within the deep interior. The locus of power now became the internal man, bequeathing authority to make sense of one's world. Second, truth was now to be found within, in one's inner experiences. While truth was once grounded in the external world and knowledge was obtained only through studied observation, the individual and his or her internal reality became a higher and more authoritative form of knowledge. Inspiration was tapped by one's imagination and inner perception, not by reason or logic. Third, the inner, unseen forces, whether conceived of as the soul or something else, attained a heightened reality, becoming more real to the romantic than anything his or her senses could present. All of the things that one could see, taste, hear, smell and touch were still genuine, but they no longer held the sacred place of exclusive reality. The universe opened to include a reality that existed beyond scientific observation, and so the epistemological certainty that once accompanied the judgments of rational thought was significantly undermined by inner experience.

---

[1] J. Richard Middleton and Brian J. Walsh, Truth is Stranger Than It Used to Be (Downers Grove, IL: InterVarsity Press, 1995), 27.

[2] Gergen, The Saturated Self, 87.

[3] Middleton and Walsh, Truth is Stranger Than It Used to Be, 41.

[4] Albert Borgmann, Crossing the Postmodern Divide (Chicago: The University of Chicago Press, 1992), 22.

[5] Middleton and Walsh, Truth is Stranger Than It Used to Be, 14.

[6] Gergen, The Saturated Self, 29.

[7] Middleton and Walsh, Truth Is Stranger Than It Used to Be, 16.

[8] Borgmann, Crossing the Postmodern Divide, 23.

[9] Gergen, The Saturated Self, 29.

[10] Middleton and Walsh, Truth Is Stranger Than It Used to Be, 17.

[11] Gergen, The Saturated Self, 20.

[12] Ibid., 95.

[13] Robert Webber, Signs of Wonder: The Phenomenon of Convergence in Modern Liturgical and Charismatic Churches (Nashville: Abbott Martyn, 1992), 16.

[14] Middleton and Walsh, Truth Is Stranger Than It Used to Be, 14.

[15] John A. Buehrens and F. Forester Church, Our Chosen Faith, 4-5; quoted in Alan Gomes, Reformation & Modern Theology Course Syllabus (La Mirada, CA: Biola University, 1998), 186.

[16] Gergen, The Saturated Self, 20.

CHAPTER 2: FROM MODERN TO POSTMODERN (PART I)   45

[17] Donald Jay Grout, A History of Western Music, 3d ed. with Claude V. Palisca (New York: W.W. Norton & Company, 1980), 551.

[18] Grout, A History of Western Music, 548.

[19] Gergen, The Saturated Self, 20.

[20] H. G. Schenk, The Mind of the European Romantics (Oxford: Oxford University Press, 1979), 3-7.

[21] Gergen, The Saturated Self, 19.

[22] Ibid., 20.

[23] Lillian R. Furst, Romanticism in Perspective (New York: Humanities Press, 1970), 220.

[24] Gergen, The Saturated Self, 21. See also Hume's Treatise of Human Nature, Bk 2, Pt 3, Sec 3.

[25] Ibid., 23.

[26] William James, The Varieties of Religious Experience (New York: The Modern Library, 2002), 85-86.

[27] Furst, Romanticism in Perspective, 220.

[28] David Hume, Treatise of Human Nature; quoted in Lillian R. Furst, Romanticism (London: Methuen & Co Ltd, 1969), 27.

[29] Schenk, The Mind of the European Romantics, 6.

[30] Gergen, The Saturated Self, 20.

[31] Furst, Romanticism in Perspective, 220.

[32] Ibid., 221.

[33] James, The Varieties of Religious Experience, 415.

[34] Ibid., 369.

[35] Ibid., 249-250.

[36] Ibid., 469.

[37] Ibid., 414.

[38] Ibid., 415.

[39] Ibid., 462.

[40] Ibid., 83, 86.

[41] Schenk, The Mind of the European Romantics, 5.

[42] Furst, Romanticism in Perspective, 129.

[43] Colin Duriez, The J.R.R. Tolkien Handbook (Grand Rapids: Baker Books, 1992) 126.

[44] Coleridge, Biog. Lit., 1202; quoted in Lillian R. Furst, Romanticism in Perspective, (New York: Humanities Press, 1970), 120.

[45] John Keats, The Selected Letters of John Keats, selected and with an introduction by Lionel Trilling (Garden City, NY: Doubleday & Company, Inc., 1956), 99.

[46] Northrop Frye, ed., Romanticism Reconsidered: Selected Papers from the English Institute (New York: Columbia University Press, 1963), 16.

[47] Duriez, The J.R.R. Tolkien Handbook, 126.

[48] George MacDonald, "The Imagination: Its Function and its Culture," in A Dish of Orts [book on-line]; available from http://www.er90481.dial.pipex.com/imagination.htm; Internet; accessed 23 March 2004.

[49] Schenk, The Mind of the European Romantics, xvii.

[50] Alethea Hayter, Opium and the Romantic Imagination (Berkeley, CA: University of California Press, 1968), 29-30.

[51] Ibid, 17, 30.

[52] Ibid., 73.

[53] Ibid., 70.

[54] Schenk, The Mind of the European Romantics, 90.

[55] Henri Peyre, What is Romanticism?, trans. Roda Roberts (University, Alabama: The University of Alabama Press, 1977), 114.

[56] Gergen, The Saturated Self, 27.

CHAPTER 3

FROM MODERN TO POSTMODERN (Part II)

Behind the Curtain

One of my favorite movies from the 1990s was the runaway box-office hit, *The Matrix*. This sci-fi thriller is one of those incredible films that perfectly reflect culture, dynamically capturing the zeitgeist of the age. *The Matrix* is a unique twist on the post-apocalyptic tales of the 70s and 80s, like *Planet of the Apes* or *Bladerunner,* because of the manner in which the characters (and by extension, the viewers) evaluate and interact with reality. In the first scene, we meet computer hacker Neil Anderson—Neo to his cyber acquaintances—in his dark and angst-ridden apartment. All of his contacts with the outside world are sketchy and superficial, as he is isolated by his preoccupation with technology, as well as by his aloof and guarded temperament. He is contacted by an other-worldly type character named Morpheus, who seems to manifest himself at will through Neo's computer terminal, as well as through the most convenient telephone line.

When Neo does finally meet him, Morpheus becomes a veritable spiritual guide to Neo, attempting to convince him that the world he experiences is a species of virtual reality constructed by computers. The machines have taken over society, and a virtually omnipotent, computer network has created a cyber-reality, the "matrix" in which Neo is imprisoned. Moreover, these entities are growing humans and harvesting their energy in order to power the system. Everything that Neo trusts around him is a creation of that system. Reality, as Neo knows it, is a cyber-construction of some virtual-

other, and the majority of humans are oblivious slaves to this technological reality.

One of the most powerful scenes occurs when Neo agrees to be extracted from the matrix. Morpheus offers Neo the choice of either a blue or red pill, one of which will allow him to continue in anesthetized oblivion, and the other of which will give him an objective seat on the fifty-yard line of reality. The viewer is trapped in the suspense of the moment, not wondering whether or not Neo will accept, but entranced rather by what he will find when the curtain is drawn back. Neo chooses reality, and awakes from his existential nap to find himself naked and harnessed to a machine that sucks the energy from his body, bathing in a pod surrounded by thousands of similar human cocoons.

What makes the scene so powerful is that it confirms the suspicion that incipiently lurks within each one of us, that there is a powerful reality behind the curtain, and that the reality we cling to in our lives is a beguiling construction of someone else's invention. It is the ultimate conspiracy theory of existence. As authors Middleton and Walsh assert, "worldviews provide the best orientation to life when we are not aware of them."[1] When the suggestion of another possibility of reality is seriously entertained, suspicion forever eradicates certainty in *any one particular worldview.* Indeed, suspicion is perhaps the key attitude of the postmodern consumer. The question of truth and reality, especially as it relates to social constructions, is artfully shoved down the throat of the viewer. One is forced to entertain the strange, epistemological suggestion that the truths standing behind one's worldview are only perspectives on reality,[2] and that a deeper, absolute truth, although conceivable, might be either inaccessible or unknowable. This kind of epistemological uncertainty is wildly destabilizing for the average person, who still basically believes, along with Descartes, that rational thought is the most reliable approach to truth and knowledge.

The movie posits the question, what if I cannot trust my receptors of knowledge to be accurate, given that they are operating on the basis of flawed information? What if my approach to knowledge and truth is grounded in a construction that is disconnected with reality? What if the only way to know something is to take a leap of faith—the red pill that Morpheus offers—and to finally experience reality in order to know it? This is not unlike the approach recommended by Huxley and others within the drug culture of the 60s, who recommended using mind-altering drugs to order to arrive at a "first-order experience."[3] Perhaps what I propositionally believe about the universe is informed by and inferior to what I experience about the universe. Perhaps even my experience of the universe will not reflect ultimate truth, but will prove only to be the most convenient and pragmatic way to navigate life in a coherent and reasonably safe manner. The viewer has just been forced into the shoes of the postmodern.

The Puzzle of Postmodernism

In Evangelical circles, characterizing something as *postmodern* these days has become almost synonymous with simply describing contemporary culture, a trend that tends to blunt the intent of the word. Consequently, what is actually meant by the term can be a big question mark. Initially, the term was employed in the field of architecture, and over time has accumulated various other associations.[4] However, the philosophical usage and understanding of "postmodernism" is primarily related to epistemology, that is, how one approaches and appropriates beliefs, knowledge, and ultimately, truth. The term "postmodernism," for the purposes of this work, will be employed to reflect the current tendency to view one's approach to knowledge as something that need not be connected with an objective reality. The rest of this chapter will attempt to briefly summarize that disconnection, exploring the resources that the postmodern has called upon in its place.

While it is convenient to say that postmodernism involves the absence of absolutes, it is surely a simplistic and problematic identification. Rather, it would be better to say that with the proliferation of perspectives, it is difficult for a postmodern to see any one worldview or explanation as having a complete and exclusive lock on reality. The question is not so much are there any absolutes, but is there one grand story or narrative that fully explains reality, or is reality actually a composite or pastiche in which all of the explanations share? If reality is a bistro glass (a cup with eight flat sides), then perhaps each surface is a perspective on reality, but none comprehensively account for the entire glass. It is not that postmoderns have lost absolutes, but that they have shattered them into perspectives, and are comfortable in the knowledge that they have the freedom to reassemble them in the manner that best coheres with their experience. They willingly accept many perspectives on reality,[5] but vehemently maintain the absolute authority to determine how they should be pieced together in their private worldview. If there is one "absolute" in postmodernism, it is that no one has the right to compose another's reality.

The Proliferation of Perspectives

Perspective is the first piece of the puzzle of postmodernism. The postmodern has allegedly removed the goggles of his or her all-consuming worldview,[†] and granted that all worldviews are basically perspectives on reality. They all share in a representation of reality, but none encompasses it. In this regard, Brian McLaren has described all truth as "contextual" in the postmodern mindset,[6] which suggests that something is only "true" if it carries with it a specified background. With a myriad of backgrounds, the postmodern assumes many truths. The multiplicity of voices claiming authority, but disagreeing with one another has resulted in an intellectual quandary.[7] The individual is saturated with all the worldviews and their claims, and answers the dilemma not by choosing one, but by essentially choosing from them all.

[†] This has been called a central fallacy of postmodernism. Postmodernism seeks to maintain an objective seat on the sidelines of truth and reality, judging the various perspectives from outside a particular allegiance to any one perspective. However, this is manifestly impossible to do, and deconstructionism makes exactly that point. Middleton & Walsh agree: "Postmodernity, as the master discourse which guides our understanding that all stories are mere human constructs, does not appear on the table. It is the table on which all the other dishes are served. Postmodernity thus functions as the larger interpretive frame that relativizes all other worldviews as simply local stories with no legitimate claims to reality or universality....The postmodernist is thus caught in a performative contradiction, arguing against the necessity of metanarratives precisely by (surreptitious) appeal to a metanarrative." Middleton & Walsh, Truth Is Stranger Than It Used to Be, 77.

CHAPTER 3: FROM MODERN TO POSTMODERN (PART II)   51

Kenneth Gergen identifies this as "the saturated self," and attributes this predicament to the technological explosion of the 20th century. He points out that the expanding globalization forces the individual to be continually exposed to a variety of competing worldviews, making it difficult for one to maintain any exclusive claims.

> The expansion of telephonics, air travel, television, radio, computer networks, fax systems, and the like are dramatically increasing our exposure to others, and we absorb opinions, beliefs, attitudes, and values from all points of the globe. It is precisely this exposure that undermines commitments to objectivity. For as the range and variability of reactions to any condition are increased, so does "the truth of the matter" become increasingly cloudy.[8]

Whereas worldviews once could hide in their respective kingdoms, insular and isolated from one another, that species of intellectual protectionism is no longer acceptable. One of the tacit tariffs of world commerce is the cognitive dissonance that occurs from regular exposure to other worldviews, and that tension creates real issues for those who seek to maintain exclusive loyalty to any one particular perspective.

One of the byproducts of this open-ness to all perspectives is that there is not really supposed to be any perspective that is "off the table." Whether this is actually the case in practice is another question.[‡] However, there is a certain legitimacy extended to all perspectives, and so those worldviews that involve supernatural explanations are now appropriate once again. Whereas modernism developed an anti-supernatural bias and shunned explanations that relied upon supernatural realities, the postmodern is open to these possibilities as another in the smorgasbord of choices.

Indeed, society is increasingly fascinated with the supernatural, along with the somewhat nebulous concept of "spirituality." Consider the popularity of the television show *Crossing Over,* which features medium John Edwards conducting spiritualistic interviews with the dead on behalf of their

---

[‡] In theory, postmodernism embraces all perspectives, but in practice, any perspective that is considered to be intolerant or exclusive is not welcomed. Gergen is seemingly consistent with his view, and validates some perspectives that others would shun. He remarks "rather than shutting out the voices of drug dealers, Mafiosi, and the KKK from the public forum, it is important to expand the possibilities for dialogue." Gergen, The Saturated Self, 257.

loved ones. The séance, which was once a romantic preoccupation, has now been resurrected in postmodern garb. Indeed, spiritual interests have seen a remarkable resurgence. "Far from the erosion or even eclipse of religious belief that the Enlightenment so confidently predicted, the Enlightenment itself has been eclipsed, resulting in a veritable smorgasbord of religions and worldviews for our consumption."[9] Ideally, the postmodern realizes that if his or her perspective is only a partial glimpse or fragment of reality, then there must be other perspectives that do not necessarily synthesize with his or her own. On the positive side, this intellectual position invites a lot more cognitive humility than that of the hyper-modernist; on the negative side, humility is not always the inevitable response.

The Curious Authority of the Splinter Narrative

Second, there is a suspicion of "meta-narratives" and a heightened interest in "marginalized" perspectives,[10] meaning those explanations of reality that have been suppressed by the predominance of the primary meta-narratives. A meta-narrative is a grand story, or an explanation of reality that is all encompassing in its focus and intention, like the Bible or the Koran. This is the kind of perspective that either claims, or is used by its adherents to claim some kind of highly authoritative, comprehensive explanation of reality, particularly one that is manifestly exclusive of other perspectives. Postmoderns reject these types of exclusive explanations, whereas they are interestingly attracted to more "localized" or marginalized narratives, what I have called "splinter narratives," for their existential value.[11] For example, the narrative of the oppressed, native American is championed against the meta-narrative of American imperialism and expansion; likewise, the once grand story of Columbus instead becomes about his cruel subjugation of native peoples, not his navigational feats.[12]

Truth is fractured into perspectives, and so the splinter narrative is affirmed, while any meta-narrative that makes broader truth claims is shunned. In a post-Nine Eleven address at Georgetown University, ex-president Bill Clinton remarked:

CHAPTER 3: FROM MODERN TO POSTMODERN (PART II) 53

> We are incapable of ever having the whole truth. They [the terrorists] believe they got it. Because we don't believe you can have the whole truth, we think everybody counts and life is a journey....They believe that because they have the truth you either share their truths or...you're a legitimate target.[13]

As is evident from this quote, the postmodern is motivated in his or her approach to knowledge by a sort of hypersensitivity to all perspectives, and by the conviction that *truth is a puzzle that can never be fully completed.* He or she allegedly welcomes the inclusion of all narratives that do not demand exclusivity because they fit nicely in the puzzle, highlighting those that are most marginalized and affirming their contribution to a composite perspective on truth. In actuality, every grand story—including those in the Bible—begins as a local narrative, and is transformed by culture into a meta-narrative.[14] Regardless, for a postmodern, the individual narrative becomes a sort of truth-assigning vehicle or mechanism, as each story carries a unique and valuable perspective on and contribution to reality in the details it relates.

Middleton and Walsh note that human beings have a peculiar need for meta-narratives, as stories that make sense of their lives. Hence, they gravitate towards the exaltation of certain stories for their personal interpretive value.

> Humans, it seems, constitutionally need metanarratives. We require some overarching framework that makes sense of the totality of life and that gives meaning to our place in the grand scheme of things. Hence even local narratives pertaining initially to even a small tribe or community end up being treated as if they were universal.[15]

We see this phenomenon at Christmas, when the Capra classic *It's a Wonderful Life* is broadcast as religiously as the Christmas story. The story has an overarching theme about community and grace that touches each of us because it connects with the search for meaning in our own lives. Stories give meaning to our lives.

A "Pastiche" Approach to Reality

Thus, the postmodern tends to choose his or her picture of reality not from one over-arching story or meta-narrative, but from a variety of narratives, based upon an approach to knowledge that is sometimes called the "narrative structure." A narrative structure is "a set of propositions describing a possible world which we have constructed that is more or less exhaustive."[16] It is a picture of reality that is organized and framed by our imagination. Individuals assemble a personal worldview or construction of reality by selecting aspects of stories that, when incorporated into their personal narrative, empower them to make sense of the significant details and events of their lives. These narratives are constructions that represent "a way things are or could be,"[17] and end up becoming reality or "truth" as the postmodern affirms it. No longer does the grand story or meta-narrative that is passed down over generations embody truth, but instead the mosaic that the postmodern has assembled from a variety of sources.

Furthermore, stories are selected as "true," that is, meaningful, based upon the degree of coherence that one finds between them and one's own personal experience. By experience, in this case, I mean both the external events of one's own life as well as the inner sensations, mystical episodes or personal presuppositions that are intimately related to them. For example, a Christian friend of mine—who incidentally is a poster child for postmodernism—was considering converting to Judaism. She struggled with the fact that there is suffering in the world, and found it difficult to accept that a good God could send people to hell. Because some Jews do not believe in hell, she ideally would have liked to lift that aspect of their narrative and include it in her own. She wanted to borrow aspects of another narrative and incorporate them into her own construction of reality in order to explain her own preferences and experiences.

Hence, one can overlap a narrative onto one's own life, like the plot of a good movie, and it can function in the same way that a novel does: it can provide an analogy for thinking about one's own partial worldview, that is believed and then lived.[18] A story becomes an animation of truth, and aspects of stories that are especially meaningful stick to the flypaper of one's narrative structure. Ergo, society is profoundly preoccupied with the telling of stories, not because the stories are necessarily true or false, but because they appear true and are personally validating when experienced in juxtaposition with one's own life. Indeed, the force of one's formulated narrative depends more upon the exercise of the imagination than it does upon the cognitive concern about what to believe.

As a result, the narrative structure results in a deliberately and imaginatively constructed worldview, and the individual self becomes fragmented, what Gergen calls a pastiche personality, composed of bits and pieces of other worldviews.[19]

> As social saturation proceeds we become pastiches, imitative assemblages of each other. In memory we carry others' patterns of being with us. If the conditions are favorable, we can place these patterns into action. Each of us becomes the other, a representative, or a replacement. To put it more broadly, as the century has progressed selves have become increasingly populated with the character of others. We are not one, or a few, but like Walt Whitman, we "contain multitudes."[20]

Imagination and Meaning

Imagination retains a pivotal role in the postmodern worldview and epistemology, just as it did in the romantic one. Imagination recombines and interprets the features of reality in order to explain the world, and hopes to arrive at a sum of truth that transcends the primary parts. Truth is as much in the reordering and interpreting of reality as in the pieces themselves. Imagination is like an editor of reality, reassembling the happenings of life in order to portray truth in a certain manner.

Although not typically linked with postmodernism, C.S. Lewis had plenty to say about the imagination that was remarkably neo-romantic, and showed great influence from George MacDonald in this respect. He linked the imagination with the "making of meaning,"[21] and believed that both reason and imagination were integral to knowledge. He wrote: "Reason is the natural organ of truth; but imagination is the organ of meaning. Imagination, producing new metaphors or revivifying old, is not the cause of truth, but its condition."[22] Lewis thought that the imagination, in reorganizing reality, was a viable partner with reason, and could arrive at a more complete picture of deeper truth than rationality alone might grasp. Therefore, Lewis felt that myths, for example, had explanatory value and were therefore true in a special sense in bringing meaning to propositional or theoretical truths.[23] Imagination reframes truth with meaning.

In the process, however, the essence of truth as a concept can change for the postmodern. "True" no longer strictly signifies consistency with objective reality, but rather implies that something has been found to be meaningful to someone as a way of interpreting his or her experiences. As a result, a story can be true, that is, consistent with someone's experience, without being factual at all, and so becomes true in a special sense. For example, a cartoon movie like *The Lion King* can provide certain truth for a particular individual, not because it was in any sense coherent with reality, but because they could select aspects from the narrative that were meaningful and consistent with their experience and preferences, and thus, true. Imagination anthropomorphizes lions, giving them uniquely human father/son relationships, and leaving the viewer to affirm what the story affirms—that one's deceased parents are always watching over them. In essence, a narrative can provide material for thinking about one's own life, whether or not one actually believes it to be consistent with an objective reality. It becomes true primarily on the basis of one's imagination.[24] Meaning has replaced truth.

The Source of Authoritative Knowledge

Finally, the narrative structure as a worldview-forming apparatus moves authority back into the experiences of the individual. Whereas in the modern worldview, truth was located in the accumulated knowledge of experts, the postmodern redefines truth and measures it by his or her own experiences or "inner truth." The recent shift in advertising reflects that this kind of approach has become far more persuasive to the average consumer. Marva Dawn comments "the new generation places the locus of authority within the self....A person at this pole understands spirituality in terms of a journey or quest as she seeks truth and meaning within herself."[25] The subtlety of this shift should not be underestimated. If reality is constructed by selecting aspects from whatever stories are the most agreeable, then the various experiences of the person become the prime arbiter of truth. If some person has "sensed" their deceased parents looking down from above, as in *The Lion King,* then who would argue with their inner experiences? In postmodernism, as in romanticism, experience equals power.

Experience as Power

In summary, the collapse of objective truth in postmodernism has resulted in the exaltation of experiential knowledge as the prime medium by which truth or meaning is assessed. The removal of the ability to know something objectively makes experience the only possible alternative as knowledge. "If all that we can know is in our experience, then we can know nothing beyond it—which would exclude the possibility of knowledge of an external, or nonexperiential, world."[26] Hence, personal experience, whether internal or external, becomes the most authoritative kind of knowledge.

Moreover, doing away with an objective reality that one can know leads to a divided knowledge of the soul, in which an experience of faith is divided from rationality as two irreconcilable forms of knowing.[27] This is an existential approach to knowledge, a "leap of faith" as opposed to a step of reason. Since reason is effectively sidelined as a way of knowing something—at least as far as spirituality is concerned—then the existential leap of faith is the only other option. The two paths to knowledge of faith and reason, popularized by Aquinas, have suffered road closures, and a yawning chasm has opened in their place. An individual's fragmentation as a result of exposure to innumerable cultures, when put to its logical extreme, must mean that he or she can *only* arrive at truth through personal experience, and not by the authoritative voice of any one particular approach. Whatever perspective or cultural voice comports with his or her experience is allowed to contribute to his or her peculiar construction of truth. The narrative structure, as it intrinsically borrows from other perspectives, is fabricated upon the framework of one's own experience.

Although this is not an exhaustive treatment of postmodernism, it serves to highlight several significant aspects, aspects that are remarkably similar to the romantic worldview. First of all, experience of all kinds becomes an exalted type of knowledge. It is given a subtle authority over other ways of knowing, a reaction against rationalism as well as some of the questionable values of the modern worldview. Just as the romantic found experience so much more persuasive than reason and logic, to a certain degree, so does the postmodern.

It is not surprising that having an experience becomes especially profound and desirable in this day and age, and the drive to generate experiences begins to consume the inhabitant of postmodern culture in a myriad of different ways. Francis Schaeffer credits much of the serious drug use of the 1960s to this quest for meaning, noting that the individual hoped "that by taking them he would experience the reality of something which would give his life some meaning."[28] The increased spirituality of the current generation is a fascinating marker of the same quest. Leonard Sweet writes "postmoderns are constantly putting their hands and the rest of themselves where God may have visited; hoping it's still warm. They are hungry for experiences, especially experiences of God."[29] Thus, experience-yielding activities—whether extreme sexual relationships, extreme addictions, extreme spirituality or even extreme sports—become especially significant in postmodern culture and priorities. More to the point, Christian worship begins to be pursued as a similar quest.

Second, experience equals power. Granted, this is a different kind of power than that which knowledge bequeathed during the Enlightenment. The power of experience is not the power to assert control over nature or leverage one's place in society; rather, it is existential power, that is, *the power to make meaning.* Because personal experience of all kinds is conceived as higher knowledge, the authority to define truth has moved back into the deep interior of the individual, just as in romanticism. The postmodern will struggle with the meta-narrative that claims to be authoritative, regardless of the expertise or knowledge base that backs its acceptance, because it involves disempowerment.

He or she seeks to construct his or her own narrative of reality, placing himself or herself in the authoritative position as the arbiter and measurer of truth. This is the authority or power that the postmodern craves, the authority to make true whatever they find compelling and meaningful, because it is meaning that drives their epistemology. He or she represents the splinter narrative, and it is the splinter narrative that is affirmed in the postmodern worldview. Imagination also retains an epistemological role in their formation of truth, because it is imagination that reframes truth, largely based upon its coherence with one's experience. As Keats submitted, what is imagined is a genuine perception of truth, because the authority to make it so has now moved back into the individual.

Finally, the naturalistic world of the modernist is now opening up again to explanations that are beyond what the scientific method can convincingly explain. The supernatural world has reappeared as a viable explanation among the variety of choices. There is plenty to say on this topic, and it certainly deserves a much broader discussion. Perhaps of more importance to this work, however, is the resurgence of the romantic idea that the presence of God is to be found within. The postmodern does not search for God quite as openly in the external world, retaining a basic suspicion to external phenomena, but is more philosophically predisposed to search for God within himself or herself. The supernatural life force, however one conceives it, now is sought within the deep interior.

Is Postmodernism a Neo-romanticism?

It is more than fascinating that there are myriad similarities between romantic sensibilities and those of the 21st century postmodern. Although modern values certainly live in full force alongside postmodern ones in the new millennium,[30] romantic tendencies are in such full bloom in postmodern culture that one cannot help but notice its essential neo-romantic characteristics. Gergen recognizes this point, writing that the postmodern perspective is, in some respects, a "resuscitation of romanticism."[31] Writing in the 1970s, the literary critic Henri Peyre predicted "in the last third of the twentieth century there will occur a romantic cataclysm unparalleled at any time except during the preromantic period of 1760, when men were weary of rational understanding and intense analysis."[32] While there are certainly epistemological considerations in the transition from modernism to postmodernism that cannot be categorized as particularly romantic, the clear similarity of values certainly cannot be overstated. They suggest that what is happening in postmodernism is another swing of the cultural pendulum, a swing to neo-romanticism.

Just as the romantics reacted to modernism, so have the postmoderns. Unfortunately, cultural reactions often become "reactionary" and unbalanced in their quest for change, invariably resulting in excesses to the other extreme. Many positive aspects of the modern worldview are unwittingly sacrificed, while questionable aspects of postmodernism are uncritically accepted. To maintain a balance, one must recognize the currents from which cultural movements sprang, and then consider how those cultural ideals are being reincarnated. This is especially critical where culture intersects with Christianity.

The postmodern, Evangelical experience of worship is essentially a return to a romantic sensibility, where passion or overwhelming thirst for a romantic ideal—the unseen, mysterious and transcendent lover of our souls—is magnified. Moreover, this orientation lends itself to a fairly all-consuming quest for experience, as was realized by our romantic predecessors. By no means is this categorically a negative development in our churches and culture. On the contrary, the swing of the cultural pendulum often eliminates the excesses of a previous period, acting as a corrective movement of culture, and perhaps even a corrective movement of the Spirit. A pendulum swings to extremes, however, because that is the nature of a pendulum, and so balance is always the inherent struggle. The Evangelical paradigm, which is an especially enthusiastic ideology, can tend to either embrace or shun cultural movements far too quickly in the energy of the pendulum swing. Much can be lost that was valuable, and much can be embraced that is lamentable,

CHAPTER 3: FROM MODERN TO POSTMODERN (PART II) 61

unless the basic philosophical shifts are clearly explored, particularly the manner in which they inhabit our cultural forms. As William James remarks "the philosophic climate of our time inevitably forces its own clothing on us."[33] His comments are more than poignant in this generation.

Understanding the philosophical shift is the first step towards ascertaining its penetration, and redeeming it to meaningfully influence our culture without twisting or distorting our theology. In order to avoid the mistakes of cultural reactionism in the Evangelical world of worship, we must now critically examine how postmodern culture has specifically influenced our understanding and practice of worship. Before we can conduct this investigation, however, we must study how postmodernism has invaded broader culture, which will be the effort of the next chapter.

---

[1] Middleton and Walsh, Truth Is Stranger Than It Used to Be, 36-37.

[2] Gergen, The Saturated Self, 120.

[3] Francis A. Schaeffer, The God Who is There (L'Abri Fellowship, 1968; reprint, Downers Grove, IL: InterVarsity Press, 1982), 43 (page citations are to the reprint edition).

[4] Fredric Jameson, foreword to Jean-François Lyotard, The Postmodern Condition: A Report on Knowledge, trans. Geoff Bennington and Brian Massumi (Minneapolis: The University of Minnesota Press Press, 1984), xvii.

[5] Middleton and Walsh, Truth Is Stranger Than It Used to Be, 31.

[6] Brian D. McLaren, A New Kind of Christian (San Francisco: Jossey-Bass, 2001), 106.

[7] Gergen, The Saturated Self, 87.

[8] Ibid., 85.

[9] Middleton and Walsh, Truth Is Stranger Than It Used to Be, 42-43.

[10] Ibid., 73.

[11] Ibid.

[12] Ibid., 9.

[13] President William Jefferson Clinton, (speech delivered at Georgetown University, Washington D.C., 7 November 2001); available from http://www.Georgetown.edu/admin/publicaffairs/protocol_events/events/clinton_glf110701.htm; Internet; accessed 5 January 2004.

[14] Middleton and Walsh, Truth is Stranger Than It Used to Be, 76.

[15] Ibid.

[16] R. Douglas Geivett, interview by author, 12 June 2003, Brea, California.

[17] Ibid.

[18] Ibid.

[19] Gergen, The Saturated Self, 71.

[20] Ibid., 71.

[21] Duriez, The J.R.R. Tolkien Handbook, 128.

[22] C.S. Lewis, Rehabilitations; quoted in Duriez, The J.R.R. Tolkien Handbook, 131-132.

[23] Duriez, The J.R.R. Tolkien Handbook, 130-131.
[24] Geivett, interview by author.
[25] Marva Dawn, Reaching Out Without Dumbing Down (Grand Rapids: William B. Eerdmans Publishing Company, 1995), 83-84.
[26] Gergen, The Unsaturated Self, 101.
[27] Schaeffer, The God Who is There, 43.
[28] Ibid.
[29] Leonard Sweet, "A New Reformation: Re-Creating Worship for a Postmodern World," in George Barna, et al., Experience God in Worship (Loveland, CO: Group Publishing, Inc., 2000), 174.
[30] Middleton and Walsh, Truth is Stranger Than It Used to Be, 41.
[31] Gergen, The Saturated Self, 248.
[32] Peyre, What is Romanticism?, ix.
[33] James, The Varieties of Religious Experience, 471.

CHAPTER 4

THE POSTMODERN WORSHIPER

Modernism Demythologized

The fall of the Berlin Wall was one of those rare moments in cultural and political history that came to signify so much more than the actual event itself. The experience of a barrier being torn down, even a wall that divided a nation in two, could not compare with some of the currents it would inspire. It was like a stone dropped in a still pond that generated endless concentric rings. As the cameras rolled and crowds climbed upon the crumbling edifice, the world watched with a sense of thrill and expectation, aware that the immensity of the event contained ramifications that could not be fully realized by any single person in attendance. The collapse of the stone bulwarks foreshadowed the demise of the Iron Curtain and the Soviet Union, signaling the conclusion of the Cold War and temporarily lessening the imminent threat of nuclear annihilation. I remember feeling a sense of jubilant optimism as I witnessed the images projected on the television screen.

Was there a similar deathblow to modernism? Given that modernism as a worldview is far from comatose, speculation might be premature. There certainly have been a variety of factors that created the climate in which postmodernism has flourished. However, one historical event stands out as a definitive moment in which the modern myth of progress by science and technology was seriously called into question. The beginning of the end likely came over the skies of two towns in Japan—Hiroshima and Nagasaki—names of which most Westerners had probably never heard, but would never be able to forget. Although two world wars might not have been able sufficiently to shake the foundations of the modern paradigm, the dropping of two atomic bombs over Japan certainly could. As Robert Webber remarks, "The mechanistic worldview of the Enlightenment and the high estimate of human reason to understand the way the world works began to break down with the smashing of the atom."[1]

Although modernism did not crumble with that action of the American government, the children of that generation were the ones who became the nuclear protesters of the following generations. All of a sudden, the principles of modernism—progress by science and technology—were no longer steering the world towards a better tomorrow, but towards the possibility of *no* tomorrow.[2] Science became an entity that no longer merely provided meaning, but conceivably could completely annihilate meaning. The modern meta-narrative began to be seen as violent and brutalizing in its manipulation of people and the environment.[3] Post-apocalyptic films pictured the world of tomorrow as a disaster-stricken remnant of a once great civilization, and both the Cold War and the Vietnam War catalyzed the growing fear and unrest. The "tomorrowland" of modern values was a bewildering anachronism to many individuals, and the answers provided by the prevailing modern worldview, particularly as this meta-narrative was embraced by Western governments, became increasingly unsatisfactory.

While these historical events undermined the modern worldview, the essential transition was actually philosophical in nature. Caught in the crosshairs of a worldview intent on either domination or annihilation, the Western world began to reach for a neo-romantic, postmodern perspective. Singer/songwriter Sting, who was basically a child of the atomic era, wrote a hauntingly beautiful, pre-apocalyptic love song that championed the essence of the romantic ideal, in contrast to the violence of modern principles run amuck. Although this song was written in the 1980s, it captured the philosophical reaction to the Cold War, and the basic worldview shift from modernism to neo-romanticism. In the song, Sting sings longingly of his love for his newborn child, an inherently romantic gesture, in the face of the impending doom of civilization by the hand of science and technology. While he appeals to reason in his protestations, the persuasive content of the song relies heavily upon a revitalized romanticism:

CHAPTER 4: THE POSTMODERN WORSHIPER 65

> How can I save my little boy from Oppenheimer's deadly toy?
> There is no monopoly in common sense on either side of the political fence.
> We share the same biology, regardless of ideology;
> Believe me when I say to you, I hope the Russians love their children too.
>
> Sting, "Russians"[4]

Reacting to the excesses of modernism, a countercultural movement began to grow during the 1950s and early 60s that was decidedly romantic in its perspective, and these sensibilities flourished as a result of the basic instability of the modern paradigm. This countercultural group reached for a new approach to truth and knowledge that was inherently experiential in nature, relying upon divergent basic premises. The psychedelic culture of the 1960s followed the intellectual and epistemological tendencies of a century and a half earlier, and the ripples from that philosophical move are still being witnessed upon the still waters of society. Postmodernism is a perfect companion and offspring of that change, and the current cultural climate of the new millennium undoubtedly the next generation of that revolution. Thus, the development of the postmodern worshiper cannot be understood, unless one grasps the intellectual and philosophical currents of the 1960s and 70s, particularly as they resulted in the phenomenon of the Jesus movement. The cultural climate of those decades decisively set the table for the changes that have been since subtly incorporated into Evangelical worship.

The Rise of Experience

The psychedelic movement of the 1960s was really the cutting edge of a neo-romantic revival,[5] now connected in this work with postmodernism, and the central pillar of this movement was an *epistemology of experience*. Although there were many cultural changes that accompanied this grass-roots movement, a primary shift concerned one's basic presuppositions about the acquisition of knowledge, just as in the romantic period of the previous century. Experience, particularly inner experience of a spiritual, mystical or "psychedelic" sort, was conceived to be the most desirable and profound approach to knowledge and truth.[6] The exalted quest was for an inner state of consciousness that bestowed a clearer perception of reality, as reality was no longer believed to be deeply or vividly apprehended through "external empiricism or deduction."[7] Just as the romantic poets were fascinated with dreams, so the psychedelic culture sought the deep interior as a window into a more fundamental reality. Experience, particularly inner experience, was exalted as a higher way of knowing.

The Enlightenment moorings of logic and reason were unceremoniously abandoned in favor of inner experience, and the rationality that is central to Western civilization was essentially disparaged. Enroth, Ericson and Peters highlight how the counterculture reacted to the predominance of reason in the Western tradition, seeking a variety of approaches to knowledge.[8] They further note how youth culture was "obsessed with feeling and passion as opposed to intellect and reason," desperate for some kind of "visionary experience" that would give meaning to life.[9] Indeed, there was a species of nascent anti-intellectualism pervading much of the movement, not for lack of intellectual ability, but a result of the exaltation of inner experience to a higher epistemological plane. John Lennon, in the Beatles' psychedelic song "Tomorrow Never Knows," intoned a lyric borrowed from *The Tibetan Book of the Dead.* He borrows from a version of the text which had been prepared by Timothy Leary as a "handbook for people wanting to achieve spiritual enlightenment by taking LSD":[10]

> Turn off your mind, relax and float downstream.
> It is not dying. It is not dying.
> Lay down all thought, surrender to the void. It is shining. It is shining.
> That you may see the meaning of within. It is being. It is being.
> That love is all, that love is everyone. It is knowing, it is knowing.
>
> Lennon/McCartney, "Tomorrow Never Knows"[11]

Psychedelic experience and a spiritually enlightened journey into one's deep interior "defined the fundamental vision of reality,"[12] and this pursuit excited those in the psychedelic culture to search for a variety of pathways that would access this exalted inner knowledge. Just as the opium-eaters of the romantic period had discovered, mind-altering drugs provided a convenient avenue for those who sought truth and meaning through inner experience and higher states of consciousness.[13] These individuals avidly pursued experimentation with acid and other hallucinogenic drugs in order to arrive at a quintessential high or "peak experience,"[14] † viewed as a moment of supreme perception. In combination with these substances, imagination functioned as a psychedelic avenue to inner truth, just as it had in the romantic paradigm, "for all that the mind imagines is equally 'real'—and the experience which may be the wellspring of philosophy can be induced through the minutest quantity of a chemical."[15] Accessing this inner vision of reality through experience became the preoccupation of the psychedelic culture.

While radical drug experimentation was not practiced throughout the entire countercultural movement, the epistemology that it proposed functioned as a common denominator for the generation as a whole, witnessed by the rise of involvement in Eastern religions, yoga, mysticism, the occult, meditation, etc.[16] A basic understanding of the Eastern approach is that truth or God is to be found within, that all are one with the nonmaterial universe, and that the goal is transcendence of the material plane through the inner self. This concept harmonized beautifully with the psychedelic culture, and tacitly pervaded the entire movement.[17] The quest was for a vivid and powerful experience of inner consciousness, so any procedure that allowed the individual to bypass reason and the cognitive judge in order to penetrate the deep interior was an appropriate pathway. Robert Ellwood summarizes the basic presupposition of the movement: "Reality is known by unleashing subjectivity to its highest ratio."[18] His comments vividly reiterate the epistemological dynamic that "truth," which had become synonymous with "meaning," was intrinsically linked with inner experience.

For those youth who were separated from Haight-Ashbury or Greenwich Village by distance or life experience, this philosophical approach radically penetrated the music of rock icons like the Beatles, so that the ideology was carried on the wings of what was simultaneously a pop music

---

† The term "peak experience" was coined by psychologist and author Abraham Maslow to describe the cognitive happenings associated with moments of "highest happiness and fulfillment." These moments were very flexible, encompassing experiences that were mystical, creative, aesthetic, athletic, orgasmic, etc.

phenomenon. Perhaps for the first time on this scale, pop culture became an incredibly powerful and pervasive vehicle for an ideology and philosophical worldview, and few were isolated from its influence. Even if they were not die-hard advocates of drug culture, the youth culture began to feel an alliance with the attitudes of the psychedelic movement, taking a definitive turn away from the modern worldview of their parents' generation. "The drug experience was the sacrament which bound together the new culture with a sense of community. It gave them the experience of a reality seen as supremely valid, even by those who rarely or never took drugs: a timeless now, infinitely deep and rich in texture, ineffable glory."[19] This underlying philosophy effectively penetrated youth culture as a whole. With the weakness of the political climate and the crumbling modern paradigm, the underlying message of the psychedelic culture found a generation eager for its influence.

The kind of existence that the psychedelic culture inevitably created was radically destabilizing. There were a plethora of so-called pathways to reality, but many of them turned out confusing and empty in the final analysis, and the lifestyle of the drug addict was one that typically resulted in even greater despair and destruction. Although drugs had been popularized as a means to apprehend deeper truth and meaning, the addiction that invariably followed led not to spiritual fulfillment, but to deeper disillusionment and greater existential crisis.[20] Ellwood argues that by 1968, the psychedelic culture had begun to burn out under the weight of its own excesses,[21] leaving many desperate young people hungry for a spiritual experience that would actually result in a degree of inner harmony. They craved experience, yearning for something real that was powerful and transcendent, but also ultimately satisfying on the deepest level. Into the political and cultural malaise of the 1970s came a strangely congruent and profoundly romantic reply: the Jesus movement.

The Jesus Movement

Although the psychedelic culture could not provide the answers that it promised, it did significantly predispose its adherents for the spiritual movement that was to follow. On so many levels, the individuals set adrift in their search for reality through experience were primed and prepared for the Jesus movement. The shift from an experience of the inner self to an experience of God was not a far leap, as the epistemological premises were basically the same, and the locus of investigation and transformation was still the inner self. Central to this shift of attention, however, was the overwhelming thirst for experience that pervaded the worldview of the psychedelic culture.

Experience was still a profound avenue to truth and meaning in their worldview, but the object of the Jesus people's pursuit now became a personal experience with Jesus as God.[22] However, truth was no longer solely about meaning, but about a real person, Jesus, who lived and died as an objective reality. There was a degree of authenticity in this experience that could not be matched by any chemical or pseudo-spiritual substitute. They could identify with this narrative, as it reflected their own sense of cultural alienation, and they could validate Jesus' experiences—a marginalized, splinter narrative of Judaism—as truth.

Moreover, those involved in the drug culture had experienced the overwhelming power of drug interactions. They craved the same kind of "high" experience, the same vital empowerment, and the Jesus they experienced in the power of the Holy Spirit was a viable and less destructive answer. Enroth et al. remark "when those in the counter-culture talk about being turned on to Jesus, they are referring to an emotional experience that, for them, has striking similarity to the emotional experience induced by drugs."[23] The difference between a mystical experience and a psychedelic one is not really a long trip. This comparison is not intended to call into question the Jesus people's authenticity as believers, as if they simply sought Jesus as another kind of trip, but rather to illustrate their predisposition towards experience as an authoritative form of knowledge. Armed with a basic sincerity and radical commitment to a given worldview, the Jesus people experienced a vitality of transformation that was powerful and life-altering, and the movement seemed to take the country by storm. The enthusiasm of the psychedelic culture was easily translated into the vigor of the Jesus movement, but several other factors were of considerable importance in the transition.

First, converts into the Jesus movement were already convinced by their vivid experiences with mind-altering chemicals that spiritual issues were real, intense, powerful and subversive. The anti-supernatural bias of modernism had long ago been swept away in their worldview, and so there was little or no cognitive transition needed to understand and accept the primary spiritual reality of Christianity.[24] Indeed, those drug addicts who had experienced bad trips were especially aware of spiritual forces, having witnessed phantasmagoric delusions first hand, and perhaps this is—at least in part—why the Jesus people were always so overtly preoccupied with the demonic realm.[25]

Second, the plurality of pathways to truth exalted by the psychedelic culture made the "One Way" movement particularly attractive to a movement burned out on existential dead-ends. Ellwood notes:

> The unconverted life is described as confused by countless options, symbols, and alluring paths. It is the world of innumerable beckoning experiences, too many for any one person to taste, except perhaps by living for a new one every day—drugs, easy sex, political involvement, overadvertized possessions and products…The Jesus movement's clear, direct answer to all this is the slogan 'One Way!' One shining alternative in the midst of all the confusing phantasmagoria stands out—Jesus.[26]

The "One Way" dynamic was a basic reaction against pluralism, and it was inherently appealing for its simplicity. The Bible provided a one-stop shopping center of truth for many of the complicated questions of existence.[27] The many confusing alternatives offered by society were replaced by a simple plan of salvation.[28] Instead of many roads to truth, there was One Way, and it was both objectively true and existentially powerful. While the collapse of objective truth had led to existential burn-out, the reconstruction of truth in the affirmation of Jesus and Christianity still allowed the Jesus people to pursue a powerful and transcendent experience.

Interestingly, the swing of the cultural pendulum resulted in a religious movement that was profoundly exclusive in its perspective, unlike the mainline denominations, and quite unlike postmodernism in that one aspect.

The boldness of the Jesus movement in proclaiming hellfire for those who did not accept the One Way did not fit the perspective that had been proposed by the psychedelic culture, although it did reflect the reactionary nature of a cultural pendulum swing. Predictably, the enthusiasm of the first movement was translated into a religious vigor that was equally enthusiastic, though deeply sincere. As a result, the passion of preachers like musician Keith Green was found by many to be both winsome and frightening in its enthusiastic, yet exclusive appeal. Even his record label struggled with some of his lyrics that seemed to press passion into extremes.

Pentecostalism

Third, and most importantly, their epistemology of experience was completely coherent with the basic approach of the Pentecostal movement, to which they gravitated. The Pentecostal church, which had existed for probably a century in one realization or another, emphasized a visceral experience of the power of God through the Holy Spirit. Conversion was accompanied by a powerful and tangible manifestation of the Holy Spirit in the sign gifts of tongues, healing and prophecy, and worshiping God meant continuing to experience the power and presence of His Spirit in the worshiping assembly. While Scripture was exalted, the spontaneous work of the Holy Spirit, particularly through the experience of tongues, was equally so. Signs and wonders, a hallmark of the Pentecostal movement, were particularly persuasive evidence of the power and presence of God to those who had already experienced the power of both narcotic and spiritual forces. For those with an epistemology of experience, these spiritual manifestations were undeniable.

In addition, the ecstatic nature of the worship style reinforced the value and attraction of a mystical and emotional worship experience. The Vineyard churches, although not Pentecostal per se, were a significant, charismatic outgrowth of the Jesus movement, and actually grew out of a Quaker worship experience.[29] Quaker theology and practice emphasize the "Inner Light" of the Holy Spirit, and make inner experience the most authoritative revelation and guide in the believer's faith and practice. "Friends generally believe that first-hand knowledge of God is only possible through that which is experienced, or inwardly revealed to the individual human being through the working of God's quickening Spirit."[30] Indeed, Quakers actually place inner experience on a higher revelation than the Bible, claiming that "divine revelation is not confined to the past. The same Holy Spirit which has inspired the scriptures in the past can inspire living believers centuries later."[31] While Quaker theology was not necessarily wholly imported into the Vineyard movement, one can see how this approach was particularly consonant with the values of the psychedelic culture and the Jesus people. Thus, a high value was placed upon inner experience over revealed truth as an authoritative form of knowledge.

Furthermore, there was already a basic anti-intellectual strain in the Pentecostal movement, suggesting that rational processes were somehow antithetical to the workings of the Spirit. This tendency was not unlike the same tendency in the psychedelic culture, which advocated subverting the reason and intellect in order to arrive at a more profound experience or state of higher consciousness. Both movements understood the cognitive processes to be essentially inferior to the power and transcendence of mystical, spiritual forces, which is a classic romantic response. However, the tendency in the Pentecostal worldview could also be to see reason as the doorway of the devil. Ellwood narrates a first-hand example in which the speaker asserts that the devil finds entrance into the individual through the natural mind and thoughts.[32] While this is surely an extreme example, it does illumine the tendency within the Pentecostalism of the period to denigrate the intellect and the rational processes, seeing them as a barrier to the sometimes non-rational movements of the Spirit.

As a result, the basic anti-intellectualism of the Jesus people, which grew out of their psychedelic subculture, predisposed them towards Pentecostal denominations. "It is transforming power, not rational answers, they want...those in the Jesus movement have found, or rather have been given, transforming power and absoluteness through the old American evangelical and Pentecostal lineages."[33] While both movements were reacting to different tendencies in culture, both found themselves in a position that involved an anti-intellectual and/or hyper-experiential epistemology.

Finally, the Pentecostal movement featured expressions of worship, particularly in music, that were highly consonant with the experiences of the psychedelic culture. Music was an essential piece of this countercultural movement, allowing a popular expression of its fundamental ideologies. For many in this movement, music was the medium by which they were to experience a higher consciousness, and would allow them, in the words of Jim Morrison, to "break on through to the other side."‡ Music is always an essential piece of a people group's identity, particularly in countercultural movements, for it expresses their passion in a depth of manner that nothing else can. The importance of the rock and folk music of the psychedelic culture for its own adherents cannot be underestimated, and neither can the resulting music and worship styles of the Jesus movement. These musicians brought their music cultures together with their Christian faith, and wrote songs that reflected their own cultural experience, just as Martin Luther did in his own day.[34]

Missionaries who are ethnomusicologists* recognize the importance of writing new Christian songs in the musical idioms of the cultures they strive to reach, rather than simply translating Christian hymns for use in worship. Ethnomusicologist Tom Avery calls the primary musical idiom of a culture its "heart music," and comments that it is a "gateway into the heart of a people."[35] He further remarks that "using the heart music of a people can be a way of connecting the gospel message with the authority of their ancient traditions."[36] This is exactly the situation that occurred with the Jesus people, who became indigenous missionaries by virtue of their music connection.

Many older Evangelicals are able to identify with this concept of heart music, as they often find the hymns with which they were raised to connect with them on a level that can never be matched with newer,

---

‡ Even the name of his band, "the Doors," was borrowed from a Blake poem of the romantic period, stating that "when the doors of perception are cleansed, man will see things as they truly are, infinite." David V. Erdman, ed., <u>The Poetry and Prose of William Blake</u> (Garden City, NY: Doubleday & Company, Inc., 1970).

* An "ethnomusicologist" is a missionary who specializes in learning the indigenous music of a particular people group in order to incarnate the gospel into their cultural languages.

contemporary music. Hymns are their heart music. One encounters the same phenomenon every year at Christmas, when believers and unbelievers alike cling to hymn-like Christmas carols that they recall from their youth. Christmas carols are the heart music for a majority of people in the Western culture. In the same manner, the need for heart music caused the Jesus people to write worship music that connected with their own cultural styles, constituting such a huge piece of their identity.

The jump from rock culture to the Pentecostal worship culture was actually a rather short step. People who were culturally geared to creative freedom of expression began to write about their new experiences with Jesus, and icons of the Christian rock movement like Larry Norman and Keith Green were born. These individuals flowed in and out of the local church in an organic manner, and Christian worship labels like Maranatha were formed under the auspices of large, local churches.[37] A repertoire of praise and worship music began to be written that would radically infiltrate and alter the future of Christian hymnody and worship practice.

Even the rock concerts of these musicians began to feature characteristics of worship assemblies, including the use of worship repertoire and group participation. The context and content of these worship experiences were highly charged, intensely personal and deeply emotional, and many of the first praise songs were simply direct settings of the Psalms. Moreover, the converts from the Jesus movement carried their Pentecostal traditions into the music that they penned, as well as the worship experiences that they enjoyed. One of the fundamental characteristics of the Pentecostal worship time was that the worshiper encountered the real presence of God in a supremely immanent manner as he or she engaged in praise and worship.[38] While this statement might not seem radical or profound today, it was a wholly different paradigm from most Evangelical worship in the 70s. Worship, for those who formed the Jesus movement, was essentially an encounter with God, an experience of His presence.

CHAPTER 4: THE POSTMODERN WORSHIPER

The Postmodern Worshiper

Evangelical worship in the new millennium is the heir of the Jesus movement legacy, particularly as it has been influenced by the Pentecostal approach to worship as an experience of the power and presence of God. Pentecostalism itself is considered to be the "fastest-growing and most important religious movement of the 20th century," and Leonard Sweet credits this growth to the manner in which the church's basic philosophy connects with the postmodern's desire for experiential knowledge.[39] It is no wonder that the Evangelical church as a whole has been slowly adopting the values and approach of the Jesus movement, particularly as it stands in direct lineage from some of these original founders of Christian praise and worship music.

Indeed, the most dramatic manner in which this movement has impacted Evangelical worship is the degree to which Evangelical songwriters and worship leaders of succeeding generations have adopted their repertoire and basic philosophy of music. The praise and worship material from the 1970s generation have become the "standards" in Evangelical worship today, just as the hymns of Martin Luther became the standards of the church throughout the history of Protestantism. Moreover, their style of songwriting, which highlights the experience of the worshiper, has been assimilated into the mindset and approach of worship composers. While there are certainly other historical currents that have influenced this paradigm shift in Evangelicalism—like the manner in which the Vineyard churches have committed themselves to fashioning new music—the energy and enthusiasm of the Jesus movement basically catalyzed and empowered all that was to follow. Thus, viewing worship as an experience of God's presence is now becoming central to the Evangelical paradigm of worship across a wide range of denominations.

The emphases of postmodernism, particularly an epistemology of experience, are completely consistent with the move towards worship as an experience of the presence of God. What the Jesus people brought to Evangelical worship was intricately related to the postmodern culture in which they had been saturated, and those cultural influences have continued to penetrate Evangelical worship ever since. Under the growing influences of the Jesus movement, the postmodern worshiper was born. The influences of this culture do not necessarily predispose the postmodern worshipers to be any more or less biblical than their modern forebears. However, the philosophy of this work has been to uncover the cultural and historical influences of the current Evangelical philosophy of worship, so that no cultural paradigm is uncritically accepted without first evaluating the extent of its penetration by secular culture.

While we are undeniably products of our own cultures, it is essential to understand both the positive and negative aspects of that influence, so that we can harmonize with the positive ones, and reject those that are negative. In order to do so, it will be necessary to evaluate this postmodern or neo-romantic worship paradigm in practice, as well as to describe the existing modern paradigm as a foil for the discussion. This task will be the focus of the next two chapters.

---

[1] Robert E. Webber, Ancient-Future Faith: Rethinking Evangelicalism for a Postmodern World (Grand Rapids: Baker Books, 1999), 21.
[2] Barbara Hargrove, Reformation of the Holy, 281; quoted in Ronald M. Enroth, Edward E. Ericson, Jr., and C. Breckinridge Peters, The Jesus People: Old-Time Religion in the Age of Aquarius (Grand Rapids: William B. Eerdmans Publishing Company, 1972), 224.
[3] Middleton and Walsh, Truth is Stranger Than It Used to Be, 34.
[4] Sting, "Russians," published by Magnetic Publishing Ltd. (PRS), represented by Regatta Music, administered by Irving Music, Inc. (BMI) in the U.S. and Canada.
[5] Robert S. Ellwood, Jr., One Way: The Jesus Movement and its Meaning (Englewood Cliffs, NJ: Prentice-Hall, Inc., 1973), 12.
[6] Enroth, Ericson, and Peters, The Jesus People: Old-Time Religion in the Age of Aquarius, 165.
[7] Ellwood, One Way: The Jesus Movement and its Meaning, 11.
[8] Enroth, Ericson, and Peters, The Jesus People: Old-Time Religion in the Age of Aquarius, 165.
[9] Ibid., 226.
[10] Tim Riley, Tell Me Why (New York: Alfred A. Knopf, 1988), 199.
[11] Lennon/McCartney, "Tomorrow Never Knows," 1966 EMI Records Ltd.
[12] Ellwood, One Way: The Jesus Movement and its Meaning, 11.
[13] Enroth, Ericson, and Peters, The Jesus People: Old-Time Religion in the Age of Aquarius, 226.
[14] Abraham H. Maslow, Toward a Psychology of Being, 2d ed. (New York: D. Van Nostrand Company, 1968), 73.
[15] Ellwood, One Way: The Jesus Movement and its Meaning, 9.
[16] Walter Houston Clark, et al., Religious Experience: Its Nature and Function in the Human Psyche (Springfield, IL: Charles C. Thomas Publisher, 1973), 5-6.
[17] Ellwood, One Way: The Jesus Movement and its Meaning, 16.
[18] Ibid., 8.
[19] Ibid., 5.

[20] Enroth, Ericson, and Peters, The Jesus People: Old-Time Religion in the Age of Aquarius, 228.

[21] Ellwood, One Way: The Jesus Movement and its Meaning, 18.

[22] Enroth, Ericson, and Peters, The Jesus People: Old-Time Religion in the Age of Aquarius, 164.

[23] Ibid.

[24] Ibid., 201.

[25] Ibid., 202.

[26] Ellwood, One Way: The Jesus Movement and its Meaning, 54-55.

[27] Enroth, Ericson, and Peters, The Jesus People: Old-Time Religion in the Age of Aquarius, 162.

[28] Ibid., 224.

[29] Andy Park, To Know You More: Cultivating the Heart of the Worship Leader (Downers Grove, IL: InterVarsity Press, 2002), 248.

[30] The Religious Society of Friends Website; available from www.quaker.org; Internet; accessed 5 January 2004.

[31] Ibid.

[32] Ellwood, One Way: The Jesus Movement and its Meaning, 79-80.

[33] Ibid., 133.

[34] Andy Park, To Know You More: Cultivating the Heart of the Worship Leader, 242.

[35] Tom Avery, "Music of the Heart: The Power of Indigenous Worship in Reaching Unreached Peoples with the Gospel," Mission Frontiers Bulletin 18, no. 5-8 (1996): 14.

[36] Ibid.

[37] Andy Park, To Know You More: Cultivating the Heart of the Worship Leader, 247.

[38] Sheldon Sorge, "The Surging Spirit and Reformed Worship: Liturgical Implications for Pentecostal-Presbyterian Dialogue" (paper presented to the Office of Theology and Worship Pastor/Theologian Consultation, San Antonio, 28 February – 1 March, 2000, pg. 6); quoted in Robb Redman, The Great Worship Awakening (San Francisco: Jossey-Bass, 2002), 42.

[39] Leonard Sweet, Soul Tsunami (Grand Rapids: Zondervan, 1999), 208.

CHAPTER 5

TWO WORSHIP PARADIGMS (PART I)

"I wasn't able to worship"

As a worship leader, I find it interesting to inquire of people leaving a worship gathering their impressions of the service. It is fascinating to hear the reactions—what things grabbed their attention, what things were particularly meaningful, and what things irritated them. While there are typically a whole host of responses, there is one comment in particular that I have heard on a number of occasions, an elusive expression that has always intrigued me: "I wasn't able to worship." From the way this comment is phrased, it sounds like the worshiper was somehow actively prohibited from participating by some external force. Is the act of worship some feat to be accomplished that depends upon a variety of external factors or conditions? "I was not able to worship" might as well be "I was not able to climb Everest."

Can the choice to worship be prevented by something outside of oneself? Is the activity so outside of the worshiper's control? Can one be prevented from worshiping, when worship simply involves the choice to magnify the Lord, and lift up a sacrifice of praise? These questions betray the fact that I was raised with a well-developed worship paradigm, and in my formative years developed discrete expectations regarding what I should "experience" in a worship setting. A worship service was not so much an intimate interaction with God, but more of a concert of praise that we chose to enact. As long as I was physically present at the gathering, only a natural disaster or some other activity-stopping cataclysm could prevent this program from taking place. The experience of worship was not something mystical that happened inside of me, something that might be inhibited or derailed, but rather a series of external, "corporate" or group activities in which I participated.

Conversely, worshipers in a "neo-romantic" paradigm expect an inner experience of worship as they offer praise to God, an internal interaction with His special revealed or "manifest" presence. They think of worship as a mystical, supernatural "conversation" with God, in which they are able to express their deepest thoughts and emotions to Him as they offer a sacrifice of praise. They hope for a corresponding sense of His blessing in their worship, an emotional response of deep satisfaction—like David felt—in their souls. The worship service is expected to enable this deeply mystical and subjective interaction. With these expectations in mind, the comment "I wasn't able to worship" makes a great deal more sense. With such subtle, specific and profound expectations for worship, a worshiper in this paradigm could easily be preventing from worshiping for any number of reasons.

I will label this approach a neo-romantic or experience-oriented worship paradigm as it emphasizes many of the romantic values that were explored in the previous chapters, including a much greater reliance on an epistemology of experience. While the neo-romantic approach to worship cannot simply be equated with postmodern culture, the experiential values of this paradigm are still particularly enticing to the postmodern worshiper. Hence, I will tend to refer to the neo-romantic paradigm as an offshoot or a subset of 20th and 21st century postmodernism. It is rapidly replacing another approach which I will label a modern worship paradigm, as this worship orientation is typically more consistent with the modern worldview which was detailed at length in chapter two.

Of course, these are particularly broad categories, and so one always finds exceptions to the parameters or boundaries that one creates. Postmodernism has undeniable similarities to romanticism, particularly in terms of epistemology, but by no means do all individuals of postmodern leanings prefer a neo-romantic approach to worship. Individuals are still products of nature and nurture, and so may lean to one worship paradigm over another simply as a result of temperament or training. Moreover, just because someone belongs to a particular time period does not mean that he or she agrees with the prevailing worldview. Indeed, there are currents of modernism and romanticism present in any culture or time. However, it is the contention of this work that broad, gradual shifts in epistemology have resulted in correspondingly broad cultural changes, and that one of those changes has been a paradigm shift in the Evangelical approach to worship. Understanding this shift requires that one grapple with what are clear and categorical differences in expectation of worshipers on either side of the cultural chasm.

While many wage "worship wars" over the style and substance of worship, the deepest divide is an unspoken one, a rift between sets of values that are played out within these two worship paradigms. While the differences are surfaced in the worship activity itself, the underlying philosophical and categorical assumptions are not always obvious. Hence, a great deal of attention is often garnered by those changes that are only superficial to the much more basic shift. The conflict over hymns versus praise choruses, for example, is only instructive as it reveals much deeper differences, differences that are emblematic of a completely divergent worship philosophy. These chapters will attempt to describe how these two approaches contain different expectations for the worship service as well as for the personal experience of the worshiper. A clear understanding of both perspectives is essential, otherwise the paradigm-shift will be disorienting, frustrating and confusing.

The Difficulty of Definitions

In this postmodern era, placing a label on any movement and attempting to define it from an external perspective always feels a little suspicious. The intellectual stance of historian and cultural cartographer implies that one is in a position to accurately describe something from an objective perspective, and that one's evaluations are formed outside of an interpretational framework. Furthermore, it implies to the reader or listener a tacit reassurance that the writer somehow stands in a hierarchical position to his or her data. Not only is this position predictably self-selective, it is thoroughly modern. Describing data and categorizing it as a "movement" simply means that one has chosen to notice certain trends, highlighting particular details and omitting others.[1] The evolutionist will read the fossil record in a particular way, because he or she is fitting the data into his or her own peculiar paradigm, as will the "creation scientist." While I might not be able to claim absolute objectivity as an historian, however, hopefully good research and a wide cross-section of samples in this work can result in sufficient relative objectivity.

The difficulty of describing a movement is further complicated when the changes are occurring in one's own generation, for there is little hindsight to evaluate cultural and historical trends. The first chapters of this work are intended to lay as much groundwork along these lines as possible; but as these changes in Evangelical worship are currently in process, it is difficult to ascertain which ones will end up being central, and which will be peripheral. I am acutely aware that I am stretched between several different perspectives in this effort—the way things were, the way things are, and the way I think things should be—and this dilemma will certainly color my selection.

Furthermore, what this paradigm-shift exactly looks like depends upon who is describing it, and I am certainly limited by my own experience. There are incarnations of this neo-romantic approach that I have never seen, though I have witnessed quite a variety of worship experiences. Moreover, there are probably features of the modern paradigm that are skewed by my own church experience, though I was exposed to a wide cross-section of Evangelical churches in my childhood travels with my parents. Regardless, I certainly hope that I am not erecting a kind of straw man in either of these descriptions in order to immolate him with my argumentation. I would like to describe them in such a way that actual adherents to both approaches could at least own them intellectually, though I hope that both will make us all feel a little uncomfortable. While I am not unbiased, I do hope that the reader will not assume that I give unqualified support to either paradigm.

Another challenge of this undertaking has to do with defining and understanding the relationship between modernism and Evangelicalism, particularly the various strands of the Evangelical movement. While much of Evangelicalism embraced the principles of modernism and modern Christianity, Mark Oestreicher comments that other segments—specifically the

CHAPTER 5: TWO WORSHIP PARADIGMS (PART I)

African-American church—clearly did not.[2] This was certainly the case with the Pentecostal churches, whose experiential inclinations were suggested in chapter four to have made them very attractive to the Jesus movement. Modernism never defined Evangelicalism, and yet, a great majority of Evangelical churches adopted a distinctly modern approach in worship philosophy and practice. Hence, it is necessary to examine a few characteristics of the modern worship paradigm, in order to provide a foil for what will be a much lengthier discussion of the neo-romantic one.

The Modern Paradigm: Worship as Edification

An Intellectual Enactment of Praise

While the driving purpose behind the Evangelical worship service of the modern paradigm is undoubtedly to exalt the Lord, the intended result for the worshiper is probably not an experience of God's manifest presence. Instead, *the modern paradigm highlights the worshiper's edification,* and the worship service is prepared in order to accomplish this goal. This statement is not meant to suggest that an inner experience of God in worship is not edifying or transformational, nor is it intended to imply that the modern paradigm would not welcome this occurrence as a byproduct of the service. Rather, the concept of "edification" has basic cognitive overtones and suggests a pursuit of spiritual growth that is founded upon rational processes. The modern paradigm exalts reason and the intellect as the best and most reliable tools of character formation, investing more confidence in them as the viable instruments that the Holy Spirit catalyzes in the worship service.

Hence, in the modern paradigm, virtually everything that is included in the service can be understood as a method of teaching truth, connecting first and foremost with the intellect. I do not intend to take away from the fact that these services contain prayers and praises that are earnestly intended as an offering to God, an authentic sacrifice of worship, and not simply a method of transmitting doctrine to the people. However, I seek to highlight the fact that the elements of the modern service contain an inherent dual purpose as both sacrifices of praise to God and implements of edification or teaching for the believer.[3]

The philosophy behind this approach, while not unbiblical, is likewise founded upon a modern approach to knowledge and spiritual growth. For the offspring of the Enlightenment, reason is perceived as the only *reliable* way in which to know something.[4] Cognition—not sensation or vague inner experience—yields true beliefs. Moreover, this perspective assumes that "truth"—specifically the objective reality of God's revealed will—accurately perceived, results in authentic inner and outer change, i.e., being and doing something new. Thus, the *content* of the worship material is of the utmost importance, greater than whether or not the worshiper felt that he or she had "experienced" God, because truth, rightly understood, will change lives.[5] Edification is the name of the game.

The spiritual journey of the Christian is to grow in the knowledge of God and in obedience to His will, and these changes happen by hearing, understanding and practicing truth, a process that is basically rational and objective. That is the essence of a modern approach to spiritual growth: people become more like God by finding out from His written Word what exactly He expects of them, and then doing it. Truth must be transmitted so that the congregant can comprehend and comply, and the worship service becomes the flagship event in which this critical information is authoritatively disseminated.

Experience—meaning emotion, intuition, inner sensation, or any kind of non-rational perception—is not viewed as a reliable source of the knowledge of God in this modern paradigm; in fact, it is more likely viewed as a highly questionable approach to faith. Experience is clearly meaningful in confirming knowledge, but the intellect always precedes inner experience in the acquisition of beliefs. Experience follows intellect, if at all, and so the major emphasis of the worship service is placed upon informing the mind. Robert Webber comments on this philosophy: "I question the Enlightenment adage that a person arrives at experience through knowledge. This view has the cart before the horse and has resulted in a highly intellectualized worship which appears closed to any of God's actions other than the enlightenment of the mind."[6]

This assertion is not intended to suggest that worship in the modern paradigm is highly "intellectual," as if all modern worshipers are rocket scientists, nor does it imply that experience has no function in the modern worship service. Rather, experience is simply not endowed with the same authority as reason or the intellect. Christians are edified through their rational apprehension, not through their inner experiences, and the worship service provides the appropriate venue for that to occur. Although not the supreme purpose of the worship service, cognitive "edification" is at least an overriding goal.

Music as Teaching

This philosophy plays itself out in several ways. First of all, the music involved in the service is evaluated first and foremost on its *content*, and is programmed in order to teach or reinforce something about God or theology for the worshipers. The affect of the music in relationship to the worshiper's experience is a secondary consideration. This is a broad generalization, of course, and certainly not absolute in every instance of modern worship, but consider the data. The music in a modern service is typically chosen with the express purpose of highlighting the sermon. It is included in a given service because of its content, and its thematic unity with the teaching, the prime instance of edification in the service. The teaching within the service is the controlling factor, and music is incorporated based upon its coherence with the whole.

Moreover, the music of this paradigm is usually hymns and gospel songs, with a smattering of praise choruses in recent years. While hymns are frequently poetic and poignant creations, they often tend to specialize in content, highlighting much more theology than other types of worship music. In generations past, hymns have even been employed as a type of catechism, utilized to teach people the truths of the faith.[7] This does not mean that hymns as a genre are distinctively modern in approach, any more than praise choruses are purely postmodern. Arguably, the composition of hymns has followed the trends of culture, with the works of composers like Wesley following the more neo-romantic trends of the period.[8] Rather, I am suggesting that hymns as a form have become a beloved tool of the modern paradigm because they are able to convey content more effortlessly than other forms. Their lack of syncopation, simple strophic structure and on-the-beat melody lines allow the lyrics to carry much more complex content, well serving the didactic approach.

One notices that the function of participation in the service is different as well, not geared primarily to facilitate an experience of God, but to reinforce some fundamental truth for the people. Singing in these services is as much about communicating correct theologies to *one another* as it is about offering praise to God, for the service is heavily focused on enriching the mind. Worship leader Craig Allen points out:

> In these traditional settings the principal function of music was presentational. Music was for the edification of believers....The lyrics were intended to inculcate doctrine into the lives of the singers. Hymns were not sung so much to God as to one another.[9]

"Presentational" is an accurate word, as the music—whether congregational hymns, choir anthems or special music—is carefully chosen to "present" something true about God to the people, which they in turn offer back to Him as praise. The worshiper's experience of God in the service is not really an explicit part of the equation.

Although proponents would respond that God is thus carefully kept "the subject and object" of worship in this approach,[10] the result of this philosophy is that the worshiper has to make his or her own point of personal or experiential connection with the music. Marva Dawn gives this feature a slightly different spin, noting "the advantage of texts that focus on objective truths instead of subjective feelings is that we bring to them our own honest emotions."[11] A different perspective on this approach, however, is that the worshiper's experiential or inner connection with God is intended to be a byproduct of what is first and foremost an intellectual exercise.

In this paradigm, the methodology is to present truth about God in an appealing package, because the assumption is that the heart will doubtless be captivated by the content. Target the mind with truth about God, and the worshiper's experience will be drawn along in its wake. This approach makes sense when one views reason and the intellect as the only reliable pathway to knowledge. When worship is about edification, then the doctrinal content of the worship material—particularly the fact that it focuses on "truth" about God and not on the worshiper's emotions or experiences—is critical to the entire paradigm.

The Path of Spiritual Growth

Obviously, the topic of how spiritual growth occurs is much broader than the scope of this work, although it will be addressed again in later chapters. What is the interaction of the mind, emotions and volition in authentic heart change? Must the intellect have supremacy over the other two resources for change to happen? Do emotions or experience naturally follow cognition in the process of change? As I have suggested, the modern paradigm has some of these assumptions regarding spiritual growth, and they influence the paradigm of worship in a broad manner. However, they flow as much from Enlightenment principles as they do from biblical ones, and subtly differentiate this paradigm from other approaches more than one might expect. Indeed, the differences in how these paradigms understand spiritual growth—particularly in terms of epistemology—are not incidental to how they approach worship as a whole; rather, they are fundamental to the entire conversation.

In contrast to the modern understanding, perhaps the mind, emotions and volition must function *in tandem* for an individual to be deeply and profoundly changed? Indeed, some would claim that change which does not penetrate the heart—meaning the whole of the human constitution—is not authentic change at all. Perhaps the inner experiences of sensation, emotion or non-rational perception are more fundamental than we might think? Does the Holy Spirit initially work through the intellect alone in transforming the individual, or does He sometimes target the emotions first? Often it would seem that the emotions must first be affected in order for the mind to be opened to change, at least as one surveys a variety of conversion experiences. If this is the case, then it might suggest that the path of spiritual growth is actually from the emotions through the intellect to the volition, which is critically different from what I have described as a modern approach.

Obviously, temperament plays into this discussion as well. A longer book on the process of spiritual growth would include a lengthy discussion of personality types, and how they influence our approach to the world, let alone knowledge. Myers-Briggs has well documented how some individuals lead with "feelings" and others with "thinking." Undoubtedly, there are those who primarily approach spiritual growth either with their emotions or their intellect in both of these worship settings. The point, however, is that the approach and assumptions of these two paradigms broadly diverge along the lines of how spiritual growth happens, and that it is a bedrock issue. The choices that are made in worship are only superficial to what is a mammoth issue hidden below the waterline.

A regrettable outcome of the modern paradigm is that the driving goal of edification sometimes can tend to exalt reason and the intellect but disregard the importance of the emotions to spiritual growth. If the rational processes are the primary receptors of the Holy Spirit's activity, then the direction of spiritual growth in the modern paradigm could be described as through the intellect into the emotions. Given that the worship service is largely about teaching, then it makes sense to center the main substance of the service, including the music, on the intellect. Unfortunately, the material can tend to focus on content at the expense of the worshiper's experience. The worshipers' emotions can be neglected by the service, with the result that they become accustomed to praising God with their minds, and little else.[†]

Unfortunately, intellectualized worship does not engage the whole person, tending to bifurcate the self into the intellect and emotions, and missing what is really the deeper essence of spiritual transformation. While some claim that a focus on feelings in worship limits the development of spiritual

---

[†] Certainly this situation differs from church to church in the Evangelical world, and even from service to service. My point, however, is that the philosophy of the modern paradigm by default can tend to highlight the mind and marginalize the emotions.

character,[12] the absence of vital engagement with the emotions also misses one very critical area of spiritual growth. Marva Dawn does appeal for a balance when she comments "we must avoid the dangers both of intellectualism and of emotionalism. To focus on the mind alone won't engage people's will and heart so that they act on what they know. To focus exclusively on training the emotions encourages faith without substance."[13] However, the balance of material in the modern paradigm often tends to marginalize, rather than target the emotions.

One can understand why an excessive focus on emotions is considered a little suspicious in this paradigm. Recall from chapter two that in the modern conception, the passions and the "deep interior" of the individual were pictured as unpredictable, fickle and even misleading, and so inner experiences were not really considered a viable path to knowledge. Dawn, who leans toward something of a modern approach, writes "since feelings are so easily swayed by the circumstances of the moment, they cannot be reliable guides for knowing God. Yet they are important for our response to God and cannot be repressed, ignored, or forced."[14] Rereading the last four words of this quote, I am struck by how emotions are almost made to sound like an annoying habit that one can't quite shake. Her book, *Reaching Out Without Dumbing Down,* has plenty of important things to say about worship, but the title reveals her essential orientation: worship must have a high intellectual value, meaning a high quotient of content, or it is not optimal. Indeed, I have heard the same criticism from the mouths of myriad modern worshipers. In a modern paradigm, content is everything because the intellect is the bulls-eye.

The Sermon as the Goal of the Service

The philosophy of edification over experience plays itself out in a second significant manner. Because edification is a primary goal of the worship service, the entire structure of the service is geared towards the sermon, which is understandably perceived as the pinnacle, weekly event of edification. The message is the main reason for the worship service, because that is the venue in which the minister opens the Bible for the people. He is that preeminent, authoritative figure, the repository of knowledge that figured so prominently in my description of the modern worldview. The minister is supposed to experience God first-hand through the Word, and he explicates his "contact" with God each week during the worship service. It is the primary venue of edification for the worshiper, and the authoritative forum in which he or she comes to know God. Everything else in the worship service, particularly the music, is a preliminary to the sermon. Thus, the service is structured in order to highlight the text and themes of the message—the main content of the service—and to prepare for the central moment of edification that the minister will deliver. If the worship is primarily about edifying by engaging the intellect, then it makes sense to highlight the sermon.

As Webber comments, "Many pastors turned worship into teaching."[15] Instead of an experience of worship in which edification is occurring, the entire service easily begins to revolve around teaching, including the prayer and praise elements. This dynamic is often explicitly played out in the pastoral prayer. At the end of the sermon, the pastor typically will pray to close his teaching. More often than not, however, the prayer is a summary of the message, and not actually a conversation with God at all. The pastor has taken an element of worship and condensed it to teaching. Instead of communing with God, he is passively communicating to the people, "Here is what you need to take away from this message!" Growing up, we used to joke about one of our pastors who would even give the announcements in his pastoral prayer. "Lord, please bless the men's prayer breakfast that will take place at 7:30 this Saturday morning in the Fellowship Hall." He reinforces the idea that worship is people-directed, an element of teaching, and not an authentic interaction with God.

Furthermore, this philosophy of worship also tends to insure that congregational involvement and participation in the service will be much lower than in churches with an experience-oriented paradigm. If the worship service is a complete program that the church staff presents for the onlookers, and the first-hand experience of God is not a primary component of that assembly, then there is much less motivation to participate in the singing or the liturgy. The responsibility of the worshiper is to listen and be edified, because experiencing God in this setting comes through hearing and understanding the proclamation of His Word, not through singing or raising one's hands. When worship is seen as teaching, then the worshiper becomes a student, and so the task of the student becomes taking down notes from the lecture. They are here to receive instruction, and that comes from the preacher, not from the worship and music. The emphasis is on what the pastor will say, not what the people will do, and this limited focus tends to discourage participation. The worshiper easily devolves into a spectator. Webber continues "whenever I worship or speak at a church where the pastor is the focal point, I feel dominated and stifled."[16] In this paradigm, the main task of the worshiper is to receive instruction, and so participation can become particularly passive.

I realize that this point will be controversial with those readers who support this modern perspective, because this is probably not the manner in which the paradigm was intended to operate. Presumably, practitioners of the modern paradigm hope that presenting truth in an arresting manner will engage the mind and then penetrate the heart. Perhaps this kind of participation does happen on an internal level. However, the expectation of experiencing God's presence seems to invigorate the participation of the congregation in a much more dynamic manner. As someone who leads worship around the country and in a variety of settings, I have witnessed this dynamic work out in practice time and again. I have even seen it in churches that have both a "traditional" and a "contemporary" service, one immediately after the other, where each service tacitly pursues a different paradigm of worship. I have seen it in my own church as well, which leans towards a modern approach.

The sum of congregational participation—singing, clapping, praying out loud, etc.—in churches that major in an experience-oriented approach is astoundingly higher, because the underlying philosophy *by definition* requires the involvement of the worshiper. Edification or instruction as a goal of the service only requires that one listen or read, whereas an experiential approach demands that one participate in a much more extroverted manner. Unfortunately, the participation of the worshipers in a modern service can easily become passive and introverted, with little external engagement, because their worship philosophy can lend itself to that result.

A One-Way Interaction

Not only is worship about edification in this paradigm, it can become a one-way interaction in which the worshipers expect to bless God with their sacrifice of praise, but do not necessarily anticipate a blessing from God in exchange. The suggestion that someone might approach worship with an expectation of gain, positioning themselves to receive a blessing that rightly ought to be offered to God, seems rather utilitarian, more than a little self-centered, and less than pious from this perspective. Although God certainly blesses true worshipers, whether of a modern or neo-romantic approach, this kind of expectation in worship is often distasteful to the modern worshiper, and smacks of narcissism. Dawn, incorporating the remarks of Leander Keck in her argument, illustrates this persuasion: "Since the worship of God is an end in itself, 'making worship useful destroys it, because this introduces an ulterior motive for praise. And ulterior motives mean manipulation, taking charge of the relationship, thereby turning the relation between Creator and creation upside down.'"[17] For many modern worshipers, expectations of blessing or *pleasure* in worship compromise the purity of that worship.

This philosophy is more "modern" than one might realize, having directly descended from Enlightenment values. John Piper points to the teaching of Immanuel Kant in this regard, who affirmed that an action is moral "only if one has no desire to perform it, but performs it out of a sense of duty and derives no benefit from it of any sort, neither material nor spiritual."[18] Receiving a blessing from worshiping God, in a purely modern conception, would seem to make it "immoral" in a philosophical sense. Certainly this application of Kant's characterization is an extreme one, for no modern worshipers would find the reception of a blessing "immoral." However, it does explain why modern worshipers highlight *honoring* God, but are sometimes puzzled by the process of *delighting* in Him. The modern worshiper usually emphasizes that we primarily come to "give unto the Lord" in the worship service, rather than to receive. "Reciprocal blessing" is not an idea that the modern worshiper easily entertains.

CHAPTER 5: TWO WORSHIP PARADIGMS (PART I)

In the modern paradigm, worship is a sacrifice of praise *intended not for the people but for God to experience*, just as he had received the sacrifices of the Israelites in the Old Testament generation. It would be considered somewhat inappropriate to expect a corresponding blessing, because worship is about blessing God. Any sense that the worship has become about the worshiper and not about God will become a problem for many of the modern paradigm. This explains in part why they are often the ones who are most sensitive to the use or overuse of first person pronouns in the worship repertoire. Any derived benefit from the worship service is considered highly suspect; any sense that the worshiper takes something away from the worship service borders on impiety. As strange as it may seem, I have seen this dynamic play out in practice again and again.

Unfortunately, there is a significant down side to this understanding. While this dynamic certainly differs from place to place, I have found that the worship service of the modern paradigm is sometimes not characterized by the same sense of joy, excitement, expectation and anticipation as in an experience-oriented service. Indeed, it can sometimes come to reflect more of a sense of duty and obligation, at least as I perceived it.[19] While I do not desire to generalize from my experiences or preferences, I can meaningfully comment on what I have seen in practice over a swath of congregations, including my own. While this certainly differs from congregation to congregation, there is sometimes much less expectation of pleasure on the worshiper's part, and for some, a lackluster sense of delighting in God.[20] Perhaps there is even a perfunctory or transactional sense to worship in these settings, for God receives the praise due Him, and the worshiper acknowledges the gift of grace already received. As glum as it may sound, it is an understandable result of a philosophy that can err on the side of denying benefit to the worshiper.

As might be expected in a one-way spiritual interaction, there is also little or no expectation that God will communicate in the service, except through the preaching and the hearing of the written Word. There are certainly many factors that might contribute to this attitude, some theological and some cultural. If an individual believes that signs and wonders are best relegated to the New Testament era, then his or her expectations for the service will be radically different. Of greater concern, however, is the fact that there has been a palpable anti-supernatural bias pervading much Evangelical worship, which seems to stem from the same current in modernism. Webber explains: "Conservative intellectuals adopted the Enlightenment method of science, reason, and evidence as they set out to prove their faith. 'This is a supernatural world,' they said, 'but because God does not intervene in the world today, we do not look for anything supernatural to happen in worship.'"[21] While Webber might be oversimplifying the issue, his application is still well taken. If there is little or no expectation of tangible supernatural activity in a worship service, then worshipers will tend to stop looking and listening for it.

As a result, the Holy Spirit can seem a veritable non-entity in many Evangelical churches, along with any expectation of supernatural phenomena occurring in the service. Clearly this condition excludes charismatic churches on the whole, whose preoccupation with experience was shown to align them much more with a neo-romantic paradigm. In non-charismatic churches, there is less attention given to the moving of the Spirit in the service, and virtually no spontaneity in response to His activity. Indeed, active listening for God, like certain Quaker churches pursue, falls outside of this paradigm for obvious reasons.[22] Exercises like waiting on God or listening for the Spirit in an active manner would seem nonsensical, because God's voice emanates from His Word. The "listening" that one pursues in this paradigm is largely connected to the reading and exposition of the Word, and so the experience of God easily can become correspondingly cognitive.[23] For all practical purposes, the pastor's voice becomes the voice of the Spirit, and the Spirit's role in the service becomes invisible.

A Lifestyle of Worship

Finally, worship is conceived as more of a lifestyle than an activity, following the Romans 12 model, and the significance of the worship activity becomes incorporated into a broader tapestry of worship. I am not certain why, but authors with a modern perspective on worship invariably will highlight this aspect with much greater fervor than their neo-romantic brethren. In this paradigm, the worship service becomes the arena in which believers hear how God wants them to live, and so it becomes a sort of preparation or encouragement time for the tough work of living in the real world. It is spiritual training, a "building-up" or edification program for the lifestyle-worship one pursues during the week. Advocates of the modern paradigm typically will draw attention to the fact that one cannot worship on Sunday morning without worshiping throughout the week.[24] Thus, one's "reasonable act of worship" of Romans 12 is realized in obedient life choices—the "living sacrifice" of worship—and is catalyzed by the cerebral renewal of one's mind that occurs through the activity of worship. The transformation of the worshiper's life does not primarily occur by experiencing God in the worship activity, but by hearing His Word and then fearing and obeying Him in his or her daily walk.

Thus, the modern worshiper is much less concerned with his or her experience of the worship service, and is more focused on the edification that it contains. The service is not evaluated in terms of whether one "met" with God there—an interesting and increasingly popular phrase—but on the basis of what one "got out of it," and how it will impact his or her daily life. He or she is far less preoccupied with the details of singing of his or her love for God through the worship activity, and more concerned with showing love for God through acts of obedience. Showing one's love takes precedence over singing or speaking of it, and keeping Jesus' commandments is conceived of as the primary manner in which one does so. Peterson summarizes this approach: "When Christians become preoccupied with the notion of offering God acceptable worship in a congregational context and thus with the minutiae of church services, they need to be reminded that Paul's focus was on the service of everyday life."[25] As Peterson highlights, the tiny and inscrutable details of why I "wasn't able to worship" are much less significant than the worship one pursues outside of the worship assembly.

There is no question that the worship activity is truly a small piece of a much larger worship lifestyle. However, it might be that much more could and should be occurring along the lines of spiritual growth and inner transformation than is adequately prompted by the modern worship service. Given that spiritual growth lies at the heart of the issue, it will be important for us to revisit this issue as this work continues. Yet for the moment, we will continue in the next chapter by examining the neo-romantic paradigm in greater detail.

---

[1] Gergen, The Saturated Self, 94.
[2] Mark Oestreicher, sidebar to Dan Kimball, The Emerging Church (Grand Rapids: Zondervan, 2003), 48.
[3] David Peterson, Engaging with God: A Biblical Theology of Worship (Downers Grove, IL: InterVarsity Press, 1992), 220-221.
[4] Dawn, Reaching Out Without Dumbing Down, 70.
[5] Ibid., 206.
[6] Webber, Signs of Wonder: The Phenomenon of Convergence in Modern Liturgical and Charismatic Churches, 74.
[7] James F. White, A Brief History of Christian Worship (Nashville: Abingdon Press, 1993), 71; Ralph P. Martin, The Worship of God (Grand Rapids: William B. Eerdmans Publishing Company, 1982), 46, 57.
[8] Furst, Romanticism in Perspective, 216.
[9] Ronald B. Allen, The Wonder of Worship (Nashville: Thomas Nelson Publishers, 2001), 170.
[10] Dawn, Reaching Out Without Dumbing Down, 76-80.
[11] Ibid., 190.
[12] Dawn, Reaching Out Without Dumbing Down, 111, 175.
[13] Ibid., 72.
[14] Ibid., 70.
[15] Webber, Signs of Wonder: The Phenomenon of Convergence in Modern Liturgical and Charismatic Churches, 19.
[16] Robert E. Webber, Worship is a Verb (Peabody, Mass: Hendrickson Publishers, 1992), 3.
[17] Leander Keck, The Church Confident (Nashville: Abingdon Press, 1993), 35; quoted in Dawn, Reaching Out Without Dumbing Down, 88.
[18] John Piper, Desiring God: Meditations of a Christian Hedonist (Sisters, Oregon: Multnomah Publishers, Inc., 1986), 89.
[19] Ibid., 16.
[20] John Coe, interview by author, 18 September 2003, Biola University, La Mirada, California.
[21] Webber, Signs of Wonder: The Phenomenon of Convergence in Modern Liturgical and Charismatic Churches, 19.
[22] Coe, interview by author.
[23] Peterson, Engaging with God: A Biblical Theology of Worship, 35.
[24] D. A. Carson, ed., Worship by the Book (Grand Rapids: Zondervan, 2002), 24.
[25] Ibid., 187.

CHAPTER 6

TWO WORSHIP PARADIGMS (PART II)

The Neo-Romantic Paradigm: Worship as Experience

A Supernatural Conversation of Praise

In the second paradigm, experiencing God in worship becomes the implicit goal of the worshiper in the worshiping assembly. Exalting God with praise is still the explicit purpose, but the intended result of the sacrifice is not really the cognitive "edification" which the modern worshiper envisioned. Rather, it is an inner experience or "encounter" with God's presence and a blessing that is imparted to the worshiper as a result. Make no mistake: the edification of the worshiper is critical in both paradigms, as both would certainly hope and expect worship to be transformational.[1] However, the basic means of transformation and the expectations of the service in this regard are quite different, a direct result of a different epistemological understanding of spiritual growth. Because the neo-romantic tends to highlight the inner experience as a more profound path to knowledge, the resulting paradigm of worship focuses more on the emotions and an inner experience of God as the path to heart change.

Worship becomes a mystical interaction in which the worshiper lifts a sacrifice of praise to God, and is deeply ministered to on an internal level by an immanent experience of the "manifest presence" of God. Worship is no longer practiced as a one-way transmission of praise, but becomes instead a "supernatural exchange."[2] As one praises and worships, he or she experiences the special, revealed presence of God, receiving a blessing of consolation (or emotional well-being). Moreover, this exchange facilitates a continuing work of inner transformation from interaction with His divine presence.[3] In this paradigm, the activity of expressing one's deep adoration for God opens a window in which one's heart is yielded to the Spirit, allowing Him to reposition one's thoughts and emotions so that they are congruent with His purposes. Intellect tends to follow experience or emotions on the path of spiritual growth. In essence, *the heart is transformed by delighting in God.*

As a whole, this profoundly mystical contact strives for a communication of love between God and the worshiper, connecting the creature with the Creator on an intensely personal, emotional and experiential level. The dynamic is one of heightened intimacy, emphasizing both the immediate immanence and supreme transcendence of God, and suggesting a pursuit of God that involves the whole person. No one has captured this dynamic better than Sally Morgenthaler in her text *Worship Evangelism;* her comments present a clear neo-romantic response to the modern paradigm. She writes:

> Worship is a two-way communication between believers and God, a dialogue of response involving both actions and speech...real worship provides opportunities for God and God's people to express their love for each other. It is not just a room full of people thinking inspired thoughts. Nor is it human beings speaking and acting as if God were incapable of reply. In real worship, we carry on an exchange of love with the God who is present, the God who speaks to us in the now, who has done and is doing marvelous things.[4]

Worship becomes a conversation with God that implies an intrinsic give-and-take interaction, and features a real expectancy on the part of the worshiper that God really wants to communicate with the whole person in an immediate manner. Craig Allen agrees: "Ideally a worship service includes elements of 'conversation' going both directions. In any loving human relationship both parties make opportunities to listen and to speak, and in healthy dialogue one interacts with communication from the other person."[5] Thus, a dynamic of listening and responding pervades both sides of the interaction, representing a healthy and communicative exchange of love between an attentive Father and His responsive children. Webber writes "if God really does speak and act in worship, then worship is an act of communication from above. In worship then, there is not only divine action but the actual experience of divine presence."[6] The worshiper both speaks and waits on God, expecting to hear Him.

Furthermore, God's communication with His people is not limited to the preaching of the Word alone in this worship paradigm, but in many denominations involves additional manifestations of the Spirit. (Indeed, the activity of the Spirit is often much more emphasized in churches that pursue this approach to worship.) Not only does the Spirit communicate with the worshiper through the revealed words of Scripture, He is often thought to commune with worshipers through a variety of other means, including "non-audible" words, a felt presence, visions and direct address. William James attests that these phenomena are regular features of mystical interactions, and they seem to be in keeping with the variety of supernatural experiences that he quotes in his text *The Varieties of Religious Experience.*[7] Evangelicalism as a whole is categorized by psychologists of religion as an intrinsically experiential movement that features a special experience of God at the moment of so-called "conversion."[8] The difference is that in this paradigm, these interactive experiences come alongside the Word as a normative feature of the individual's worship conversation with God.[9]

"Manifest Presence"

The special, revealed "presence of God" in the worship activity deserves some special attention at this point. Many describe this phenomenon as the "manifest presence of God," although this is basically "a human attempt to describe how the presence of God is experienced in worship."[10] The idea of manifest presence is intended to suggest that somehow a special revelation of God's presence comes upon the worshiping assembly in a real, metaphysical manner as they praise Him, bringing an abiding sense of consolation, transcendence, enlightenment, etc. Although God's omnipresence inhabits all places by definition, there is thought to be a special kind of presence that comes upon the assembly, not manifested in a glory cloud, but demonstrated through the senses, felt experience and emotions of the worshipers. John Frame explains:

> Throughout redemptive history, however, God has, from time to time, made his presence particularly overwhelming and intense. Something very unusual and important happened when Moses met God in the burning bush, when Israel met God at Sinai, and when the glory of God descended on the tabernacle. And something similar happens when God draws near to the New Testament Christian meeting, even though there may be no visual spectacle, as there often was in the Old Testament.[11]

The point is that the worshipers' emotions and experience are treated as special receptors of the presence of the Lord, and thus, one ends up measuring the presence of God by the degree of consolation or emotional exaltation that he or she experiences.[12] Worshipers of this orientation essentially explain their emotional experiences and heightened awareness of the transcendent as the visitation of a localized or intensified instantiation of God's presence.

Therefore, writers or worship leaders—particularly those of a charismatic belief system—will often describe God's presence as coming upon a worshiping assembly as they praise Him, and will characteristically utilize language that invokes His presence. Many will resort to the Old Testament language and paradigm of worship in which the worshiper approached the localized presence of God at the temple or tabernacle. This language is then transported into the New Testament era, including the idea of the temple courts as stages of worship,[13] to suggest that God's manifest presence is something that can be nearer or farther depending upon the orientation or attitude of the worshiper. John Wimber notes "the call to worship is a message to God inviting Him to visit us."[14] There is a dynamic involved in this approach that suggests that God's special, revealed presence manifests itself on the basis of the receptivity of the worshiper. Thus, the task of the worshiper becomes to excite the requisite enthusiasm or whatever is necessary to experience the emotional high connected with God's special presence.

This concept of "presence" has truly become widespread throughout Evangelical worship and the upcoming worship repertoire, even though I would guess that few who employ the terminology have carefully thought through some of the ramifications of their theology. Indeed, this statement from Michael Coleman, president of Integrity Music, is included on the back of many of their worship CDs, with no clarification as to its meaning: "Our commitment is to help people worldwide experience the manifest presence of God." Underlying the use of this phrase, there is a specific belief regarding the presence of God, an understanding that is basically epistemological in nature, one that needs serious investigation.

"Numinous"

At heart, the concept of manifest presence represents a "numinous" event, that is, a mystical interaction with the person of God in which the worshiper is allowed a brief, mitigated or shielded glimpse into God's glory. Moses experienced a kind of numinous event as he saw God passing by, as did Peter, James and John at the transfiguration of Jesus. Morgenthaler writes "in corporate worship, God desires to remove our blindfolds and give us an extraordinary, breathtaking glimpse of divine radiance."[15] Of course, the Christian today does not experience the same kind of numinous event as Moses, as he or she is not actually observing God first-hand, at least with visual perception. However, the concept suggests that the individual perceives God today in a vivid and profound manner through other means of spiritual perception.

"Numinous" was a term used by Rudolf Otto in his seminal work *The Idea of the Holy* to describe an experience of the non-rational aspects of God, that is, those mysterious and incomprehensible attributes of God that cannot be perceived with one's cognition, but are vitally experienced nonetheless. He writes: "The truly 'mysterious' object is beyond our apprehension and comprehension, not only because our knowledge has certain irremovable limits, but because in it we come upon something inherently 'wholly other', whose kind and character are incommensurable with our own, and before which we therefore recoil in wonder that strikes us chill and numb."[16] This numinous interaction is thought to manifest itself in several specific human emotions, including awe and fear on the one hand, and rapture and wonder on the other.

At the core, however, the numinous event is supposed to represent some brush of one's sensations by God's manifest glory. Thus, a great deal of experience-oriented worship repertoire will refer to experiencing God's glory in worship, even though the actual experience of God's glory would, as one speaker commented, turn the worshiper into ash immediately. Still, the concept of a numinous event suggests a window into God's glory, a realization of His manifest presence that God allows and filters according to the constraints of one's frail humanity.

Much of the literature on the subject of manifest presence is murky and highly subjective, because it is by definition not something of which the intellect can definitively lay hold. For example, the literature does not clarify whether the manifest presence of God is thought to be in addition to the indwelling of the Spirit, or whether it represents the Holy Spirit simply being enlivened in the worshiping community. Regardless, the term "manifest presence" is used to characterize more of what is going on inside of the worshiper by way of emotional exaltation than it is to describe the proximity or intensity of God's presence. Morgenthaler emphasizes "it has more to do with what is going on inside us, then in His presence moving closer or further away."[17] Essentially, the so-called manifest presence of God is a way of describing the heightened feelings of the worshiper that result from his or her participation in the worship activity.

Obviously, these concepts present some huge red flags to anyone in orthodox Christian circles, as well they should. In the next chapter, we will discuss conceptions or misconceptions regarding the presence of God from a biblical perspective. For the purposes of this chapter, however, it is enough to point out how emotions and experience are connected with the idea of manifest presence in the neo-romantic paradigm.

CHAPTER 6: TWO WORSHIP PARADIGMS (PART II)

Emotions and Pleasure in Worship

Euphoria, the release of emotions and an experience of ecstasy, is certainly a desired result of the worship encounter in this paradigm. The consolation, which the Holy Spirit is thought to bring, is frequently used by the worshiper as a barometer to measure whether or not he or she has "really worshiped," including whether or not he or she has truly experienced the presence of God. What this dynamic subtly suggests is that one of the driving motivations for experience in worship is pleasure, both the pleasure of emotional release and the pleasure of worshiping God.

While the pursuit of pleasure in this context might sound altogether unlike true worship, it is not something that should necessarily be considered antithetical to worship. Renowned worship theologian Ronald Allen agrees: "When worship brings pleasure to the Lord, it also brings pleasure to the worshiper! In true worship we bring pleasure to God, and that brings us the greatest pleasure of all!"[18] John Piper reflects the same conviction; in fact, it is the central thesis of his important text *Desiring God.* He writes: "The pursuit of pleasure is a necessary part of all worship and virtue."[19] Piper argues that one praises and adores that which one finds the most pleasure in,[20] and that the goal is to find ultimate pleasure in the fount of all joy, God Himself.[21] Indeed, his comments reflect material throughout the Psalms, in which David and others write about delighting in God and finding the experience of worship satisfying to the soul. (Ps 63:3-5) The neo-romantic paradigm suggests that the correct context or venue of this pursuit is the activity of worship.

While it is certainly not intended to be the purpose of worship, pleasure is also a legitimate motivation that God utilizes in order to draw the new believer into a deeper relationship with Himself. John Coe argues that God uses the new believer's drive for pleasure to create spiritual growth, by replacing previous carnal desires with spiritual ones. He writes "the truth is that spiritual infants do not as yet have the characterological growth to love God with a more mature love. They require spiritual pleasure in their love in order to grow."[22] Thus, the spiritual disciplines are like the bottle of spiritual pleasures that God gives to new believers in order to slowly and tenderly invite them into deeper spiritual growth.[23] Worship is one of those disciplines.

Though some might reject as impious the idea that worship could legitimately be motivated by pleasure,[24] it is fully in keeping with the writings of the church fathers that pleasure in the spiritual disciplines—including the emotional exaltation that comes through worship—is a viable tool of the Holy Spirit to seed spiritual growth.[25]

Music and Experience

Music becomes critical to the worship experience, as the central medium by which God is praised and the worshiper experiences both an emotional release and an inner awareness or communion with God. Whereas in the modern paradigm the music is more of a preliminary to the sermon, the musical presentation now joins the sermon at center stage in the worship activity, with a significantly increased portion of the service devoted to the pursuit. The reason that music receives such an exalted place in this paradigm is because music resonates with the postmodern worshiper on a deeper and more intimate level than the reasoned sermons of yesteryear. As in the romantic period, music and aesthetic experiences connect with the emotions and inner experience of these worshipers in a nebulous, yet profound manner, and thus have a greater power than the rational processes to deeply move them. In truth, the quiet, neo-romantic leanings of the postmodern worshiper begin to be manifested as the role of music in the second paradigm begins to unfold.

Music also maintains a seemingly more profound relationship with the sacred, the mysterious and the transcendent than reason ever could. Music seems to touch the divine in a sort of mystical experience that is non-rational and incomprehensible by definition. There is a numinous element to music that is recognizable to all, but difficult to evaluate in an analytical manner. Otto also reflects this conviction, noting "music stands too high for any understanding to reach, and an all-mastering efficacy goes forth from it, of which, however, no man is able to give an account."[26] It is a mysterious quantity that feels to the senses like it connects more directly with God, and given that many are affected by truth in this garb, it is clearly one road through which the Spirit draws people into a more intimate experience of

CHAPTER 6: TWO WORSHIP PARADIGMS (PART II) 105

God. This was certainly the case with the Jesus movement, and the phenomenon has only grown as postmodern culture has become more deeply imbedded in culture as a whole. Bono, the lead singer for the Irish rock band U2, comments on his own experience of this dynamic in his introduction to *Selections from The Book of Psalms:*

> Words and music did for me what solid, even rigorous, religious argument could never do, they introduced me to God, not belief in God, more an experiential sense of God. Over art, literature, reason, the way in to my spirit was a combination of words and music…My religion could not be fiction, but it had to transcend facts. It could be mystical, but not mythical and definitely not ritual.[27]

In keeping with this emphasis on the experience of music in worship, aspects of the worship repertoire have changed as well. It has already been noted in chapter four how the worship repertoire began to see new additions with the advent of the Jesus movement. This trend continued, and a form of music was created that was more conducive to an experiential approach: praise songs. Songs have become similar to extended prayers and praises, as songwriters are no longer as concerned with theology or doctrinal truth,[28] but rather are more interested in the experience of the worshiper in his or her life and in the worship service. Praise songs tend to be "more sing-able" than hymns, written in contemporary styles so that one can immediately enter into the worship experience, without having to navigate the intricacies of unfamiliar musical terrain. Indeed, praise songs are one of the major changes in this paradigm.

In essence, praise songs are like meditations on Scripture that are set to music, and they epitomize the entire philosophy of worship music in this approach. When one meditates on Scripture, one does not take an entire chapter and read it over again and again. Rather, one takes one or two verses and slowly repeats them in prayer, asking the Spirit to open one's heart to the truth He wants to reveal. Repetition and simplicity are endemic to the spiritual discipline of meditation, because the Spirit is thereby given space and freedom to position one's heart, making it congruent with the heart of God. Richard Foster in *Celebration of Discipline* notes "what happens in meditation is that we create the emotional and spiritual space which allows Christ to construct an inner sanctuary in the heart."[29]

Although I am portraying a very idealistic version of this worship paradigm, this statement reflects the overall approach of the experience-oriented worship service. The worshiper in this paradigm desires to open his or her heart to God, inviting Him to speak into that reflection. However, the worshiper or worship leader might recognize that sometimes the multiplicity of words actually can crowd out their reflection. The content must be simpler and more focused. Hence, the songs tend to be simpler—at least in terms of the lyrics—and there also tends to be significantly more repetition. Content is evaluated in a very different manner from in a modern paradigm, as it must serve the flow of worship or it is seen as inhibiting the experience. I had a friend who grew up within this paradigm question me about the use of responsive Scripture readings in the service. It wasn't that he questioned their legitimacy as worship; rather, he simply saw them as inhibiting the flow of worship, and in this paradigm, the *flow trumps content.*

Whereas the modern service is often structured around a series of events, the neo-romantic paradigm focuses on creating a *worship flow*, using "unending melody"[†] to weave a worship atmosphere. More than anything, the worship leader desires to create an environment that is conducive to a worship experience, with no elements that will jar the worshiper out of his or her concentration. Worship leaders will seek to avoid awkward transitions at any cost, using music to seamlessly bridge from one song to another, in order to maintain the aesthetic continuity. I have heard renowned worship lecturer LaMar Boschman compare the music presentation to an airplane engine. Once the engine has been started and the plane takes off, the music had better not stall or the worship will crash and burn. Such is the commitment of this paradigm to the worship flow.

Increasingly, the position of worship leader has become more important in this paradigm. In many cases, the worship leader is as crucial to the growth of the church as the speaking pastor, and churches will hunt high and low for one who can deliver a worship experience. In essence, the worship

---

[†] I am indebted to Dr. Barry Liesch for this phrase and comparison.

leader has become something of a shaman who is expected to deliver a worship experience. As strange or as pagan as it may sound, that can easily become the function of the worship leader in this paradigm. Gary Burge remarks "my students and friends are migrating, looking for pastors who can be priests, liturgists who can evoke divine encounters."[30] It is unclear whether Mr. Burge actually means "evoke" or "invoke" in this quote, because of the nature of what he has described. Just like a shaman, a worship leader in this paradigm creates a worship environment, and by his or her planning, preparation and presentation is expected to help the worshiper "enter into worship." He is one of the critical factors who will help the worshiper experience the presence of God, which is the basic role of a shaman. We will deal with this interesting development more in the next chapter.

The focus of these changes is to create a worship experience that is much deeper, more intimate, and in touch with the whole person, ideally including both emotions and intellect. Craig Allen recognizes this synthesis, remarking "new expressions are based on the idea of the wholeness of human personality, with an emphasis on heart and body rather than just in intellectual assent and volitional commitment."[31] A.W. Tozer, a stalwart neo-romantic from the peak of the modern era, champions a similar dynamic in many of his works, drawing together the emotions and intellect in his approach to God. He remarks how "real worship is, among other things, a feeling about the Lord our God,"[32] but also comments how worship involves the cognition, explaining "as God dwells in your thoughts, you will be worshiping, and God will be accepting."[33] ‡

Representing a modern perspective, it is interesting that Marva Dawn asserts that the biblical word for "heart" refers to "will and intentionality," seemingly in contrast to feelings, wanting to remove worship from too close a link with emotions. She suggests that worshiping from the heart sometimes involves praising in spite of one's emotions.[34] While her point is well taken, this approach dismisses the wholistic nature of the heart, particularly in worship. Piper comments:

---

‡ Interestingly, he highlights the emotions first in this quote, which is in keeping with what I have emphasized as a neo-romantic approach to spiritual growth.

> It is not a mere act of willpower by which we perform outward acts. Without the engagement of the heart, we do not really worship. The engagement of the heart in worship is the coming alive of the feelings and emotions and affections of the heart. Where feelings for God are dead, worship is dead.[35]

Presumably, the heart is engaged by a more vital coordination and interpenetration of the intellect and emotions in the worship. Indeed, the neo-romantic worship paradigm ideally invigorates all of one's emotions, not just the positive ones, as well as one's thoughts, in order to fully experience God in the depth of one's being—the heart. Whether this is actually the case in practice is another matter.

In keeping with this dynamic, the participation of the worshiper in the singing and liturgy receives a much more elevated emphasis,[36] as the worshiper expects by actively participating in the service to experience the blessing of God's special, revealed presence. Jonathan Edwards, in his text *The Religious Affections,* expresses his belief that "true religion lies very much in the affections,"[37] and "the duty of singing praises to God seems to be appointed wholly to excite and express religious affections. No other reason can be assigned why we should express ourselves to God in verse rather than in prose, and do it with music, but only that such is our nature and frame that these things have a tendency to move our affections."[38] Indeed, the emotions of the worshiper are now perhaps highlighted more in the music than his or her cognition, because they are the primary way in which he or she experiences the ecstasy, the reassurance of God's presence, and the consolation of the Spirit.

The Quest for Intimacy with God

Along these lines, a relationship of heightened intimacy with God, perhaps even hyper-intimacy, is emphasized by the experiential approach. The music is clearly the most obvious area in which this passion can be noted. Whereas the desire for intimacy with God is sometimes a secondary feature of some modern worship, this romantic longing for intimacy with God becomes a central pillar of the second paradigm. One of the early and most popular praise choruses, "As the Deer," was drawn from Psalm 42, which expresses a deep desire on the part of the worshiper to draw near to the presence of the Lord in the temple.[39] The song employs the first phrase of the psalm, "as the deer pants for the water brooks, so my soul pants for You, O God," and then turns it around by saying "You alone are my heart's desire and I long to worship Thee."[40] This same longing for an immanent and more intimate relationship with the transcendent God characterizes the entire approach to worship in the neo-romantic paradigm.

The new worship repertoire also features increased use of first and second-person pronouns, speaking directly to God, attempting to increase intimacy by adopting more familiar language. John Wimber recognized that this kind of familiarity in language created a more intimate worship experience, and so the Vineyard churches made this a regular feature of their burgeoning worship music. Andy Park quotes the remarks of Carol Wimber:

> "We realized that often we would sing about worship yet we never actually worshipped—except when we accidentally stumbled onto intimate songs like 'I love you, Lord and I lift my voice.' Thus, we began to see a difference between songs about Jesus and songs to Jesus." Ever since then, Vineyard worship has placed an emphasis on singing to the Lord. It's like having a conversation with someone in the privacy of your own home.[41]

The songwriters and worship leaders desired a deeper intimacy with God in worship, so they moved towards more familiarity in language and in expression of emotions. As I mentioned in the previous chapter, some have criticized this approach, particularly the use or overuse of first-person pronouns. However, the use of "I" in worship repertoire would seem to be very appropriate, as it is only through personal experience that one is able to experience God in the first place. Moreover, this practice is absolutely in keeping with the pattern established in the Psalms, in which the psalmist elaborates upon God's qualities within the context of what God has already personally done for him. (Pss 116, 138, 145, etc.) Indeed, isn't there always an "I" involved in thanksgiving? Ronald Allen writes: "The use of 'I' and 'me' in many of these praise songs is not because the songs are about the singer; it is because they follow the biblical models fully established in the Book of Psalms to be personal in one's response to God."[42] Intimacy with God requires that there is both an "I" and a "you," and so using first-person pronouns to describe one's experience of God's works and attributes is altogether natural and fitting.

This approach has taken an even more radical turn, as songwriters increasingly have begun to substitute language for their relationship with God that one would use for a lover. In this neo-romantic revival, the passions and deep interior are emphasized once again, but now God has become the lover in the scenario. Kenneth Gergen recognizes this change as he discusses the neo-romantic currents inherent within postmodernism, remarking that one feature of this resurgence is "torch songs for Jesus, a genre in which romantic musical idioms encourage religious devotion. One cannot be certain whether the object of such songs is Jesus or a lover."[43] This description certainly characterizes a song entitled "Falling"[44] by worship songwriters Paul Baloche and Brenton Brown. They pen the ambiguous chorus "I am falling in love with you," an idiomatic expression that has always strictly denoted romantic affection. The desire for an expression of intimacy with God, when taken to its extreme, collapses the relationship between creature and Creator into that of romantic lovers.

In addition, a hunger and thirst for God—which are also classic romantic expressions—are common themes in the worship literature and repertoire. They are closely connected to themes of intimacy and desire for God, and are really just poetic ways of making the same statement. John Piper has epitomized this longing in his text *Desiring God*,[45] but he is neither alone nor original in his appetite, as Jonathan Edwards before him had some of the identical things to say. "Holy desire, exercised in longings, hungerings, and thirstings after God and holiness, is often mentioned in Scripture as an important part of true religion."[46] Indeed, the concept of a hunger for God is often described as a response to the numinous event. C.S. Lewis, one of only a handful who have written on the subject, calls the sensation a "romantic" experience:

> The experience is one of intense longing. It is distinguished from other longings by two things. In the first place, though the sense of want is acute and even painful, yet the mere wanting is felt to be somehow a delight...This hunger is better than any other fullness; this poverty better than all other wealth.[47]

In the worship repertoire, one finds material such as the song *We Are Hungry,* which expresses this longing for God in a slightly less articulate manner than the psalmist did in Psalm 63 or 84. "We are hungry, we are hungry, we are hungry for more of you. We are thirsty, oh Jesus, we are thirsty for more of you."[48] The hunger and thirst for God typical of this movement could not be more literally expressed.

This longing of the worshiper can best be explained as an authentic heart attitude that is critical to experiencing God in worship. The worshiper cannot simply go through the motions, whether intellectual or external, and still have actually "worshiped" in an appropriate and authentic manner.[49] John Piper agrees: "In the pew, the heart is ripped out of worship by the notion that it can be performed as a mere duty."[50] Indeed, there must be a heart penetration—meaning the wholistic coordination of the worshiper's intellect and emotions with his or her outward participation—in order to have honestly offered a sacrifice of praise and experienced the blessing of God's presence. "True worship happens only when both heart and action are right before God."[51] While this value certainly would be claimed for an ideal, modern service as well, the neo-romantic approach emphasizes emotional congruity as a *non-negotiable* aspect of worship. In this paradigm, one worships with one's emotions, not in spite of them.

The "Spirit and Truth" Question

For most worship theologians, this dynamic can best be summarized as a "spirit and truth" connection. "Spirit and truth" is an oft-repeated worship phrase lifted from the passage in John 4, in which Jesus instructs the Samaritan woman about the kind of true worshipers that God is seeking. The woman engages Jesus about a local debate between Samaritans and Jews regarding the correct location for worship, whether it was their holy mountain in

Samaria or the temple in Jerusalem. In characteristic fashion, Jesus jumps right to the heart of the issue by telling her that a time is coming when location will not matter. Rather, true worshipers will worship God in spirit and truth, for God is spirit, and they must worship him in this manner.

There are certainly many interpretations of this passage, and just about every writer will nuance it in a slightly different manner. In general, those writers of a more experiential approach will tend to emphasize the aspect of authenticity, which has a very winsome feel. Kendrick writes "to worship in truth is to stand before God with the words on our lips matching the actions in our lives, living a life in which belief and behavior are integrated."[52] Other interpreters will take a more explicitly exegetical approach, claiming that "truth" refers specifically to Jesus as the new ground of worship, and "spirit" refers to the Spirit of God in his unique role.[53] Along these lines, Frame writes "worship 'in Spirit and truth,' then, is Trinitarian worship—worship that is aware of the distinctive work of the Father, the Son, and the Spirit for our salvation."[54] *

Ronald Allen makes a refreshingly balanced interpretation by bringing these two aspects together. He notes the need for authenticity, pointing out that "on one level the words 'in spirit and truth'…[speak] of the internal genuineness of the worshiping person. These words point to the heart, to the inner man."[55] However, he also comments that the relationship must not only be sincere, but "empowered by God's Spirit and in accord with truth."[56] At the end of the day, he delightfully synthesizes these approaches: "While the phrase 'spirit and truth' certainly includes our mind, heart and emotions, I believe this is referring to a dynamic interaction in which the true worshiper is so deeply moved by truth about God that there is a stirring of the Holy Spirit within him or her that then elicits a worshiping response."[57] Interestingly, his description of the spirit and truth interaction reflects what I have called a modern approach to spiritual growth, but he incorporates the aspect of authenticity that is so highly prized in postmodern culture. This dynamic suggests

---

* One of the interesting things about this interpretation springs from the fact that the oldest Greek manuscripts were written in uncials—all upper-case letters—and so whether the "spirit" of "spirit and truth" refers to the Spirit of God or the spirit of man is always determined contextually.

that there is undoubtedly a high degree of overlap in these artificial paradigms, and that a "middle road" certainly exists between the two approaches. This middle road will be addressed more at length in later chapters.

Aesthetics as a Cultural Language

A final critical component of the experiential approach is the importance of aesthetics in the worship service. While it would seem that aesthetics were more closely associated with worship in the more "classical" traditions, aesthetics has truly become a non-negotiable in the experiential approach. However, this preoccupation with aesthetics is centered far less in architecture or visual stimuli than it ever used to be, and is now strongly grounded in the musical presentation. Music cultures and styles are one of the key denominators that separate one church from another, for the variety of music styles has increased exponentially over the past fifty years. This factor alone is very telling, and its relationship with postmodernism could receive an entire treatise.

Music is of central importance to culture, and becomes the key ingredient of the aesthetic presentation in the worship experience. Rudolf Otto writes "religious worship cannot therefore do without music. It is one of the foremost means to work upon men with an effect of marvel."[58] This connection is true for both the modern and neo-romantic service alike, but Robert Webber notes the overwhelming significance of music for the experience-oriented approach. He stipulates that "this [praise and worship] tradition has always valued music as a major vehicle for an immediate sense of the Spirit, and this tradition has always sought to provide people with an experience of God, not merely a reason to believe that he exists."[59] Music and aesthetics in this approach maintain a critical connection with experience, and therefore, knowledge.

Aesthetics is conceived of as a cultural language that either inhibits or catalyzes worship from the heart. When the worship presentation does not speak one's cultural language, then it becomes nearly impossible to worship from the heart, because worship has to undergo a kind of cultural translation that limits its impact. Richard Niebuhr, in his seminal text *Christ and Culture*, underscores this truth:

> Christ claims no man purely as a natural being, but always as one who has become human in a culture; who is not only in culture, but into whom culture has penetrated. Man not only speaks but thinks with the aid of the language of culture…the forms and attitudes of his mind which allow him to make sense out of the objective world have been given him by culture.[60]

Worship is a transcendent activity that is bound up in the earthly dynamics of culture, because it involves languages and basic cultural expression. Aesthetics is one of those languages. Given that language allows one to experience truth about God and respond in worship, aesthetics rightfully will affect one's worship expression and experience of God in worship.[61] To deny this cultural aspect of worship is to deny one's humanity. Just as language reveals the truth of the gospel, so culture and aesthetics in the medium of music can either allow people to hear and experience the truth about God in worship, or shut them out from the profundity of that experience.

Sally Morgenthaler emphasizes that churches thus become barriers to revealing who God is when they refuse to learn cultural or aesthetic languages.[62] Missionary and ethnomusicologist Tom Avery agrees: "No matter how much a hymn, Gospel song, or praise song means to me, it will not mean the same thing to a person raised in another musical culture."[63] Experiencing God in worship is facilitated by one's senses as well as by the degree to which the worship accurately reveals truth about God; but one's senses can only receive truth when it is translated into one's own cultural language. Music and aesthetics are such a language. Hence, the neo-romantic paradigm of worship places a huge emphasis on speaking aesthetic and cultural languages in the music that it uses.

While aesthetics is certainly a very important cultural language, it is interesting how aesthetics has become an *all-important* language in churches that subscribe to the neo-romantic paradigm. Indeed, it would seem that the worshipers in these venues are not "able to worship" at all unless the aesthetics perfectly conform to their needs and expectations. The worshiper essentially finds himself or herself under the control of the worship environment, and the aesthetics end up exerting something of an abnormal controlling influence on whether or not he or she has connected with God. Worship leader Darlene Zschech of Hillsongs betrays the fact that aesthetics must be perfectly executed in order to facilitate a great worship experience. "Human beings are amazing creatures who seem to need everything 'just right' in order to have an excellent church service."[64][+] The reason for this emphasis is because aesthetics are foundational to experience, and experience is the driving force of the neo-romantic paradigm.

At this point, aesthetics become less of a necessary cultural language, and more of a necessary stimulant in order to invoke a good experience. Aesthetics—particularly in music—can become much like the drugs that were needed by those in the psychedelic culture in order to experience a higher sense of transcendence or consciousness. Graham Kendrick writes "it is also far too easy, within the current upsurge of creative input in the realm of worship, to find ourselves chasing spiritual or aesthetic experiences, as if the highest achievement of our whole pilgrimage on earth was to enter some kind of praise-induced ecstasy!"[65] In this paradigm, any little disturbance might disrupt the worship experience and derail the worshiper from being able to worship. Some of these things might be a song that one does not know, too much direct address from the worship leader, or awkward musical breaks between songs. I hesitate to say that there is something wrong with this fixation on aesthetics, but it does give one pause when so many things can hinder the worshiper's experience, and the sacrifice of praise on the part of the worshiper begins to rely too heavily upon external conditions.

Individualism in Worship

Finally, the worship experience of the individual is highlighted over the worship experience of the community in the second paradigm. While this

---

[+] In all fairness, Ms. Zschech is not making this point to illustrate the point that I am making, that aesthetics exert a controlling influence on the experience of the neo-romantic worshiper. However, her comments demonstrate the basic attitude of the worshiper who "wasn't able to worship."

might not be the intent of the worship service, individualism is certainly one of the results of the approach. This assertion can be demonstrated by simply looking around at individuals worshiping under this particular paradigm: most often, their eyes are squeezed shut, oblivious to others in the room. While I certainly commend the worship postures and concentration that this suggests, it also *symbolizes* that the worship experience is much more individualistic than community-oriented. The worshiper is essentially seeking to experience God first-hand, which is a wonderful thing, but it is not basically a corporate sensation. In truth, they are pursuing God after the manner of a private spiritual discipline. While some might argue that the manifest presence of the Lord can be corporately experienced, the receptors of this experience have been shown to be essentially personal in nature, with the result that the worshiper finds the blessing of this experience purely on an internal basis. More will be said on this subject in later chapters.

Two Cultural Paradigms

In the final analysis, worship is as much about a lifestyle as it is about an activity. It is as much focused on an experience of God as it is on the edification of another. It is simultaneously a sacrifice of praise and a divine blessing of God's presence. It is both an intellectual engagement with the truth of God, and a supernatural connection with His Spirit. While the pendulum of culture will swing, our efforts must go towards retaining the balance. Interestingly, both approaches have tended to emphasize aspects of worship that are consistent with their own worldview. Aspects of both perspectives are clearly represented in Scripture. However, both paradigms are also the result of what is neither biblical nor absolute in its authority—a cultural worldview—and both tend to dissect what should be a wholistic, biblical view of worship. The stakes are high, because there is certainly the opportunity for right or wrong in this discussion, but neither paradigm is wholly right nor wrong. Furthermore, there are more or less culturally relevant aspects to each paradigm, and as long as they do not abrogate Scripture, the culturally relevant aspects should certainly be embraced for the furtherance of the Gospel.

Ultimately, the pendulum will always swing between the reciprocal energies inherent in culture, and that is not a bad thing, as we are creatures of culture. Our responsibility in light of Scripture is to understand how our culture has penetrated our lives, and either to accept or reject those accommodations on the basis of the revealed truth of God. As Niebuhr remarks "the problem of culture is therefore the problem of its conversion."[66]

It is of critical importance to this work that the neo-romantic paradigm be evaluated in light of Scripture, particularly some of its basic presuppositions, and be converted to a biblical perspective. The rest of this work will focus on evaluating the neo-romantic paradigm in depth. One of the most critical presuppositions of this second paradigm that desperately needs reconsideration is its basic approach to the presence of God. The idea of experiencing God in worship is built upon underlying beliefs about how we experience God, and how His presence is revealed in worship. Thus, an intensive biblical examination of the presence of God will be undertaken in the next chapter.

---

[1] Morgenthaler, Worship Evangelism, 52.

[2] Ibid., 48.

[3] John M. Frame, Worship in Spirit and Truth (Phillipsburg, NJ: P&R Publishing, 1996), 85.

[4] Morgenthaler, Worship Evangelism, 48.

[5] Allen, The Wonder of Worship, 211-212.

[6] Webber, Worship is a Verb, 17.

[7] James, The Varieties of Religious Experience, 81.

[8] Ellwood, One Way: The Jesus Movement and its Meaning, 28.

[9] Frame, Worship in Spirit and Truth, 90.

[10] Sally Morgenthaler, phone interview by author, 22 September 2003, Los Angeles, California.

[11] Frame, Worship in Spirit and Truth, 32.

[12] Coe, interview by author.

[13] Allen, The Wonder of Worship, 122-125.

[14] John Wimber; quoted in Park, To Know You More: Cultivating the Heart of the Worship Leader, 254.

[15] Morgenthaler, Worship Evangelism, 97.

[16] Rudolf Otto, The Idea of the Holy, trans. John W. Harvey (Oxford: Oxford University Press, 1923), 28.

[17] Morgenthaler, phone interview by author.

[18] Allen, The Wonder of Worship, 90.

[19] Piper, Desiring God, 23.

[20] Ibid., 49.

[21] Ibid., 20.
[22] John Coe, "Musings on the Dark Night of the Soul: Insights from St. John of the Cross on a Developmental Spirituality," Journal of Psychology and Theology 28, no. 4 (2000): 296.
[23] Ibid., 295.
[24] Peterson, Engaging with God: A Biblical Theology of Worship, 17.
[25] Coe, "Musings on the Dark Night of the Soul: Insights from St. John of the Cross on a Developmental Spirituality," 296.
[26] Otto, The Idea of the Holy, 151.
[27] Bono, introduction to Selections from the Book of Psalms (New York: Grove Press, 1999), ix.
[28] Allen, The Wonder of Worship, 172.
[29] Richard Foster, Celebration of Discipline (San Francisco: Harper Collins Publishers, 1978), 20.
[30] Gary Burge, "Liturgical Worship: Using Ritual to Inspire True Worship," in Barna, et al., Experience God in Worship, 70.
[31] Allen, The Wonder of Worship, 171.
[32] A.W. Tozer, Whatever Happened to Worship?, comp. & ed. Gerald B. Smith (Camp Hill, PA: Christian Publications, 1985), 84.
[33] Ibid., 127.
[34] Dawn, Reaching Out Without Dumbing Down, 109.
[35] Piper, Desiring God, 81.
[36] Craig Allen, The Wonder of Worship, 172.
[37] Jonathan Edwards, The Religious Affections (reprint, Edinburgh: The Banner of Truth Trust, 2001), 47.
[38] Ibid., 44.
[39] Earl Radmacher, Ronald B. Allen, and H. Wayne House, eds., Nelson's New Illustrated Bible Commentary (Nashville: Thomas Nelson Publishers, 1999), 676.
[40] Martin Nystrom, As the Deer 1984 Maranatha Praise, Inc. (Admin. by The Copyright Company)
[41] Carol Wimber, quoted in John Wimber, "Worship: Intimacy with God," in Worship Conference Resource Material Handbook (Anaheim, CA: Mercy Publishing, 1989), 5; quoted in Park, To Know You More: Cultivating the Heart of the Worship Leader, 250-251.
[42] Allen, The Wonder of Worship, 142.
[43] Gergen, The Saturated Self, 118.
[44] Paul Baloche and Brenton Brown, "Falling," 1998 Integrity's Hosanna! Music/ASCAP & Maranatha! Music (administered by the Copyright Company, Nashville TN) ASCAP.
[45] Piper, Desiring God, 19.
[46] Edwards, The Religious Affections, 32.
[47] C.S. Lewis, The Pilgrim's Regress (Grand Rapids: Wm B. Eerdmans Publishing Company, 1933; reprint, 1977), 7 (page citations are to the reprint edition).
[48] Brad Kilman, We Are Hungry 1999 Brad Kilman Publishing (admin. by The Loving Company)/(admin. by The Loving Company)
[49] Allen, The Wonder of Worship, 86.
[50] John Piper, Brothers We Are Not Professionals: A Plea to Pastors for Radical Ministry (Nashville: Broadman & Holman Publishers, 2003), 50.
[51] Allen, The Wonder of Worship, 85.

⁵² Graham Kendrick, Learning to Worship as a Way of Life (Minneapolis: Bethany House Publishers, 1984), 97.

⁵³ Frame, Worship in Spirit and Truth, 6-7; and Peterson, Engaging with God: A Biblical Theology of Worship, 100.

⁵⁴ Frame, Worship in Spirit and Truth, 6-7.

⁵⁵ Allen, The Wonder of Worship, 93.

⁵⁶ Ibid.

⁵⁷ Ibid., 184-185.

⁵⁸ Otto, The Idea of the Holy, 151.

⁵⁹ Robert Webber, Signs of Wonder: The Phenomenon of Convergence in Modern Liturgical and Charismatic Churches, 21.

⁶⁰ Richard H. Niebuhr, Christ and Culture (New York: Harper Torchbooks, 1951), 69.

⁶¹ Morgenthaler, phone interview by author.

⁶² Ibid.

⁶³ Avery, "Music of the Heart: The Power of Indigenous Worship in Reaching Unreached Peoples with the Gospel," 13.

⁶⁴ Darlene Zschech, Extravagant Worship (Minneapolis: Bethany House, 2001), 176.

⁶⁵ Kendrick, Learning to Worship as a Way of Life, 32.

⁶⁶ Niebuhr, Christ and Culture, 194.

CHAPTER 7

THE GOD WHO IS THERE

Bridging the Distance

On occasion, I participate in "worship nights" at a local coffeehouse. These events are open-mic situations in which local Christian artists will share either their own, original worship literature, or commonly known standards. The owner of the coffeehouse is a wonderful Christian lady, outgoing in her evangelistic efforts, and a very committed member of a local, charismatic church. I respect and admire both her enthusiasm for the gospel and her desire to see people worship the Lord. Without a doubt, she has a heart that is deeply seeking to praise God and experience His presence. On one occasion, she began the evening by introducing me, and then began to exhort those in attendance about their own involvement in the worship. I remember her repeating several times "we just need to bring the glory cloud down tonight. Let's just bring down that glory cloud!" My friend Mark and I looked at one another with quizzical expressions, not sure exactly what she intended by the "glory cloud," and even less sure what in particular she was thinking we could do in order to bring it down. Was she referring to some visible manifestation of God's presence? Was she really thinking that somehow we would invoke a pillar of fire at a coffeehouse in the middle of suburban Southern California? More to the point, is something that might I do or say, some enthusiasm that I can muster in praising and worshiping God, going to cause a supernatural spectacle to occur?

Obviously, her presuppositions regarding the presence of God, particularly its manifestation in worship, were somewhat different from mine, but the central issue is still very critical to this entire discussion. In what sense do we experience a special, revealed or "manifest presence" of God when we worship together as a community, and is that nearness something that can be encouraged and invoked or blocked and repressed by our own enthusiasm, piety, authenticity, or the lack thereof? Does God actually draw near His worshipers in a metaphysical manifestation as they seek Him, or do they simply open themselves to the God who is everywhere, the God who has already made His dwelling place in their hearts, the God who is there?

The "presence of God" has been receiving a lot of attention in worship circles of late, and has tended to create some confusion. At the heart of this particular paradigm of worship as an experience of God is the idea of manifest presence: a special awareness, manifestation or localized instantiation of God's glory or presence that brings a blessing of consolation and emotional rest to the worshiper. The concept of God's manifest presence is throughout Exodus, but it comes out clearly in Exodus 33, in which God says that His "presence" will go with His people in the desert, and will give them rest. Indeed, the theology behind this approach has in large part been pulled from the Old Testament, in which God tended to reveal His presence to His people through a special, visible manifestation, like a burning bush, a cloud or a pillar of fire.

Throughout a great deal of the Old Testament record, there was indeed a localized realization of God's glory in the tabernacle or temple, and David describes the experience of God's presence in worship as something that was deeply satisfying to his soul. (Pss 63:5; 84:2) Furthermore, this "tabernacle dynamic" allowed the worshiper to physically approach or come into God's manifest presence, which was encountered at a particular location,[1] as he or she was exhorted to "come before His presence with singing."[2] (Ps 100:2) To worship was to come into His presence, because that is how God manifested Himself. This language references the logistical dynamic of the temple, but also implies that there were times in which God's manifest presence was both geographically and spiritually distant.[3] This Old Testament data, when superimposed onto the current age, suggests to those of an experience-oriented paradigm that *there is an inherent distance between God and the worshiper that somehow can be bridged by the act of worship.* In the New

CHAPTER 7: THE GOD WHO IS THERE

Testament, this special manifestation was represented in Acts by the signs and wonders that fell upon the apostles as they waited for the outpouring of the Holy Spirit; thus, the sign gifts of the Spirit in the worship assembly now are often understood as a barometer of God's presence.

With all of this biblical material in view, the worshiper must ask several basic questions: how should the contemporary believer expect to experience the presence of God, and how is this presence related to Christ and the indwelling of the Holy Spirit? Secondly, is there a special, manifest presence of God that is revealed in the worship assembly, and is this presence something that can be affected by the actions, thoughts or emotions of the worshiper? This chapter will seek to uncover a biblical understanding of how both the Old and New Testament believers experienced the presence of God in worship, and how this should affect worshipers today.

God's Presence in Ancient Near Eastern Culture

Because there is such a wide historical and cultural chasm between daily life in the Old Testament and contemporary life, grasping how the ancients mentioned in the Bible understood their relationship with God or the gods becomes difficult to translate into a contemporary realization. Ancient near eastern culture featured religious ideas and presuppositions that are eons away from our own Christian ones, and their beliefs are sometimes hidden behind the all-too-familiar material in the biblical record. Christians tend to export contemporary attitudes back onto these ancient vignettes, and fast-forward biblical conditions into current culture. The manifest presence of God as it is used today is an *anachronism*, an ancient concept that has been too neatly moved into contemporary circumstances, underestimating the overwhelming significance that it held for the ancient culture and disregarding the special manner in which God's presence is manifested in our era. Without understanding ancient culture or the progress of revelation, Christians begin calling down the glory cloud, oblivious to the immensity of what they invoke. One must arrive at a clear understanding of how the biblical characters understood the presence of God to operate, and how they expected to be able to interact with His presence (or more precisely, how they expected the gods to interact with them). There are several hurdles involved in this task, but these expectations and presuppositions are critical to a faithful interpretation of biblical material.

The first major hurdle is the fact that the ancients lived in a polytheistic society, and because they had pre-scientific conceptions of life and existence, they cultivated a fundamentally different relationship with their gods. In a polytheistic culture, gods were seen to be basically territorial, and living and prospering in a certain area meant learning to appease them. The major gods required sacrifice and cultic worship in order to allow the crops to grow, bring rain in the right season, give protection from destructive acts of nature, and so forth. But there were also localized gods, and these also required special appeasement in order to be able to exist in their territory.[4] This conviction is played out in II Kings 17. When the Israelites had been taken into captivity by the Assyrian king, he sent colonists in order to repopulate the land, assimilating their culture by overwhelming it. The colonists complained to the king that they did not know how correctly to worship the Israelite God, who was in turn sending lions to kill them. The colonists requested that the king send Israelite priests to teach them how to worship the local Israelite God, which is exactly what occurred. This account reveals the basic philosophy of polytheism.

The challenge of living in this culture involved identifying where the presence of the god dwelt, and determining how to appease that particular god. David Peterson, who has done quite an impressive biblical study on the presence of God, comments "the great concern of people in the ancient world was to know where the presence of a god could be found and to know the names of gods so that they could be approached and communion with them established. Certain localities came to be identified as the dwelling-places of the gods, and here altars were erected and patterns of worship established."[5] Locating the dwelling place of a god was a critical factor, and examples of this type of mentality are found throughout the Old Testament. For example, Jacob builds an altar and names the location Bethel (literally, "house of God") in Genesis 28 when he has the dream of angels ascending and descending on a

CHAPTER 7: THE GOD WHO IS THERE 125

ladder from heaven. His comments are worth noting: "'Surely the Lord [YHWH] is in this place, and I did not know it.' And he was afraid and said, 'How awesome is this place! This is none other than the house of God, and this is the gate of heaven!" Jacob identifies the personal name of God, whom He believes can be approached at this holy location, and establishes a marker.[†] Although the dwelling place of the gods was not ultimately conceived to be a location upon the earth, the places in which the presence of a god manifested itself were still of singular importance.[6]

The second hurdle to understanding ancient culture is grasping what really drove the practice of idolatry. Making an idol was essentially an effort to localize the presence of a god, so that he could be persuaded into helping out with the especially troublesome features of basic human existence. Offering sacrifices to these idols was an attempt to achieve their favor, in a sense predisposing or cultivating them to assist with the affairs of one's daily life. In a pre-modern society, appeasing the gods was the best chance that an individual had to control his or her own fortune on earth. It was an ancient gamble for control of one's life, and the practice of idolatry sought to connect the gods with earthly facsimiles so that they could be more easily managed. Word Biblical Commentary, quoting Bernhardt, notes "such images were used throughout the ANE [ancient near east] as a means of suggesting the presence of deity, not as objects of worship: the image 'was much more something corporeal that the divine influence possessed.'"[7]

Therefore, when the Israelites made a golden calf in the desert, they were not necessarily trying to replace the one true God, but were rather attempting to localize His presence into a benign and less fearsome image that they could more easily approach. They had witnessed the cloud, fire and rumblings on the mountain, and the calf seemed much less threatening and far more agreeable. Note the proclamation of the Israelites and Aaron's response in Exodus 32, when together they beheld the idol: "'This is your God, oh Israel, that brought you out of the land of Egypt'...And Aaron made a proc-

---

[†] Interestingly, rabbinic tradition maintained that the stone on which Jacob laid his head was the "foundation-stone" of the temple, making the angelic ladder and the place of Jerusalem a kind of spiritual vortex or door to heaven. McKelvey, The New Temple, 77.

lamation and said, 'Tomorrow is a feast to the Lord [YHWH].'" There was no question which deity the idol was meant to represent. Peterson explains: "With the making of the calf-idol the Israelites were apparently concerned to provide their own means of securing the presence of the Lord. This is a pagan notion, which is offensive from an Old Testament point of view, because the living and true God cannot be manipulated by his creatures in any way."[8] The calf was an attempt to "handle" the presence of God.

Experiencing the presence of God was something that many of the ancients desired for utilitarian purposes, and so their dubious means of doing so involved trying to appease the gods with their acts of worship. With a pantheon of gods at their disposal, the philosophy of "whatever works" resulted in freestyle worship. (Indeed, this approach of freestyle worship eventually leaked into Israelite practice, causing the "high places" to be torn down and rebuilt with the ascension of each new king.) However, the glory and transcendent presence of the one true God of the universe was lethal, and dabbling with worship could be deadly. How was a holy God to establish a real relationship with sinful and fickle humans? How could He interact with His people without them continually attempting to manipulate Him for their own purposes? The answer was by making a covenant with His people by sacrifice, and the resulting relationship was realized in tabernacle worship.

Tabernacle and Temple Worship

God was apparently not interested in the worship practiced by the polytheists, and had no intention of being manipulated by anyone, particularly His worshipers. Therefore, when God first established a relationship with the people of Israel, He set about defining how and where the Israelites could worship Him, and the tabernacle was approved as the legitimate point of contact in which His people might approach Him. God took a very proactive position (which is not at all surprising), not allowing them to define willy-nilly what worship practices they would pursue, but making a covenant with them as a people and giving them specific instructions regarding worship. The core of these instructions involved how they were to approach Him, and

CHAPTER 7: THE GOD WHO IS THERE

how they were to experience His manifest presence. In order to meet with His people as well as to dwell among them, God took the initiative in circumscribing His manifest presence among His people, giving detailed blueprints regarding the tabernacle that they were to construct for worship.

God was incredibly specific in that period regarding how and where they could experience His presence, for the sake of His glory and for their own sake. They would not be allowed to manipulate Him, attempting to invoke or localize His presence with freestyle worship and the making of graven images, as these expressions were an affront to His holiness. They would not be allowed to engage in syncretistic worship practices, as a relationship with the one true God was exclusive and binding. They could not live in disobedience, as if their sinfulness held no ramifications for the community and for their relationship with Him. They could not expect to approach Him at will. These plenary restrictions, given at the inauguration of their covenant relationship, were at least in part for their own protection, a necessary barrier for those sinful humans who would live in community with God's manifest presence and absolute holiness. But these requirements were also an expression of God's character, and so He specifically outlined in the Law how He did and did not want to be worshiped.

The first point here is that God did indeed want to make His dwelling place (literally "tabernacle" in Exod 25:9)[9] among His people, manifesting His presence in their midst and accompanying them in a special way on the journey, but *the relationship had to be conducted on His own terms.* There was no experimentation with worship allowed, and the offering of strange fire received swift retribution. God would be with His people in their travail, and the tabernacle, including the parameters involved with tabernacle sacrifice, was sanctioned as the central meeting place between God and humankind, the prime venue in which He would make His presence known.

The people could approach God's "localized" presence at this structure, praising Him and communing with Him, because He created a venue in which they could meet.[10] "The tabernacle was intended to provide a portable expression of God's presence with His people, to be located at the very center of Israel's life on the march from Sinai to the promised land."[11] It was not conceived of as a structure or a dwelling place that would somehow contain God, as Solomon recognizes regarding the temple in I Kings 8:28, but as the approved site where the God who was everywhere would let Himself be tangibly experienced in some shielded or mitigated fashion. God's presence would literally be with His people on their journey and in their daily struggles, but the tabernacle was the focal point of that heaven and earth interaction.

Second, the tabernacle was central in that it would interface the special, manifest presence of God, the glory of the Lord, and would allow the blessings of His presence to come upon His people. The "glory of the Lord" in the Old Testament is a quintessential phrase that essentially prefigures the contemporary concept of God's manifest presence.[12] The word "presence" in the Hebrew is literally translated "face," so the idea of being in God's presence denoted to some degree being exposed to His glory or experiencing some kind of local manifestation first-hand. The tabernacle and the temple allowed the people to experience the blessing of His divine presence, an act of accommodation and a gesture of grace that God made to their "creaturely capacity."[13] It erected a shield, if you will, a barrier before God's revealed glory, so that the people could experience the delight and wonder of worshiping before His "face" without being consumed. In essence, the tabernacle and the temple *mediated* God's presence for the people.

Perhaps the most interesting aspect of God's glory or manifest presence upon the earth is the fact that it regularly seemed to involve some cosmic disturbance or natural phenomena, like clouds, thunder, quakes, lightning, etc. Throughout the Exodus record, the phrase is used almost exclusively with some kind of visible manifestation. Indeed, it is used in Exodus 16:10 and 24:17 almost synonymously with a cloud and consuming fire, respectively, as if the reader understood that these phenomena equaled the tangible experience of God's manifest presence. Indeed, their daily interaction with God's glory became so endemic to their desert experience that they grew accustomed to following it as it literally led them on their journey. (Exod 40:36-38) However, the cloud always lingered over the tabernacle, highlighting that the presence of the Lord was particularly tied to that singular venue of worship.

CHAPTER 7: THE GOD WHO IS THERE

The same visible manifestation occurred when Solomon dedicated the temple (1 Kgs 8:10-11), and the connection that the temple was now the legitimate meeting place with the God who is everywhere was not lost on the people.[14] For them, the cloud signified God's blessing and habitation.

These visible manifestations are not to be confused with God's glory itself. In Numbers 16:42, the coming of the cloud and the appearance of the glory are described separately, a description which could simply be a hendiadys, or a Hebraic literary figure for saying the same thing. In point of fact, the glory was perhaps even more intrinsically connected with the ark of the Covenant, for when the ark was captured by the Philistines in 1 Samuel 4:21, the glory was said to have "departed" from Israel, for "the ark of God has been captured." Moreover, God was said to dwell between the cherubim, the mercy seat representing His throne, and the ark itself the "footstool" of His throne.[15] Given that the priest only had access to it once a year, and only after a whole process of purification, it becomes fairly obvious that the experience of God's presence in the holy of holies was significantly more demanding and intense than whatever the Israelites woke up to on a Monday morning. Whatever the cloud was, it was not itself the Shekinah glory that it shielded, and everyone in the Israelite camp understood this fact. These natural phenomena were simply manifestations that cloaked God's true magnificence, so that frail humanity could experience and interact with Him.[16]

The point is that God chose to manifest Himself to the children of Israel in a particular manner—in a visible, natural phenomenon—and so His manifest presence eventually came to be connected with this sort of expectation. It was the way that He allowed His people to experience His presence, rather than suffering their attempts to localize His presence as their pagan neighbors did with their gods. With Moses, God allowed a closer look, responding to his plea in Exodus 34 by allowing him to be hidden in the cleft of a rock as God passed by. But for the people of Israel, God allowed His presence to be experienced in a different sort of way, clothed in either fire or a cloud. In surveying these Scriptures, one will note that there was always some species of visible manifestation that accompanied His manifest presence to these people. Indeed, it was probably the kind of manifestation that they could handle, given that they might have been consumed by a closer look, and it was also probably the kind of manifestation that they deeply needed. Wandering alone in the desert, the Israelites certainly needed the reassurance that a pillar of fire would bring (not to mention the illumination at night!).

It is important to note at this point, however, that God also manifested Himself through His Word.[17] The Law was perhaps a more complete and meaningful experience of God than the pillar of fire could be, because it clearly spelled out for the Israelites who this God was, and what exactly He expected of them. God had proclaimed His name for Moses (and indirectly for the people), which revealed His character and attributes, a kind of presence that is perhaps more revealing than a glory cloud.

> Now the Lord [YHWH] descended in the cloud and stood with him there, and proclaimed the name of the Lord [YHWH]. And the Lord [YHWH] passed before him and proclaimed, 'The Lord [YHWH], the Lord God [YHWH EL], merciful and gracious, long-suffering, and abounding in goodness and truth, keeping mercy for thousands, forgiving iniquity and transgression and sin, by no means clearing the guilty, visiting the iniquity of the fathers upon the children and the children's children to the third and the fourth generation.' (Exod 34:5-7)

The glory cloud may have lifted their spirits and given them a fantastic experience of the presence and power of God, but the Word gave them real substance to hold onto in their struggles regarding God's inherent goodness, faithfulness and loyal love to those who follow Him. At the end of the day, both experience and revealed truth came together in the way that God revealed Himself to His people, and the Israelites in their journey through the wilderness experienced both a visible manifestation of God and the corresponding truth of His Word.

Finally, there is one other central way in which God made Himself present to His people through the tabernacle. The tabernacle, and the ritual sacrifices involved in its presentation of God, made it possible for the people of Israel to approach God and to be in a meaningful, covenant relationship with Him. Sacrifice was truly the central purpose and function of the tabernacle, for it made conceivable a relationship with the most holy God who was everywhere, but who manifested His glory between the cherubim. Without the atoning sacrifices, sinful humans could never have approached a holy God, let alone survive Him dwelling among them. "The sacrificial system was the means by which God made it possible for a sinful people to draw near to him, to receive his grace and blessing, without desecrating his holiness and so incurring his wrath against them."[18] Once again, it mediated His presence. The temple and tabernacle existed as a mechanism whereby a God-to-man relationship could actually function, where purification would happen on the part of the people, and where God could bless them with His presence.[19] Sacrifice and the experience of God's presence in this specific venue were inextricably linked.

The End of an Era

The "glory" or manifest presence of God is described by Ezekiel as departing from the temple (Ezek 11:23), and so far as we know from the biblical material, it never explicitly returned in a special, revealed manifestation. Moreover, the destruction of the temple in 587 BCE seemed to seal the deal, suggesting that God's special presence had been taken from the nation of Israel as a result of its unfaithfulness to God. "Ezekiel insisted that the loss of the temple meant the departure of God's glory and, with the loss of his presence, the removal of his protection and blessing."[20] Some have argued that the wording of the text in Ezekiel, noting that the glory went up from the city and stood on the mountain to the east, suggested that God's glory was traveling to the east, where His people were in captivity. Regardless, many of the prophets became focused on the construction of a new temple, with specific blueprints being given to Ezekiel. (Ezek 40-48) Moreover, this new temple was to be a place where all nations would come and worship the Lord. (Mic 4; Jer 3:17) Isaiah 2:2-3 spells out this future hope:

> Now it shall come to pass in the latter days
> That the mountain of the LORD's house
> Shall be established on the top of the mountains,
> And shall be exalted above the hills;
> And all nations shall flow to it.

> Many people shall come and say,
> "Come, and let us go up to the mountain of the LORD,
> To the house of the God of Jacob;
> He will teach us His ways,
> And we shall walk in His paths."

This expectation is also behind Isaiah's statement in 40:5, when he claims that the "glory of the Lord will be revealed, and all flesh shall see it together." Hence, there was a lot of expectation when the exiles returned that a new era would be ushered in. While the text in Ezra displays this hope, the disappointment is what seems most palpable. "Many of the priests and Levites and heads of the fathers' houses, old men who had seen the first temple, wept with a loud voice when the foundation of this temple was laid before their eyes. Yet many shouted aloud for joy, so that the people could not discern the noise of the shout of joy from the noise of the weeping of the people." (Ezra 3:12-13a)

Whether or not this text actually reveals the lagging hopes, the glory never seemed to have returned. When the new temple is dedicated in Ezra 6, the glory of the Lord is conspicuously absent from the narration. While all the sacrifices and temple worship were joyfully reinstated, there was no glory cloud covering the new temple, as it did the tabernacle in Exodus 40 and the first temple in I Kings 8. This could not have been an omission on the part of the author, and it would not have gone unnoticed by the worshipers, who connected the glory cloud with God's blessing and habitation of their place of worship. They had put on the party, but the guest of honor never showed, at least, not in the manner that they expected. The second temple began to be viewed as not complete, lacking the ark and other pieces of original furniture, and certain Jewish writers suggested that the divine presence had not returned.[21] The focus increasingly was bent upon a future temple—a place of worship for all nations—that once again would facilitate God's tabernacling presence among them.

The main historical significance of the temple was that God could dwell among humans and His presence be experienced by them, but God's glory did not seem to have manifested itself in the second temple. Moreover, there is no reason to think that God's manifest presence inhabited Herod's

CHAPTER 7: THE GOD WHO IS THERE

temple either. We have no indication that when Jesus walked through the temple courts, there was any cloud of glory that hung about the place. The temple in Jesus' day was a place that was very preoccupied with teaching and with sacrifices, but there is never any mention of God's manifest presence invading or inhabiting it. When Jesus walked through that temple, the glory of the Lord was indeed revealed in it, but it did not manifest itself in a glory cloud, but in a person: Immanuel.

Immanuel

When I was child, I was fascinated with the Handel oratorio, *The Messiah*. Coming from a family of musicians, this is not at all surprising, given that my mother was the church organist. Every year at Christmas, we would all stand in rapt wonderment as the choir would sing the Hallelujah Chorus, marveling at the beauty of the music and thrilled at the incredible message that it proclaimed. As a singer, I remember that I began learning *The Messiah* in high school, when I would come home from school and sit down in front of the stereo with the score. After several read-throughs, I was fairly confident in the notes, and began to relax into the significance and magnitude of the lyrics.

There is something about the confluence of Scriptural texts in *The Messiah* that is so striking, that my spirit was drawn into the entire musical celebration. My mind lingers on the alto recitative, with the text from Isaiah 7:14. "Behold, a virgin shall conceive and bear a son, and shall call His name Immanuel, God with us." Even today, when I simply hear the name "Immanuel," my hair stands on end and I experience the shivers that I used to sense in listening to *The Messiah*. Although the music is gorgeous, my palpable reaction is not based solely on Handel's score. Rather, the concept of "God with us" will easily leave me on the brink of tears, if I sit and think about it long enough.

"God with us" invades our despair and brokenness. "God with us" dresses His divine eternity in precious, newborn fragility and humility. "God with us" takes upon Himself our sins and sorrows. "God with us" demonstrates the kind of Father that many have never known. "God with us" does not leave His people alone, but determines never to "leave nor forsake" them. Immanuel is the answer of the God who cares, the God who presences Himself to His people, the God who is there.

The Manifest Presence of God Takes on Flesh

The glory of the Lord was indeed revealed, in the third temple and elsewhere, but it was revealed in a manner that few really expected, because many were so preoccupied with the temple as the visible and tangible manifestation of God's presence. God's presence was revealed in a person, in Immanuel, as prophesied by Isaiah. The Apostle John highlights this theme as well, proclaiming that the glory of God was revealed, not through a glory cloud, but in a living person: "And the Word became flesh and dwelt among us, and we beheld His glory, the glory as of the only begotten of the Father, full of grace and truth." (John 1:14)

Jesus is the manifest presence of God having taken on flesh. Paul agrees in Colossians 1:15 that Jesus is "the image of the invisible God," and the author of Hebrews notes in 1:3 that He is "the brightness of His glory and the express image of His person." No longer does a cloud mitigate His glory, but it streams out through every pore of Jesus' being, and His disciples were overwhelmed by the experience. The Father's presence is now manifested to all people through the living being of the God-man. Moreover, John goes on to assert that in Jesus, God's presence and glory have been perfectly manifested, downplaying any of the previous theophanies that might have come to the reader's mind. "No one has seen God at any time. The only begotten Son, who is in the bosom of the Father, He has declared Him." (John 1:18)

Jesus was the "final and definitive manifestation of God's presence among His people."[22] That is the essence of His name, Immanuel. Peterson makes an insightful comment along these lines: "The point is not that Jesus ever bore Immanuel ('God with us') as an actual name, but that this title indicates the deepest significance of his coming."[23] The glory of the Lord was revealed, no longer hovering over the tabernacle or filling the temple, but

CHAPTER 7: THE GOD WHO IS THERE

through the Incarnation. McKelvey writes "the glory of God which was present in the tabernacle and (afterwards) in the temple of Jerusalem...dwells in Jesus Christ....Now at last the longstanding tension between the transcendence and the immanence of God is resolved."[24] Though some would continue to look for additional manifestations of God's presence, Jesus was the perfect revelation of God's glory. Immanuel is the manifest presence of God.

In a sense, Jesus was also the new temple, and all nations would now come to worship God through Him. His statements that compared His body with the temple, particularly those about raising it in three days, highlighted this new reality. What was unclear about Jesus' prediction at the time was the relationship He would have with the temple, particularly the nature in which He would replace it. In hindsight, however, it becomes perfectly clear: Jesus was the Lamb of God (John 1:36), the Passover Lamb (1 Cor 5:7), slain from the foundation of the world (Rev 13:8), in whom the sins of all the world could be taken away. (John 1:29) Jesus was the perfect, once-for-all sacrifice, and His death did away with the need for sin offerings, because He Himself was made an offering for sin. (Heb 9:12-14) He was the atoning sacrifice that made a relationship with God possible (Heb 4:14-16), and His blood was the entrance into the New Covenant. (Luke 22:20; 1 Cor 11:25)

No longer were the rituals needed in order to mitigate God's holiness for the people, and no longer was access limited to those forming the Jewish nation. At Jesus' death, the veil was rent in two, signifying that humankind could now approach God, not through the temple, but through the person of Jesus. (Heb 6:19-20)

> Jesus replaces the temple of Jerusalem as the source of all life and renewal for the world and as the center for the ingathering of the nations. He does this because he is the ultimate meeting point between God and humanity, by virtue of his incarnation, death and exaltation...He is, at one and the same time, the ultimate means of relating to God and is himself the object of homage or worship.[25]

His person becomes the new temple, the focal point of man's adoration and worship of God, and the vehicle of God's manifest presence among them.[26]

(Dan 7:13-14) His sacrifice replaces the endless animal offerings, establishing a New Covenant (Heb 8:6), and providing atonement for worshipers from all nations who approach God through Him. (Rev 5:9-10) No longer do worshipers experience God's presence through the temple, because Jesus manifests God's presence incarnate, and rightly will receive the worship of all people.‡

As a result, the exaltation of Christ should really be central to every Christian worship service today. Just as the offering of animal sacrifices was central to tabernacle and temple worship, the celebration of Christ's once-for-all sacrifice should be the climax of Christian worship. Christ has made it possible for the Christian to approach the throne of grace with boldness (Heb 4:14-16), and eventually will be confessed by all humanity. (Phil 2:9-11) It makes perfect sense that His adoration should be the pinnacle of the correct worship of God, and the centerpiece of our Christian worship celebrations.

Christ's Presence Manifested through the Spirit

When the manifest presence of God is experienced today in worship, it is intrinsically connected with the person of Jesus and the Spirit, for God's presence is no longer experienced in the glory cloud, but through Immanuel, "God with us." While the glory cloud was a shield that cloaked God's blinding magnificence, Immanuel is the perfect revelation of it in the flesh. He is God's glory and presence among us. Although God could certainly manifest Himself in anyway He desires, one should not expect the glory cloud or some other Old Testament manifestation in worship today, because God now dwells among His people and manifests His presence through Jesus Christ and His

---

‡ While Scripture clearly indicates that Jesus replaces the earthly temple, it is less clear how Jesus' life and death affect the heavenly temple. According to Hebrews 8:5, the earthly tabernacle/temple was simply the copy of a heavenly reality. When Jesus made atonement by His blood, He entered the Holiest Place of the heavenly version as the Most High Priest (Heb 9:11-12) and made it possible for worshipers to draw near the throne of grace. (Heb 10:19-22) However, aspects of the heavenly temple seem to show up again in the book of Revelation, posing a question whether or not they have also passed away. Ultimately, there is no temple in the new heavens and earth, because *God and the Lamb are its temple* (Rev 21:22), which would seem to support the assertion that Jesus ultimately replaces both the earthly and heavenly temples. However, there is disagreement on this point.

CHAPTER 7: THE GOD WHO IS THERE 137

Spirit. (John 14:7) Jesus takes this relationship one step further by proclaiming that He will remain with His disciples forever, promising in Matthew 28:18 that He will be with them until the end of the age.

Unfortunately, many interpreters—and worship theologians in particular—have struggled with how this presence might manifest itself, making poor choices in the texts they use to provide this reassurance. Interpreters will often turn to Matthew 18:20 in an attempt to prove the idea that Christ is especially present in the worshiping assembly. In fact, the phrase "where two or three are gathered" has become an oft-quoted hallmark of this approach, which is a regrettable development. The context of Matthew 18 is simply not discussing worship in the assembly at all, but rather the discipline of the church or covenant community.[27] The suggestion that Christ is present in the gathering of two or three should beg the question, is He not present otherwise? While many rightly ask this question, some are thrown off track by their interpretation of this verse, namely, that it supports a special presence of Christ in the worshiping assembly.

Because this text is often thrown around haphazardly in worship discussions, it becomes necessary to briefly demonstrate how it *does not* apply to Christ's presence in the worshiping assembly. In context, the "two or three" mentioned in Matthew 18:20 does not refer to a gathering of worshipers per se,[28] but to the "two or three" witnesses just mentioned in 18:16, who are gathered to confront a brother or sister. "Moreover if your brother sins against you, go and tell him his fault between you and him alone. If he hears you, you have gained your brother. But if he will not hear, take with you one or two more, that '*by the mouth of two or three witnesses every word may be established.*'" The "two or three witnesses" of both 18:16 and 18:20 actually refer back to the Law, in which the testimony of two or three witnesses was needed in order to establish a matter, thereby convicting someone of wrongdoing. (Deut 17:6; 19:15) Jesus is reassuring His disciples that when two or three come together and "agree," confronting another brother on a matter of discipline, they receive guidance and authority from Christ in their midst. "It is a promise for the church to claim wisdom and restoration for the erring brother."[29] Although this data does not deny the fact that Christ is forever present with His followers, this passage does not support the assertion that Christ manifests His presence in a special way when we worship together.

Rather, the means of Jesus' abiding presence, in the worshiping assembly or elsewhere, is through the Spirit, who is given to all who are in Christ. (Eph 1:13) The indwelling of the Spirit is really the continuation of "God with us" in the life of the New Testament believer. Therefore, the experience of God's presence and glory moves from an external "tabernacle dynamic" of God dwelling *in their midst*, to God dwelling *among them* in the person of Immanuel, to God dwelling *in them* by means of the Holy Spirit.[30] McKelvey writes "God's dwelling on earth is no longer a thing apart from his people; it is the people themselves."[31] God's presence has moved inside His people.

This Spirit connection is a concept that is being developed from the Major Prophets onward, and culminates in Jesus' ministry. When the Old Testament prophets discuss the New Covenant, the Spirit's role in the lives of God's people is particularly proactive. In Ezekiel 36:27-28, God declares "'I will give you a new heart and put a new spirit within you; I will take the heart of stone out of your flesh and give you a heart of flesh. I will put My Spirit within you and cause you to walk in My statutes, and you will keep My judgments and do them.'" This text demonstrates the remarkable immanence of the Spirit's activity under the New Covenant, taking God's presence a step beyond what had been experienced to date, and hinting at the indwelling presence of God that was to come. Paul picks up on this same theme in 2 Corinthians 3:3, remarking "clearly you are an epistle of Christ, ministered by us, written not with ink but by the Spirit of the living God, not on tablets of stone but on tablets of flesh, that is, of the heart." But the capstone of these prophecies regarding the Spirit's activity is the prediction in Joel 2:28. "I will pour out My Spirit on all flesh; your sons and your daughters shall prophesy, your old men shall dream dreams, your young men shall see visions."

Jesus is one who sets this process in motion, standing at the crossroads of the Old and New Testaments, drawing together the manifest presence of God with His internal presence in the life of the believer. First, He is the one who baptizes with the Holy Spirit (Mark 1:8), introducing the indwelling presence of the Holy Spirit into the lives of those who are true worshipers of God. (John 3:5-17; 4:23-24; 16:7) Jesus speaks repeatedly in the upper room discourses of either the Father or Himself sending to them the Paraclete, i.e., the Spirit of truth, upon His departure (John 14:16, 25; 15:26; 16:7, 10), and further prepares them to receive the Spirit on the Day of Pentecost. (Acts 1:8)

Second, Jesus characterizes His continuing presence with His disciples in John 14 in terms of the Holy Spirit. "And I will pray the Father, and He will give you another Helper, that He may abide with you forever—the Spirit of truth…I will not leave you orphans; I will come to you." Indeed, the presence of the Spirit confirms the abiding presence of Christ in His followers, so there is clearly an integrated relationship between the two in the life of the believer. (1 John 3:24; 4:13) The Apostle Paul concurs, pointing out that the Spirit of Christ dwelling in us is evidence that we belong to God, and that we have the Spirit of God within us. (Rom 8:9-11) Notice that the two phrases "Spirit of God" and "Spirit of Christ" are used almost interchangeably in this passage, and Word Biblical Commentary notes "Christ and Spirit are perceived in experience as one—Christ known only in and through the Spirit, the Spirit known only as (the Spirit of) Christ."[32] The indwelling Spirit would seem to manifest Christ's presence.

Finally, Jesus is the pivotal figure who accomplishes the Old Testament prophecies regarding the Spirit, as His redemptive work allocates His Spirit in the life of the believer. Galatians 4:4-6 is instructive in this regard: "But when the fullness of the time had come, God sent forth His Son, born of a woman, born under the law, to redeem those who were under the law, that we might receive the adoption as sons. And because you are sons, God has sent forth the Spirit of His Son into your hearts, crying out, 'Abba, Father!'" Christ's work of redemption *initializes* the indwelling presence of God, that is, the Spirit, in our hearts. The bottom line is that *the indwelling presence of the Spirit in the lives of believers is the most immanent realization of Christ's presence, "God with us," and ultimately, of God's presence.* "Through the gift of the Spirit, the glorified and exalted Lord Jesus continues to dwell in and with his disciples."[33] If Christ Himself is the final revelation of God's glory and presence, and the Spirit is given to embody Christ's presence in the lives of believers, then ultimately, the Spirit must be the means of God's manifest presence.[34] The indwelling Spirit enacts "God with us."

There is one other sense of Christ's presence in the worship service that needs to be mentioned, although I will not attempt anything close to an exhaustive discussion on the topic. Many will claim that the worshiper experiences Christ's presence as he or she receives the sacrament of communion. Indeed, this is actually the position of historic Christianity, whether or not it is a strictly faithful representation of biblical teaching, and conflict over the subject plumbs the depths of the abyss between Catholic and Protestant theology. I have sat with Catholic friends who find the reassurance of Christ's promise regarding His abiding presence (Matt 28:20) fulfilled in the Eucharist celebration. It is emotionally for them the means in which His manifest presence is transmitted to them.

Protestants have a slightly different approach, a result of the Reformation, some denominations asserting that Christ's presence is "in and under" the element,[35] and others contending that the element is rather a meaningful memorial. Robert Webber maintains a somewhat eclectic perspective, as he combines the belief that worship is a real experience of God's presence with the traditions of historic Christianity. Thus, he believes that we actively experience God in worship through the proclamation of the Word, the fellowship of the body, the prayers of the saints, and the reception of the sacrament of communion. "In worship I experience God's presence and action toward me through the sign of the Bible and through the signs of bread and wine, the Holy Communion."[36] Although the means of Christ's presence in the Eucharist will not be sorted out here, it is important to affirm what can be demonstrated biblically regarding Christ's presence in worship: God is with us, in life and in worship, through Christ and the Spirit, in the believer and the body of believers as the temple of God, to which we now turn.

Spiritual Gifts as an Experience of God's Presence

Jesus is meant to be the center of true Christian worship, replacing the temple, as He is the atoning sacrifice by which we approach God. In another

CHAPTER 7: THE GOD WHO IS THERE   141

sense, however, both the individual believer and the body of believers become the new temple of God as they each individually receive the Holy Spirit dwelling within them. Paul frequently alludes to the image of the believer as the temple of God and the domain of the Spirit as one of his favorite metaphors. (1 Cor 3:16; 6:19; 2 Cor 6:16) The individual believer is the new temple of God, in that the Holy Spirit manifests God's special presence in him or her, and maintains a unique role in his or her life.[37] This indwelling of the Spirit will invariably include ministries of interceding (Rom 8:26), directing in obedience and convicting of sin (Ezek 36:27-28), teaching (John 14:26), comforting and encouraging (Acts 9:31), etc. However, there is also a sense in Paul's theology in which the church gathered as the body of Christ (and also the larger, universal church) also represents the temple of God.

> Now, therefore, you are no longer strangers and foreigners, but fellow citizens with the saints and members of the household of God, having been built on the foundation of the apostles and prophets, Jesus Christ Himself being the chief cornerstone, in whom the whole building, being fitted together, grows into a holy temple in the Lord, in whom you also are being built together for a dwelling place of God in the Spirit. (Eph 2:19-22)

This illustration of the church mirrors Paul's discussion about the body of Christ in 1 Corinthians 12, as he describes a single entity that has been endowed by the Spirit with many parts and diverse functions. He pictures the local church coming together for worship, each member with a different gift, each gift a manifestation of the Spirit. (1 Cor 12:11) These many gifts are poured out upon the individual members for the corporate edification of the entire body (1 Cor 12:7). As members are joined to Christ as the Head (Eph 4:15-16), the Spirit gives gifts or functions to each of them to exercise "for the profit of all." (1 Cor 12:21) On a horizontal level, each member truly experiences the presence of God as they minister one to another. As Peterson remarks, "we meet God when we meet with one another."[38] God's indwelling Spirit manifests His presence through the various gifts He bestows upon the members, and makes His presence known (so to speak) as believers make their presence known. Spiritual gifts reveal God's presence in people.

Is this not exactly the point that Paul is making in 1 Corinthians 14:24? When the unbeliever comes into the worship assembly and witnesses believers using their gifts, the Spirit uses the exercise of these gifts to convict the unbeliever of the secrets of his or her heart, causing him or her to worship God and report that God is among them. The same could be said regarding the preaching of the Word, and also the leading of worship. As the Scriptures are opened wide and the Word is expounded, the Holy Spirit empowers the gift of preaching or teaching to reveal truth about God.[39] As the worship leader exercises his or her gifts, whatever they might be, he or she ideally proclaims truth about who God is and what He has done. The worshiper, who is the recipient of these gifts, is edified by the truth displayed about God and moved to a response of worship by the Spirit within.

God uniquely reveals His manifest presence in the assembly through the gifts of the Spirit that have been poured out on His people. This is not to say that God's Spirit does not commune with us individually as we come before Him in worship. However, the fellowship of believers in the assembly allows a unique, horizontal manifestation of God's presence, as there is a corporate enlivening of the Spirit when believers worship together and edify one another with their gifts. Richard Foster calls this enlivening of the Spirit in the lives of gathered worshipers the "koinonia" of the biblical writers, a "deep inward fellowship in the power of the Spirit."[40] The exhilaration that worshipers sense when the body gathers for worship is the Spirit choosing to make His presence known.

The manifest presence of God in the worship setting today is not a mysterious supernatural force that invades the room in some mystical fashion. Rather, it is the Spirit of Christ and God already residing in the lives of believers. This presence is not revealed in the assembly in a glory cloud or in a pillar of fire. God makes Himself known through the Holy Spirit in our lives, and the instruments He often chooses to use in the assembly are the spiritual gifts of His followers. The manifest presence of God has moved from a glory cloud, to the person of Christ, to His Spirit indwelling us and manifesting His presence in our gifts. It is God's presence in and through the people of God.

CHAPTER 7: THE GOD WHO IS THERE

A Final Question

The manifest presence of the God who is everywhere has been perfectly revealed in these last days in the person of Christ, and in the Spirit that indwells all believers. The presence of God could not draw any nearer than He already has through the indwelling of the Spirit, and no glory cloud or Old Testament manifestation of God's manifest presence can rival the presence of God that we experience in Christ. God has manifested His glory in Christ Jesus, and His Spirit has taken up residence in our hearts, just as Ezekiel prophesied. Jesus says that Abraham longed to see this day, for it is the most immanent and treasured experience of God that has ever been known in human history! God is with us in Immanuel, and He dwells in our midst and within us through the Spirit.

Therefore, our worship experience should not be pictured as some kind of bridge that closes a perceived distance between the worshiper and God. That separation was already decisively closed long ago by the sacrifice of Jesus Christ on the cross. Hence, we should not use language in the worship assembly that suggests that God's presence is anywhere but among us. We should not call on His presence to visit us or draw near our assembly, as if He were not already here indwelling our hearts, or use worship music that suggests that same dynamic. We should not activate Old Testament verbiage that reflects a different era in God's manifestation to His people. We should not imply that somehow the enthusiasm or sincerity of our worship activity will bring Him nearer than He already is through Jesus and His Spirit.

Immanuel: God's presence is forever with us. If He were not, is there anything we could do to coax His presence? Is there any kind of righteousness we could achieve, any kind of special excitement we could muster that would bridge the gap on our own? Sally Morgenthaler comments on this absurd scenario: "How are we going to call him down? By being holy enough? By using the right jargon? By praying hard enough?"[41] In truth, this kind of attitude is thoroughly pagan, resembling more of the ancient near eastern culture than that of historic Christianity. To suggest that we can invoke or "evoke a divine encounter"[42] by our worship activity is to believe that we can manipulate God like the ancient pagans tried, endeavoring to appease the gods by their ritual acts of worship. It is to step outside of Christianity and to seek to localize the presence of an eternal God with our own efforts at worship. There is nothing that the worshiper could possibly do by his or her own efforts to bring close the presence of God, otherwise Christ's sacrifice would have been unnecessary. The cross has achieved that relationship on our behalf, and to suggest otherwise is to basically deny its power. Rather, it is now for us to draw near the throne of grace, as the writer of Hebrews invites (Heb 10:22), but that involves a very different attitude and approach.[*]

We do not invite God into our presence. Rather, we open up our hearts to the presence of the God who is everywhere, the God who has already made His dwelling place in our hearts, the God who is there. That is the sense in which we experience the presence of God in worship today. The difference is the critical truth that God does not move, but we do. The movement occurs internally, within our hearts. As we open our hearts—the conjunction of our minds and emotions—to the truth about who God is and what He has done, we begin to experience His presence in our lives, the presence of the God who has been there all along. This awareness occurs "because we are intentionally revealing who this God is and are opening ourselves to him."[43] Sometimes, an awareness of His holiness juxtaposed with the reality of our own disobedience will cause us to fall in humble confession as we sense His presence. When we practice thanksgiving, our hearts are turned from the gift to the Giver, and we become aware of His blessings that have already been poured out on us, yielding a deeper blessing still. We begin to be astounded by the incredible attributes of our gracious and almighty God who has poured out these gifts, and so our hearts most naturally respond with joyful praise.

As we seek Him, we become aware of His presence, the presence of His Spirit who is already dwelling in our hearts. In truth, sometimes God's presence *seems* farther away, but we are not to assume that this lack of awareness means God is *actually* distant from us. Coe quotes Thomas Merton in

---

[*] Some have relied upon the language in James 4:8, noting that drawing near to God means that He will draw near to you. Confession and submission is the context of this verse, and it clearly reflects a dynamic of attitudinal change on the part of the believer, not proximity change. While the language is similar, a better passage for a model of worship interaction with God is expressed in Hebrews 10.

this regard, correcting this fallacy: "God, who is everywhere, never leaves us. Yet He seems sometimes to be present, sometimes absent. If we do not know Him well, we do not realize that He may be more present to us when He is absent than when He is present."[44] It should not cause us to pursue worship with a greater ardor, thinking that our enthusiasm will cause His presence to draw near again.[45] Through His Spirit, God's immanent presence is with us forever.

Unfortunately, many worshipers make the mistake of measuring God's presence in terms of the consolation or emotional release that they experience in the service.[46] Hence, the drive in many worship services begins to focus on what the worshiper must *do* in worship to order to invoke an awareness of God's presence and an experience of the Spirit. They begin to think that their experience or awareness of God primarily depends upon their own efforts at worship, and that they will experience more or less of the Spirit as they wholeheartedly participate. The activity of worship comes to be about generating an experience, and that is one of the many drawbacks of the approach to worship as an experience of God's presence. These drawbacks are the subject of the next chapter.

---

[1] Ronald E. Clements, Old Testament Theology (Atlanta: John Knox Press, 1978), 67.

[2] All quotations from Scripture are taken from the New King James Version (Nashville: Thomas Nelson, Inc., 1979).

[3] R.J. McKelvey, The New Temple (Oxford: Oxford University Press, 1969), 5.

[4] Walter Eichrodt, Theology of the Old Testament, vol. 1, trans. J.A. Baker (Philadelphia: The Westminster Press, 1961), 104-105.

[5] Peterson, Engaging with God: A Biblical Theology of Worship, 24.

[6] Eichrodt, Theology of the Old Testament, 103-104.

[7] K.-H. Bernhardt, Gott und Bild (Berlin: Evangelische Verlagsanstalt, 1956), 67; quoted in John I. Durham, Word Biblical Commentary, vol. 3, Exodus [CD-Rom] (Dallas: Word Books, Publisher, 1998).

[8] Peterson, Engaging with God: A Biblical Theology of Worship, 34.

[9] Ibid., 31.

[10] McKelvey, The New Temple, 2.

[11] Peterson, Engaging with God: A Biblical Theology of Worship, 32.

[12] Ibid.

[13] McKelvey, The New Temple, 2.

[14] Ibid., 4.

[15] Peterson, Engaging with God: A Biblical Theology of Worship, 31.

[16] Ibid., 32.

[17] Ibid., 35.
[18] Ibid., 49.
[19] Ibid., 35.
[20] Ibid., 46.
[21] McKelvey, The New Temple, 23.
[22] Peterson, Engaging with God: A Biblical Theology of Worship, 81.
[23] Ibid., 82.
[24] McKelvey, The New Temple, 76.
[25] Peterson, Engaging with God: A Biblical Theology of Worship, 102.
[26] McKelvey, The New Temple, 77-78.
[27] Allen, The Wonder of Worship, 37.
[28] Earl Radmacher, Ronald B. Allen, and H. Wayne House, eds., Nelson's New Illustrated Bible Commentary, 1174.
[29] Ibid.
[30] McKelvey, The New Temple, 95.
[31] Ibid., 100.
[32] James D.G. Dunn, Word Biblical Commentary, vol. 38a, Romans 1-8 [CD-Rom] (Dallas: Word Books, Publisher, 1998).
[33] Peterson, Engaging with God: A Biblical Theology of Worship, 95.
[34] McKelvey, The New Temple, 98.
[35] Luther, Larger Catechism, 91; quoted in Gomes, Reformation & Modern Theology Course Syllabus, 40.
[36] Robert E. Webber, Worship is a Verb, 66.
[37] McKelvey, The New Temple, 101.
[38] Peterson, Engaging with God: A Biblical Theology of Worship, 198.
[39] Robert E. Webber, Worship is a Verb, 71.
[40] Foster, Celebration of Discipline, 164.
[41] Sally Morgenthaler, phone interview by author.
[42] Gary Burge, "Liturgical Worship: Using Ritual to Inspire True Worship," in Barna, et al., Experience God in Worship, 70.
[43] Sally Morgenthaler, phone interview by author.
[44] Thomas Merton, No Man is an Island (New York: Harcourt, 1950); quoted in John Coe, "Musings on the Dark Night of the Soul: Insights from St. John of the Cross on a Developmental Spirituality," 293.
[45] Coe, "Musings on the Dark Night of the Soul: Insights from St. John of the Cross on a Developmental Spirituality," 299.
[46] John Coe, interview by author.

CHAPTER 8

THE DRAWBACKS OF EXPERIENCE (PART I)

The Attraction of Experience

I used to lead worship with a good friend who is a number of years older than myself, who had experienced quite a journey in terms of his perspective on the subject. Jim took his calling as a worship leader very seriously, and earlier in his life had eagerly decided to pursue a biblical understanding of worship. He was not the kind of person to do anything halfway, and really desired to have a solid grasp on the theology and practice of what he had been called to do. Given the depth of his sincerity, commitment and passion, he wanted to give everything an honest try, and to remain as open to all approaches to worship as was humanly possible.

For a period of time, Jim attended a large, charismatic church in the area, desiring to experience the heights and depths of "Spirit-led" worship. As the Spirit moved during the ministry time, he invariably found himself down on his knees in the front of the large auditorium, surrounded by a small group of people praying over him to receive the gift of tongues. Jim was ready and willing for anything the Spirit might want to do, but mainly for some tangible, supernatural experience. Minutes ticked by, and nothing happened. After a few more minutes, several people from the prayer circle quietly whispered in his ear "just start saying anything." Given that Jim is a very earnest individual, he felt like doing so would be faking it, even though "faking it" may not have been their intention. More time passed, and nothing happened. Jim could see other prayer groups out of the corner of his eye, and could hear the excitement and celebration as the recipients of their efforts each received tongues. Pressure mounted. Then Jim noticed something strange. His own group was diminishing. The members were slowly slipping away, joining other groups, apparently giving up. Nothing was going to happen here. No outpouring of the Spirit. No supernatural experience. The people apparently lost interest, because nothing had happened. Jim was basically left alone.

I do not cite this example to make any kind of statement about the legitimacy of the sign gifts, or the sincerity of those prayer servants who make themselves available for this type of ministry. Rather, I cite this example to highlight a simple point: *experience in worship is very attractive, so attractive that it easily becomes the focus of our efforts.* When people first experience the presence of God in worship, they bask in the warmth and the incredible exultation, their hearts overwhelmed with the desire to praise, as well as with the sheer joy of exalting their marvelous Creator and Redeemer. The next time that they come to worship, however, they probably don't notice the subtle change that has begun to occur. While they sincerely desire to worship God, they also are very interested in that experience of worship, that incredible consolation that they initially felt. The joy of the worship experience has become tantalizing and addictive, like a carrot dangling in front of their eyes, with the memory of that first experience driving them onward.

They begin to work harder to position themselves in that same emotional space that allowed their initial experience. They close their eyes, and concentrate on the lyrics. They raise their hands, and try to get lost in the music. They try to diminish anything that might distract them from the experience. While the experience may come again, it seems to require a lot more effort on their part this time. What they don't realize is that a quiet shift has taken them from worshiping God to *worshiping the experience of worshiping God.* Their efforts at worship now begin to be consumed with generating the experience of worship. The experience of worship, strangely enough, has become an idol.

While there is an incredible positive side to worship as an experience of God, there are also deeply distressing negative aspects, not the least of which is the temptation to generate a worship experience. It was suggested in the last chapter that the presence of God in worship begins to be something

CHAPTER 8: THE DRAWBACKS OF EXPERIENCE (PART I)

that we think we are responsible to invoke by the sincerity and enthusiasm of our worship, or by our own piety and authenticity. However, the presence of God does not move any nearer than the Holy Spirit indwelling our hearts, and so the task of worship becomes the opening of one's heart to the presence of the God who is already there. This task can be complicated by a number of drawbacks, and thus, true worship is easily diverted or derailed. These drawbacks can be categorized in terms of "characterological"[†] drawbacks, or detriments to spiritual growth, and epistemological/other drawbacks. If we are going to operate out of this approach to worship and reap its many benefits, it is essential that we also clearly understand its subtle pitfalls. This chapter and the next will attempt to uncover these weaknesses, and the following one will address some of the more positive aspects.

Characterological Dangers of Experience

The Danger of Experience Becoming the Purpose of Worship

"Gold fever" was the term that was applied to the mania that developed surrounding the gold rush of the late 1800s. When a prospector stumbled upon a small nugget of gold, his life changed as he began to be consumed by the quest for that elusive mineral that hid itself within the veins of the earth. All of his resources became focused on unearthing that tiny piece of ore, and the discovery of a few small nuggets was enough to cause someone to leave his family and to seek his fortune in the treacherous gold fields of California or Alaska. Gold fever drastically altered many lives by its all-encompassing allure, leaving the landscape littered with empty mines and empty lives in the wake of its pursuit. What motivated the miner? Was he captivated by the intrinsic beauty of the substance? Was he smitten by the grandeur of its sparkle and shape? Did he devote his life to its discovery sim-

---

[†] I am deeply indebted to Dr. John Coe, a pioneer in the field of spiritual formation, for the benefit of his insights in this chapter, and for introducing me to the word "characteriological," which I have yet to find in any other literature.

ply for the pleasure and adoration of its existence? Of course not. Gold fever enthralled thousands of regular people like you or me, not because they loved the metal itself, but because they loved what it could do for them. A few flakes of gold dust promised that their lives would change, and their destiny would be altered. Nuggets, like dollar bills, represented power. People desired gold because of what it did for them.

When people experience the presence of God in worship for the first time, they are like the prospector who has stumbled upon a few gold nuggets. They rejoice in the discovery, and are overwhelmed by the experience. However, their natural tendency as humans is to begin worshiping the experience, losing sight of the object of that wonder. Stumbling upon God's presence is so magnificent and enthralling, that Lewis describes it as being "surprised by joy."[1] The human heart barely contains the emotional exaltation that ensues, and so it is understandable that the experience of God will easily take the place of God Himself, and become the object of our desires. Graham Kendrick agrees: "One of the most serious dangers that we encounter when we seek to enrich our worship is our capacity as human beings to turn even the most Godward activity into a selfish pursuit."[2] Distracted by the vivid sensations, the heart reels from the overwhelming response that bubbles up within the soul, with the result that this visceral reaction becomes more desirable than the God who actually caused it.

The first danger of experiencing God in worship is that experience will become the driving force or purpose of worship, particularly for the spiritual beginner, and that the sacrifice of praise and the glorifying of God will become a secondary consideration. Nowhere is this heart shift better described than in the writings of Jonathan Edwards, who critiqued the revivals that occurred during the Great Awakening. Andy Park quotes from *The Religious Affections,* and Edwards' remarks are worth including at length:

> Having received what they call spiritual discoveries or experiences, their minds are taken up with self and the admiration of their experiences. What they are chiefly excited about is not the glory of God or the beauty of Christ but the thrill of their own experiences. They keep thinking "what a wonderful experience this is! What a great discovery that is! What wonderful things I have

encountered!" And so they put their experiences in the place of Christ and His beauty and all-sufficiency. Instead of rejoicing in Christ Jesus, they indulge in their own wonderful experiences. They are so caught up in their own imagination about these great and wonderful experiences that all their notion of God relates merely to them.[3]

Experience so easily begins to drive worship, drawing worshipers back again and again, though they are likely unaware that it is more the experience they adore than the God of their praises. The experience has subtly slipped into the place of the God who initially smote them with His majesty. This is the natural reaction of the human heart, which sees only dimly with barely-opened spiritual eyes, and so is easily misguided in its fledgling flights of worship. It easily swaps God for the human experience of Him, and begins to love the intensity of that experience as much it loves God.

This is a particular trap for the spiritual beginner, who has not yet learned clearly to discern the idolatries of the human heart. "Scott" has made an intuitional connection between his emotions during worship, and the immanence of the God who caused them. Aware of this supernatural presence that is foreign to him, he assumes a causal linkage between this new awareness and his emotional response, as well as his efforts at worship. His experiential knowledge is not wrong, God is indeed near him, but he has rather made a wrong assumption about the nature of God's presence. He assumes that the presence of God is always manifested in a particular way by his emotions, and that the lack of these feelings denotes His absence. His emotions become a barometer of God's presence.

Moreover, this beginner believes that his efforts at worship achieved this immanence for him, and that his praising brought this God near. He is as near to an ancient pagan in practice as possible in his perspective on worship. John Coe writes: "They were habituated as beginners in their earlier life to look to a *spiritual feeling* as the criterion for spirituality. However, God is deeply committed to helping them re-focus, to see that a feeling is not the proper measure of his presence, and to see that he has been and always will be the only true difference."[4] Therefore, it is understandable that the spiritual beginner would seek God in the emotional high of worship, the exaltation of that first experience, equating his or her heightened feelings with God's closeness. The quest for experience in worship has begun.

Contrary to what some have written, I believe that this pursuit is begun in honesty for the beginner and that the worship experience itself is a wonderful gift of the Lord to encourage his or her growth. To see this pursuit of the worship experience as a purely utilitarian preoccupation is to deny the depth and authenticity of that initial experience. If "Jane" came to a worship service looking to have a real experience of God's presence, then authenticity is endemic to what she is seeking. No one desires a fake experience of God's presence. If she then consciously sought to use the service in order to manufacture an experience, the knowledge of her plans would thoroughly undermine the possibility of having an authentic experience of God. Authenticity and utilitarianism cannot coexist in the same worshiper at the same time, for they are spiritually at odds. Piper writes: "True worship cannot be performed as the means to some other experience. Feelings are not like that. Genuine feelings of the heart cannot be manufactured as stepping stones to something else."[5] While she might be confused about the nature of the experience itself, one has to agree that this worshiper is at least seeking it in honesty.

Furthermore, what God gives by way of spiritual and emotional pleasure in those first worship experiences is designed to nurture spiritual beginners and draw them into a greater depth of relationship with their Creator.[6] Although some would argue that we should worship God for His sake alone,[7] this approach ignores the fact that there is a developmental spirituality,[8] and that God motivates every believer in different ways depending upon the depth of his or her spiritual maturity. (Heb 5:12-14) To insist that a spiritual child relate to God and love Him on the same level as a spiritual father is like demanding that an infant be fed sirloin steak, hoping that he or she will develop a taste for it.[9] Worshiping God for His sake alone first requires a degree of spiritual growth, and worship is one of many paths to that end.

A more significant concern is that the beginner might begin to worship the experience, the human emotional response to God's presence, in place of God. Without realizing it, he or she can begin to equate spiritual or emotional self-gratification with worship, as Peterson suggests.[10] Although worship leader Andy Park has what I believe is a flawed understanding of the presence of God, I believe that he describes this scenario very well: "I think that a lot of what people call the 'presence of the Lord' is actually adrenaline, endorphins and the joy of music. People are looking for a high and mistakenly measure the success of their worship time by how high they get."[11] In a strange sense, the human experience of God can be worshiped in place of God Himself!

When something other than God takes the place of God, even if it is a thoroughly spiritual and valuable thing, the Scriptures call that thing an idol. When the worship of God is replaced by the experience of worship, then it becomes an idol in the heart. It is not surprising that this would occur, as the human heart has been called an "idol factory," changing anything that is of value into an object to be worshiped. That is the essence of our fallen condition; we are prone to localize God in people or things, just as the pagans did in the Old Testament. Peter Kreeft comments on this predisposition:

> Anything—anything—can be an idol. Religion can be an idol. Religion is not God but the worship of God; idolizing religion means worshipping worship. That's like being in love with love rather than with a person. Love too can be an idol, for "God is love" but love is not God...Since an idol is not God, no matter how sincerely or passionately it is treated as God, it is bound to break the heart of its worshipper, sooner or later.[12]

In this preoccupation with the experience of worship, people are not really worshiping the experience of worship so much as they are worshiping the way that one experience of God makes them feel. They are worshiping the human physiological and emotional responses to God that sometimes occur in and through worship. In truth, they are actually worshiping themselves, and the ritual sacrifices that they lay upon the altar to themselves are the emotional responses they receive in the worship service. Worship is a gift or an offering that they both give and receive.

In high school, I used to work in the shopping mall doing Christmas wrapping in order to raise money for our choir trips. There was a rather conspicuous lingerie retailer just down the corridor, and so ironically, at least half of our customers were men. They would sidle up to the wrapping station with a sheepish grin and would toss a distinctive red box down upon our workstation, eager for the embarrassing brand to be quickly covered over with Santa and elves. As I would lift the box to slip paper under it, I would notice how light it was, as if nothing were inside. On one occasion I remarked to the customer, "is there anything in there?" He replied "not much anyway." In truth, the lingerie they gave to their wives or lovers was a gift to themselves, for in reality, they probably gave with the exclusive intent of reaping an obvious benefit.

When self becomes the object of worship, the worship experience operates in a similar way, and the emotional climax that music naturally raises is often a sacrifice to oneself. Bono comments on this scene: "Music is worship; whether it's worship of women or their designer, the world or its destroyer, whether it comes from that ancient place we call soul or simply spinal cortex, whether the prayers are on fire with a dumb rage or dove-like desire…the smoke goes upwards…to God or something you replace God with…usually yourself."[13] Idolatry is often merely a worship of self.

One can see this situation taking over on the worship scene when the majority of new worship repertoire begins to focus on the worshiper's experience of worship, instead of exalting the works and qualities of the God who deserves that worship. The difference is so subtle, that I have noticed that many worshipers and worship leaders alike are not even able to discern the serious difference. Although I fully support the use of first-person pronouns in worship music, it is so interesting to find music that is actually singing *about worship*, rather than the God who inspires worship. Truly, it is a telltale sign of this experiential approach to worship. For example, I believe that it is a completely different statement to sing "how lovely is Your dwelling place" than "I love to be in Your presence." While both are based on Psalm 84, one says something about God and the other says something about my experience of God in worship.

While there are certainly stages in the worship service, particularly preparation or response, in which it is appropriate to sing about one's experience of God, a diet of worship music that is completely centered on my experience loses God as the subject of worship, and really cannot even be called the worship of God. Rather, it becomes the worship of self, for it is now a sacrifice that we are offering to ourselves. The danger of experience becoming the driving purpose of worship is truly the danger of worshiping self before God.

The Danger of Misunderstanding the Spirit's Work

When the presence of the Lord is consistently measured in terms of emotional exaltation, as well as feelings of deep and abiding comfort, then one begins to assume that the Spirit will always manifest Himself in this particular manner. We come to expect that the presence of God equals joy and contentment, and that being brushed by the Spirit will invariably cause excitement and exhilaration. Writers on spiritual formation call this sensation and interaction "consolation."[14] However, this mindset tends to limit the variety of activities and emotions that one will accept as the legitimate work of the Spirit in worship. Is it possible that the Spirit works in ways that are not always consoling? Is it possible that He sometimes utilizes weeping in order to stimulate growth?

Although there are a great many psalms of lament, we tend to shy away from them,[15] because they fall outside our preconceived understanding of worship. When we bow before the Lord, we desire the experience to create comfort, consolation, wonder, awe, etc. We do not want to accept that an experience of God's presence might result in some other less "enjoyable" responses. When individuals in the Old Testament experienced the manifest presence of God, their reaction was rarely joy and contentment, but rather was almost categorically fear and trembling. Similarly, will an experience of the Spirit in worship always result in joy, or will it also sometimes cause sadness, grieving or repentance? Spiritual writers label this manifestation of the Holy Spirit "desolation."[16] The danger of exclusively associating God's presence in worship with consolation is that we close ourselves off to other legitimate methods that the Spirit might want to employ.

Essentially, some worshipers have learned to equate what feels good with the presence of the Lord, rather than allowing the Holy Spirit to move in any manner that He desires. If we were to evaluate all of our experiences in life in terms of what feels good, then we must take James' comments to heart: "If merely 'feeling good' could decide, drunkenness would be the supremely valid human experience."[17] It is self-evident that what feels good or comfortable is rarely how one evaluates an experience, and yet, that is often how one approaches the work of the Spirit in the worship setting. The comfort of the Spirit is often what is highlighted, and little else.

Along these lines, it is interesting that we have grown accustomed to calling the Spirit "the Comforter," even though the Greek word "Paraclete" retains more of a sense of advocacy.[18] It is clear that the Spirit is sometimes experienced in a nurturing manner, but to confine His work to consolation alone is to seriously misunderstand the breadth of His viable ministry. Years ago, I remember people asking me what I thought about the movement of laughing in the Spirit. Although I won't comment here on my theological issues with that movement, I would be much less surprised to see a genuine movement of weeping in the Spirit, because I find that confession and repentance are more often the focus of His activities than ecstasy.

The central danger becomes apparent when the Spirit chooses to move in desolation rather than consolation, because the worshiper with these preconceptions has a difficult time accepting that it is a genuine movement of the Spirit. If "Joe" has learned to connect his good feelings with the presence of the Lord, and wrongly believes that he is personally responsible for that immanence, then the absence of his emotional high will naturally lead him to the conclusion that he must not be "doing" worship correctly.[19] He might think that he is not enthusiastic or sincere enough, or that there is possibly some problem with his personal piety. If Joe no longer senses that magnificent exaltation or warm sense of consolation, he might think that God is actually distant and that he is to blame, leaving him to wonder whether God might have forsaken him. While the lack of consolation or an awareness of God's presence might legitimately draw attention to the need for repentance, that is not always the case, so exclusively linking consolation with the activity of the Spirit can be doubly damaging.

As a result, the worshiper will work harder to gear up the emotions or strive at the worship in a superstitious manner, much like a shaman or witch doctor. He or she does not understand the presence of the Lord, and does not realize that God's presence is often legitimately experienced in desolation. St. John of the Cross, the Christian mystic, wrote on spiritual formation, and notes this peculiar response:

> In ceremonies, beginners may strain to squeeze out feelings of pleasure, instead of offering humble praise and reverence to God within themselves. They are so attached to reaping a sensual harvest that when no such feelings come they think they have failed…God often withdraws sensual sweetness just so that they might turn the eyes of faith upon him.[20]

As this quote implies, the Spirit will often use desolation in order to develop the character of the believer in the manner that He desires, rather than in the way that the believer requires. John Coe notes from the church fathers that God often will withdraw that sweet sense of the Spirit, that "bottle of spiritual pleasures" in order to produce deep characterological change. He writes: "What does not feel very spiritual in a dark night, in the believer's dryness and spiritual doldrums, turns out to be a profound work of the Spirit that acquaints the Christian with the truth of him- or herself."[21] If "Melinda" has mistakenly developed this shallow understanding of the Spirit's work, then she will not be open to the spiritual growth that the Spirit has for her in desolation. She will not be open to the experience of the Spirit revealing her inner idolatries, for it is often through desolation that the Spirit holds up a mirror to the truth of our hidden hearts.[22] The deepest work of the Spirit in spiritual growth is revealing the need for inner change, and desolation is frequently the mirror that He uses. Denying desolation as a legitimate work of the Holy Spirit thus denies this work of purification in one's life.

The Danger of Trying to
Generate a Worship Experience

When worshipers have equated God's presence in worship with emotional exaltation, and have succumbed to the belief that they can invoke an encounter with God by virtue of their own enthusiasm at worship, then the driving pressures on both the worshiper and the worship leader will be to generate some kind of experience on their own. Given that the worshiper might not understand the significance of consolation and desolation in the spiritual disciplines, the pressures of this worship dynamic will rather encourage him or her towards working up those feelings in order to feel that he or she has experienced God's presence and "really worshiped."

Creating a worship experience is not at all difficult when it simply involves manipulating one's emotions. Quoting from Dr. Edwin Starbuck, renowned psychologist William James cites this rather familiar description of religious experience: "The subject works his emotions up to the breaking point, at the same time resisting their physical manifestations, such as quickened pulse, etc., and then suddenly lets them have their full sway over his body. The relief is something wonderful, and the pleasurable effects of the emotions are experienced to the highest degree."[23] This description of an ecstatic experience from the start of the 20th century seems frighteningly close to many worship experiences that are pursued in Evangelical settings in this day and age. While there is nothing wrong with the expression of emotions in the worship service, the danger is that these self-induced attempts at worship exaltation will consume the worshiper, distracting him or her from actually worshiping God. Instead, he or she will become focused on worshiping experience, and will lose sight of God as the object of worship.

For those of us who are worship leaders, the temptation to try to generate a worship experience for the people can be deceptively strong. After all, the sight of a person who is being moved and engaged by the Holy Spirit looks and feels an awful lot like they are being moved and impacted by us. The natural desire in any of us is to lead out of that need for recognition and approval, and the genuine experience of worship can often provide that. While the worship leader certainly desires to be an instrument of the Lord and a servant of the people, self-gratification can easily creep into the practice of leading worship. I speak very candidly about the practice of worship leading, because I can discern these errors in myself. I know that the worship experience can be crafted in such a manner that it manipulates the worshiper's experience, throwing glory back to the worship leader. Given the fact that music itself carries an immense, emotional impact, the choice of repertoire alone may insure that the worshiper's experience is excited.

Am I planning worship with a view primarily towards revealing truth about God, or towards exciting the worshiper's experience? Certainly the aesthetic dynamic of a worship presentation is very important for worship; it is partially through aesthetics that the worship material speaks truth about God into the worshiper's culture and experience. However, there is a difference between working with aesthetics and trying to conjure up God for the people, as Sally Morgenthaler has pointed out.[24] The danger of generating an experience is that it will not be in submission to the guidance of the Holy Spirit, but will be responding to personal desires of the worship leader. Furthermore, it might reinforce for one worshiper that God is experienced in emotional exaltation, and for another that his or her complete lack of consolation betrays a lack of spiritual connection with God. In both circumstances, we have probably led them astray.

The Danger of Experience Sidetracking Spiritual Growth

Trying to generate emotions for their sake is not only a misguided approach to worship, but there is a danger that it will actually derail the worshiper from experiencing the spiritual growth that the Spirit intends. Generating an experience can be the least worshipful thing a worshiper can do, if that is not what the Spirit desires to give him or her. It is the opposite of being open to the Spirit's activity; indeed, it seeks to manipulate the Spirit by duplicating the experience in one's own strength. Furthermore, Coe has mentioned that "the quest for experience in worship can actually deflect spiritual honesty."[25] Seeking the heights of consolation alone in the worship experience allows one to worship out of one's false self, or the plastic personality that we sometimes wear in community. It allows the refuse of one's sinful, human nature to remain buried under a polished and enthusiastic exterior, nearly inaccessible to the purifying work of the Spirit in worship. Instead of allowing the Spirit to hold up a mirror to one's hidden heart, generating an experience manufactures a mirror of the façade one has composed. It is the opposite of authenticity in worship.

Fortunately, the Spirit will not allow this kind of preoccupation to occur for long, for He empowers the spiritual disciplines, and will often deny consolation. Thus, He will force the worshiper to grow deeper in his or her faith and spiritual honesty, in order to be purified by the disciplines. When the worshiper is not open to the work of the Spirit in desolation, worship will become increasingly agonizing, confusing, exhausting and heartbreaking. Joy becomes elusive and virtually leaves the process, as the worshiper struggles all the harder to grasp it. God will *seem* wholly absent, in order for the worshiper to learn experientially that He is always present. Andy Park gives a needed corrective:

> I believe that God purposely chooses to pour out his Spirit at one moment and to withhold it at other times to show that he cannot be controlled by us. This keeps us from worshiping the act of worship instead of worshiping God. Our job is to honor him, praise him and thank him. We should be grateful for whatever degree of self-revelation he bestows on us.[26]

Both consolation and desolation are gifts of God,[27] and thus it is essential for the spiritual growth of the worshiper that he or she place himself or herself in the position of being a grateful receiver of whatever God gives.

At the end of the day, God creates the true worship experience, and determines how He will allow the worshiper to experience Himself based upon His own criteria. Coe remarks that if God so desired, He could give each of us the most wonderful and direct experience of His presence—a theophany—in every single worship experience. God clearly does not choose to manifest Himself with this frequency, however, and there is a very good reason. Coe suggests that theophanies are wonderful gifts for the moment,

CHAPTER 8: THE DRAWBACKS OF EXPERIENCE (PART I)   161

but they do not tend to produce deep spiritual change, and we always tend to want to hold onto them.[28] While mystical experiences are often used by the Spirit to create a vital desire for God, they do not by themselves cause characterological change.

In this day and age, we might ask "would not a theophany be the most powerful and confirming experience for one's faith? Would not such a worship experience deeply change the inner heart?" One would think so. However, almost any believer who reads the account of the Israelites in the wilderness will at some point ask this question: how can someone who is continually surrounded by visible manifestations of God, as well as by His incredible and supernatural providence, not trust Him to enter the promised land? The answer is simply this: *spiritual experience does not necessarily create trust, nor does it create lasting spiritual growth or sanctification on its own*, and ultimately, that is God's desire for every believer, regardless of the intensity of their worship experience.

The Danger of Individualism

A fifth danger of worship as an experience is that the worshiper will begin to practice worship in an individualistic manner, as a personal, private ceremony of praise. Undoubtedly, this is not the intent of the paradigm, but the expectations of the worshiper as he or she comes to the service are certainly personal in nature, for the experience of consolation or desolation cannot really be shared corporately. This is not necessarily a negative development, as it does provide a window through which the Spirit can achieve intimate moments of spiritual growth in the lives of individual believers. But worship as a discipline, which is really the heart of this approach, is difficult to practice in such a way that there is still a horizontal dimension of community interaction and edification.

This experienced-oriented approach tends to lose the New Testament value of worship as a time and place in which the body pursues mutual edification. Individualism can forsake that community dynamic. Peterson, quoting R.P. Martin notes: "Individuals intent on edifying themselves may 'seal themselves off from others and concentrate exclusively on their own personal experiences.'"[29] In these instances, the edification of the body ceases to be a component of worship at all, as experience takes over as a central goal of the worship experience. While the gifts of the leaders are certainly being used to edify the body, the worshiper in the pew has abandoned the exercise of his or her gifts, and is perhaps not really being used to edify others in the assembly. The focus of the worshiper has turned away from corporate edification to personal enrichment and enlightenment.

The Apostle Paul makes it clear that corporate worship must have the edification of the body in mind, and Peterson adds "self-edification…falls short of the primary goal of Christian assembly. Paul's principle here challenges the common assumption that church services should simply be designed to facilitate a private communion with God, either by spiritual exercises or ritual."[30] The individual worshiper is not called into the assembly with the express purpose of edifying himself or herself, but with the charge to offer a sacrifice of praise (Heb 13:15) and to "consider one another in order to stir up love and good works." (Heb 10:24) There is certainly a balance between edification and personal communion for which the body needs to strive, and Webber highlights that the two dimensions can actually augment one another when they are pursued as a both/and proposition. "A community of brothers and sisters in Christ is better able to experience God's transforming power in worship. Without an understanding of what it means to be the church, believers run the risk of individualistic worship, a worship that is not fully biblical nor completely satisfying to the soul."[31] At the end of the day, personal experience must not overbalance mutual edification.

The Danger of Losing Worship as a Lifestyle

An interesting trend has been occurring in Evangelical circles of late, that reveals something of our basic approach to worship. The word "worship" has begun to be used synonymously with, or rather in place of the word "music." When people talk about the music or the musical presentation that occurs in a worship service, they invariably will refer to it as the "worship time," as if music were identical with worship. This labeling is more than understandable, as the people—and often the leadership—are designating the time during the service in which they lift praises to God in worship. However, there are a number of problems with this identification, the greatest of which is that it reduces the concept of worship to an activity alone. Is there not a broader picture of worship in the Scriptures? Ultimately, worship is much bigger than music, and the danger is that our understanding of the whole concept of worship has been shifted by the experience-oriented approach.

The problem is not so much how we use the words, but how they picture our thinking on the deepest level. Our use of this terminology *simply reflects* a fundamental, philosophical shift, an understanding that worship is primarily an activity, not a lifestyle. In our minds, we have begun to shrink a biblical concept that encompassed all of life to a single activity that we pursue on Sunday mornings or Wednesday nights. Unfortunately, we use our one English word "worship," which is probably closer in meaning to "praise," and apply it to a comprehensive, biblical concept that involved many Hebrew words. The essence of worship thus becomes confused. Peterson writes "contemporary Christians obscure the breadth and depth of the Bible's teaching on this subject when they persist in using the word 'worship' in the usual, limited fashion, applying it mainly to what goes on in Sunday services."[32] Worship, for the Israelites, truly circumscribed a life relationship with God, and involved an *attitude* of fear, honor, respect and adoration, an *activity* of sacrifice and praise, and a *lifestyle* of obedience and walking in God's ways. Condensing worship to a single activity misses out on the breadth and richness of the biblical concept.

Throughout Scripture, worship was first and foremost an attitude and a lifestyle that inspired an activity, not vice versa. Worship was a life orientation of a worshiper of YHWH that combined the heart or the inner person with the lifestyle, meaning one's external actions of obedience. This attitude is perhaps best represented by the biblical concept of "fearing God," which was frequently connected in Scripture with keeping His commands. (Deut 5:29; 6:2; 17:9, etc.) Certainly this was the understanding of the patriarchs, who surely did not attend a weekly service of sacrifice and praise. Rather, their relationship with God was focused on their passion to trust and obey Him, pictured in the language of the Old Testament as "fearing the Lord." "Reverence or the fear of the Lord in the Old Testament means faithfulness and obedience to all the covenant demands of God. While this found expression in the cultic activity, the reference was normally to the honouring of God by total lifestyle."[33] Attitude and action supported the activity.

Thus, there was an obedience element to fearing God, but there was also a deep heart connection in worship, for God was definitely not interested in activities of worship that were ritualistic or unconnected with the "deep interior" of the person.‡ The prophet Isaiah, speaking on God's behalf, emphasized this heart component in 29:13, when he asserted "these people draw near with their mouths and honor Me with their lips, but have removed their hearts far from Me." Moreover, the component of obedience, or keeping the commandments of the Lord, was the most fundamental manner in which the Israelite was to express this deep passion for the Lord. The "worship conversation" included the worshiper expressing his or her love for the Lord by a lifestyle of obedience, not just by singing His praises. Thus, in Deuteronomy 6:1, the author introduces the idea of fearing the Lord by keeping His commands, and then links this lifestyle with the worshiper's inner motivation, his or her love for God. "You shall love the LORD your God with all your heart, with all your soul, and with all your strength. And these words which I command you today shall be in your heart." (Deut 6:5,6) The whole lifestyle of worship was intimately connected with the worshiper's internal motivation of love.

An interesting passage where the whole concept of worship is brought together is in II Kings 17, illustrating how biblical worship is an attitude, an activity and a lifestyle. The author of this passage is relating a cultural situation that occurred in Israel during the exile, and we discussed these events a little in chapter seven. Within the passage, he is seeking to describe what

---

‡ Worship is "ritualistic," by definition, if it highlights form without a connection with the deep interior of the individual. This is not to make a blanket statement that ritual itself inherently lacks the possibility of this deep heart connection, but rather that worship becomes "ritualistic" when form is denied the deeper attitude and heart reality.

CHAPTER 8: THE DRAWBACKS OF EXPERIENCE (PART I)

exactly God had expected of the Israelites by way of worship, and so basically summarizes the book of Deuteronomy in this effort:

> You shall not fear other gods, nor bow down to them nor serve them nor sacrifice to them; but the LORD who brought you up from the land of Egypt with great power and an outstretched arm, Him you shall fear, Him you shall worship, and to Him you shall offer sacrifice. And the statutes, the ordinances, the law, and the commandment which He wrote for you, you shall be careful to observe forever. (2 Kgs 17:35b-37)

All three concepts are faithfully represented here. True biblical worship is an attitude that results in a lifestyle of obedience, and is expressed in an activity of worship and a sacrifice. In a wholistic, biblical concept of worship, the heart and the lifestyle preceded the offering of praise and the ritual sacrifice. Indeed, an offering or sacrifice without the first two components was considered blatantly pagan and hypocritical. Notice the disobedient and syncretistic response of the individuals in 2 Kings 17:40-41. "However they did not obey, but they followed their former rituals. So these nations feared the LORD, yet served their carved images."

Worship that does not acknowledge a full, biblical understanding, but isolates only one of the aspects, is not true biblical worship. Ronald Allen agrees: "Worship of God that does not proceed from a life of obedience to God is really not genuine worship at all."[34] It is impossible to live a life of disobedience or flagrant rebellion against the Lord during the week, and then truly engage in the worship activity at church. It is essentially the same response of the pagans in 2 Kings 17. When worship becomes exclusively an activity of singing or praise in our mindsets, divorced from the lifestyle and attitude, then it is worship that is not pleasing to God.

---

[1] C.S. Lewis, Surprised by Joy (San Diego: Harcourt Brace Jovanovich, Publishers, 1955), 17.

[2] Kendrick, Learning to Worship as a Way of Life, 55.

[3] Jonathan Edwards, The Religious Affections; quoted in Park, To Know You More: Cultivating the Heart of the Worship Leader, 157.

[4] Coe, "Musings on the Dark Night of the Soul: Insights from St. John of the Cross on a Developmental Spirituality," 300.

[5] Piper, Desiring God, 81.
[6] Coe, "Musings on the Dark Night of the Soul: Insights from St. John of the Cross on a Developmental Spirituality," 296.
[7] Dawn, Reaching Out Without Dumbing Down, 88.
[8] Coe, "Musings on the Dark Night of the Soul: Insights from St. John of the Cross on a Developmental Spirituality," 294.
[9] Ibid., 295.
[10] Peterson, Engaging with God: A Biblical Theology of Worship, 17.
[11] Park, To Know You More: Cultivating the Heart of the Worship Leader, 155.
[12] Peter Kreeft, Heaven: The Heart's Deepest Longing (San Francisco: Ignatius Press, 1980), 21.
[13] Bono, intro to Selections from the Book of Psalms, x-xi.
[14] St. John of the Cross, Dark Night of the Soul, trans. Mirabai Starr (New York: Riverhead Books, New York, 2002), 54.
[15] Dawn, Reaching Out Without Dumbing Down, 176.
[16] Thomas Dubay, Seeking Spiritual Direction: How to Grow the Divine Life Within (Ann Arbor, Michigan: Servant Publications, 1993), 188.
[17] James, The Varieties of Religious Experience, 19.
[18] George R. Beasley-Murray, Word Biblical Commentary, vol. 36, John [CD-Rom] (Dallas: Word Books, Publisher, 1998).
[19] Coe, "Musings on the Dark Night of the Soul: Insights from St. John of the Cross on a Developmental Spirituality," 299.
[20] St. John of the Cross, Dark Night of the Soul, 53.
[21] Coe, "Musings on the Dark Night of the Soul: Insights from St. John of the Cross on a Developmental Spirituality," 296.
[22] Ibid., 302.
[23] Edwin Starbuck; quoted in James, The Varieties of Religious Experience, 276.
[24] Morgenthaler, phone interview by author.
[25] Coe, interview by author.
[26] Park, To Know You More: Cultivating the Heart of the Worship Leader, 171.
[27] John Coe, "Drawing Near to God When God Seems Far Away: Practicing the Presence of God Despite Feelings" (lecture presented at the Talbot One-Day Spiritual Retreat, La Mirada, California, 26 September 2003).
[28] Ibid.
[29] R.P. Martin, The Spirit and the Congregation (Grand Rapids: Eerdmans, 1984), 70; quoted in Peterson, Engaging with God: A Biblical Theology of Worship, 212.
[30] Peterson, Engaging with God: A Biblical Theology of Worship, 212.
[31] Webber, Signs of Wonder: The Phenomenon of Convergence in Modern Liturgical and Charismatic Churches, 65.
[32] Peterson, Engaging with God: A Biblical Theology of Worship, 18.
[33] Ibid., 73.
[34] Allen, The Wonder of Worship, 114.

CHAPTER 9

THE DRAWBACKS OF EXPERIENCE (PART II)

Epistemological/Other Dangers of Experience

The Danger of Experience
Under-balanced with Truth

When I was a young child, maybe six or seven, I had an interesting experience one night. My brother Jon and I shared a room, and had a bright Mickey Mouse night-light that cast a sort of red glow all over the room. I can still picture that plastic figurine throwing a circle of light across the walls and bookshelves on which it was positioned. It happened that I woke up in the middle of the night, and sat up in my bed. Standing in the shadows of our open door, just outside the reach of illumination, was my father. He was clad in a hound's tooth jacket with large black and white checkers that he used to wear, and I think some kind of gray turtleneck underneath. Even now, I can see that image so clearly in my mind's eye, as it is emblazoned on my memory. I sat there and looked at him for a few minutes, saying nothing, and then he was gone. It seemed strange at the time, but I thought nothing of it and went back to sleep.

In the morning, I asked my mother if he had come into our room last night. I don't remember her exact response, except that it was "no," and that whatever she told me made it impossible for him to have been there. He may have been on a trip, which was very possible, even away at a board meeting, but he could not have been standing in our doorway in the middle of the night. Later I checked his closet, and saw the hound's tooth jacket hanging there, the exact one that I had seen. While I would like to believe that I was dreaming, the experience was so real, so visceral that I cannot believe it was just a product of my unconscious mind. Regardless of the fact that I was given empirical evidence to the contrary, the memory is so vivid and the sensations so real, that I must believe that someone was standing in that doorway in the middle of the night. While rational thought tells me one thing, I find my experience far more convincing.

What I have described is not uncommon from what many have experienced at one time or another, some experience of special perception or inner realization that cannot be rationally explained, but which is undeniable because of its profound impression on one's senses. In these cases, mystical experience tends to trump rational thought, for it contains "a curious kind of authority," as James remarked.[1] As Christians, we should understand this interrelationship. The women at the tomb believed their corporeal experience of the resurrected Jesus in spite of their reason, which told them that dead people did not rise again. The disciples reacted more out of disbelief, which is probably more consistent with how we might have responded. The problem is that as 21st century Christians, we are stretched between our basically modern worldview, including what often amounts to an anti-supernatural approach to knowledge, and our open-ness to phenomena that are not explainable by the scientific method. We find ourselves caught between two worldviews, two epistemological paradigms, wondering how much credence we should legitimately lend to experience, and how much we should solely rely upon rational thought and the revealed truth of Scripture in our approach to knowledge.

As a result, there are many responses to the intersection of biblical "truth" and experience. Some are open to any kind of inner mystical or transcendental experience, regardless of how it might contradict Scripture, while others categorically deny any experience not specifically *prescribed* in Scripture. Some approve experiences that are *described* in the Bible, whether or not they are "normative" examples, while others assert that those experiences only belong in the New Testament age. We must ask, what is the correct relationship between revealed truth and experience? This question is critical to a discussion of the approach to worship as an experience of God's presence, because much of the inner, emotional experience that occurs in this approach is either implicitly or explicitly connected with what are supposedly manifestations of the Spirit. The danger is that this approach will cause inner experience to be uncritically accepted, and that it will be placed upon a higher and more authoritative position relative to rational thought, and ultimately, biblical truth.

We are creatures of our culture in this fascination with experience because much of postmodernism relies heavily upon an epistemology of experience, which was described in chapter three as the narrative structure. The narrative structure is an epistemological framework that seeks to make sense of experiences, redefining truth in terms of what is meaningful, and not in terms of what has an objective, external point of reference. The postmodern person assembles reality by borrowing bits and pieces from other narratives, in order to make sense of his or her particular story. Truth is cast in an existential light, as the individual makes the overriding criteria of truth to be whatever he or she finds most compelling and explanatory in light of his or her own experiences. Something is "true" by virtue of it being "meaningful" to the person, and by virtue of it being coherent with his or her established preferences. Therefore, "revealed" truth in Scripture is simply another source from which to inform one's own perspective on reality. It is no longer the measure by which one evaluates one's experiences, but rather, one's experiences become the standard in determining what is "true." Truth and meaning have become confused.

While one would hope that this dynamic has not influenced Christian thought or Evangelicalism, the reality is that we are all influenced by our cultures. This approach can be seen in many Bible study settings, for example, in which people share their "feelings" about what a passage means to them, regardless of whether or not the author intended it to carry that particular meaning. A telltale sign of this orientation is when people are unable to distinguish their thoughts from feelings in discussing a text, demonstrating that they are less interested in what the author critically "means" to say, but rather what the passage existentially "means" to them. Gergen notes "this argument is not a happy one for most teachers of literature, for it means that all readings of a text or poem—including those of neophyte students—are equally valid as insights into 'true' meaning."[2]

We are also particularly vulnerable to the domination of experience in the worship arena, given the fact that aesthetics are the domain of experience, and the manifestations of the Spirit in these settings are intrinsically experiential in nature. When "Mike" says that he sensed the presence of God descend upon the worship setting, what he is actually saying is that the Spirit ministered to him on a deeply emotional level. Instead of saying that, however, he characterizes the presence of God on the basis of how he emotionally experienced it, and not on the basis of what the revealed truth of Scripture says about the presence of God. Because experience connects with us on such a visceral level, we tend to define reality in terms of how we experience it, and not in terms of rational thought or revealed truth. We end up giving experience precedence over both.

One major problem with placing experience before rational thought and revealed truth is that reason actually provides the context in which experience is interpreted and given meaning by the individual. In order for experience to obtain meaning, it must be interpreted according to a pre-existing cognitive framework, which God has revealed for us through the biblical writers.[3] While both reason and sensation are complementary elements in our human make-up, rationality must have the authority or else experience is meaningless. For example, I recently heard a Bible teacher discuss the fact that God was "with David" in all his experiences of his life. She named a few, and then sought to make the point that God was with David "in his experiences, not his theology." While it is true that David's experiential knowledge of God helped inform his theology, he would have had no way of interpreting God in his experiences unless first he had believed in a certain kind of God who interacted with humans in a certain manner. Reason, in combination with revealed truth gave him this framework. Therefore, rationality and revealed truth precede our experiences and maintain an epistemological authority over them, whether we are aware of it or not; otherwise our experiences would be absolutely meaningless.

CHAPTER 9: THE DRAWBACKS OF EXPERIENCE (PART II)

Unfortunately, the "curious authority" of mystical experience has a particularly dangerous result, that the one who has had an experience will be removed from the reach of reason, logical persuasion or any kind of rational (versus experiential) data. Because rational argumentation, particularly someone else's argument, is implicitly recognized as inferior to his or her senses and experiences, he or she basically can become unreachable by logic or reason. For example, when "Joanne" claims to have heard from the Lord, her experiences are so visceral and powerful to her that there is really no way to evaluate them, even from the revealed truth of Scripture. Experience tends to precede dogma or doctrinal truth in this paradigm, as James argued. His dictum reflects the words of the Bible teacher who was just quoted. He writes "the mystic is, in short, invulnerable, and must be left, whether we relish it or not, in undisturbed enjoyment of his creed."[4] The radical danger of an epistemology of experience is that revealed truth will become impotent before the Goliath of mystical experience.

Is there a responsible mysticism? Can the faith incorporate mystical experiences that are actually complementary to revealed truth and rational thought? The heart of the matter is that there surely must be an honest balance between experience and revealed truth, and between faith and reason. Neither emphasis must over- or under-balance the other. Thomas Merton, in *The Ascent to Truth,* writes "reason is in fact the path to faith, and faith takes over when reason can say no more."[5] We live our lives in bodies that experience sensations, and to deny ourselves the experience of God in worship is to deny the fact that He made us as multi-faceted beings, that are equipped to intake knowledge on a variety of levels.

These intrinsic functions of reason and sensation are important, complementary elements of our personality, and should not be treated as adversarial. Denying experience in worship is to intellectualize it, making it nearly impossible for worship to be transformational, because spiritual growth blossoms at the nexus of our intellect and emotions, the very crucible of experience. However, our sensations and experiences are sometimes misleading, just as cognition can be, drawing us away from the objective truth of God's reality and into our own compartmentalized and private construction of it. Experience must not be under-balanced or over-balanced with truth.

The only way that I personally know to retain experience in worship but to safeguard it with truth is to make sure that inner experience is always grounded in the Word. Truly, this makes for a very different type of experience. Schaeffer writes "it is very important to realize, over against modern concepts of 'spiritual experience,' that the biblically based experience rests firmly on truth. It is not only an emotional experience, nor is it contentless."[6] Experience in worship should arise out of revealed truth, and the Bible should be the fertile soil in which the Spirit meaningfully communicates with us and catalyzes our transformation. Scripture should "hem us in behind and before," like the psalmist says in Psalm 139, standing both as the authoritative voice of God into our experiences and the measure by which our experiences are evaluated. Morgenthaler writes "truth, or the Word, is always a prerequisite for an experience of God's presence. It is the primary avenue through which God chooses to be revealed."[7]

Therefore, if meditation is used in worship, it should be based upon a text of Scripture. As new worship songs are composed, we would do well to explicitly link them with some biblical text or idea, whether or not it is quoted verbatim in the song. If the Word is preached, applications should be translated through the grid of authorial intent, and the speaker should attempt to relate his real-life situations to what the author had purposed to communicate. If sign gifts are used, particularly tongues and prophecy, they should be judged by the elders as to their authenticity, as well as to their faithfulness to the revealed Word of God. Culture must be transformed by the Word of God, not vice versa. On the other hand, the Word of God frees us up to live as human creatures, with experiences of many kinds, embracing culture, because we have an objective standard by which to evaluate truth. The Word of God remains our anchor, truly liberating us by granting us the freedom to float upon the currents of worship experience.

As Christians, we are caught between a modern and postmodern worldview, and live simultaneously in a supernatural and natural world. We should not be so audacious that we deny the God of the universe the right and opportunity to speak to us and through us in any manner that He chooses, and should always attempt to remain open to whatever manifestation He has desired to give. Given that we are imperfect humans, however, we are easily led astray by our own desires and preoccupations, and should use the critical thinking that God has built into us in order to judge our experiences. If God chooses to actually speak with us in worship, either through direct address, non-audible words, or any other means, His words will in no way contradict what He has said in His revealed Word. As Foster writes "the one Spirit will never lead in opposition to the written Word that he inspired. There must always be the outward authority of Scripture as well as the inward authority of the Holy Spirit."[8] I believe that this is a more balanced approach to experience and revealed truth. We will discuss a more meaningful interpenetration in the final chapter, but for now, we go on to a second epistemological danger with experience.

The Danger of the Similarity of Religious Experiences

Another significant problem with religious experience, when it is not carefully balanced with revealed truth, is that a mystical experience of questionable origin will be mistaken for a genuine movement of the Spirit of God. When experience receives the highest authority, then all experience becomes admirable, and there is no rational judge to question the source of the experience. Jonathan Edwards, who critiqued a great deal of experiences in his *The Religious Affections,* makes the same point. I quote him at length because of the incredible insight of his comments:

> There are some who make this an argument in their own favour; when speaking of what they have experienced, they say "I am sure I did not make it myself; it was a fruit of no contrivance or endeavour of mine; it came when I thought nothing of it; if I might have the world for it, I cannot make it again when I please." And hence they determine that what they have experienced must be from the mighty influence of the Spirit of God…What they have been the subjects of may indeed not be from themselves directly, but may be from the operation of an invisible agent, some spirit besides their

own: but it does not thence follow that it was from the Spirit of God.[9]

Whether Christians like to believe it or not, the majority of religious experiences the world over are remarkably similar. In fact, William James catalogued a whole variety of such experiences at the turn of the 20th century and found this to be the case.[10] Peter Kreeft, a renowned Catholic philosopher, makes the same observation in this generation: "The mystical experience is strikingly uniform throughout time and place, though the religious, theological, moral, and personal interpretations of it are different, especially between Eastern and Western religions."[11] If similar mystical experiences are happening from religion to religion, but Christianity is the only road to God, then there must be a variety of spirits that are not the Spirit of God manifesting their presence in a similar manner. This fact alone should give the Christian pause, and should cause him or her to evaluate experiences very carefully and according to the revealed truth of God in the Bible. If experience has been given carte blanche over the revealed truth of God, however, those who uncritically trust mystical experience might find themselves at the mercy of any spirit that decides to invoke their imaginations.

The Danger of Losing Our Critical Thinking Ability

A third danger of over-emphasizing experience at the expense of rational thought is that we do not develop our critical thinking ability. While this might seem like a minor point, its long-range impact on the community of the church is perhaps more important than one might initially realize. God created us with brains to think and analyze, and with sensations to feel and experience. Neither is unimportant, nor is one less important than the other. Critical thinking involves using our brains to ask questions about things, particularly the things we experience, in order to determine if something is beneficial or dangerous.

When we begin uncritically to accept experience of any kind, then we basically turn off our brains and categorize them as unimportant to religious life, as if any kind of experience we encounter is inherently positive. If we took this approach in the physical world, we would not long survive our disastrous choices. Instead, Scripture regularly exhorts us to sharpen our minds, particularly in the Word of God (2 Tim 2:15), but it never encourages us to have experiences simply for the intrinsic value of experience. Critical thinking is the essence of discernment, and discernment is something the church needs always intentionally to develop in order to separate truth from error in all of life. Having laid that important foundation, we turn in the next chapter to some of the positive aspects of this approach to worship.

---

[1] James, The Varieties of Religious Experience, 425.
[2] Gergen, The Saturated Self, 105.
[3] Schaeffer, The God Who is There, 142.
[4] James, The Varieties of Religious Experience, 462.
[5] Thomas Merton, The Ascent to Truth (New York: Harcourt, Brace and Company, 1951), 29.
[6] Schaeffer, The God Who is There, 176.
[7] Morgenthaler, Worship Evangelism, 101.
[8] Foster, Celebration of Discipline, 188.
[9] Edwards, The Religious Affections, 68-69.
[10] James, The Varieties of Religious Experience, 318.
[11] Kreeft, Heaven: The Heart's Deepest Longing, 241-242.

CHAPTER 10

THE STRENGTHS OF EXPERIENCE

The Delight of Worship

Every summer, my wife and I spend a week vacationing with my family on the Oregon coast. We rent a large cabin in Manzanita, situated on Neahkanie Mountain and overlooking a gorgeous beach. The cabin is nestled in a heavily wooded area, the back porch extending into an old growth forest, and so the secluded spot is perfect for times of solitude with the Lord. Reflection and contemplation with the Lord were exactly what I needed this last summer, as I was coming off of a somewhat frustrating and exhausting time of ministry. As a result, my heart was filled with all kinds of things that I needed to tell the Lord. I intended to fill Him in on all these difficult situations, and let Him know the pressing needs that were assaulting my mind. I desired to fill His ears with a shopping list of what I required from Him. I wanted to speak and have Him listen, but I was not prepared for Him to expect the same.

As I sat on the back porch that first afternoon, I did just that. I came to Him with my list of requests and began ponderously going over it for Him, drawing His attention to all the things we had discussed, making sure that He had not forgotten. The tumult of my own heart began to fill my ears, and I became overwhelmed by the immensity of my own desires. At that moment, I sensed what could only be described as an urgent sensation to just stop. Stop talking. Be quiet. I felt then that I sensed the Lord saying, "Stop. Be still. I know all these things. Be still. Delight in me. For two weeks, just delight in me." It goes without saying that I did as I was asked. I stopped. I thought about delighting in God, and then began to wonder what exactly that meant. I quickly realized that I did not know what it looked like in a practical sense to delight in God. I had read the Scriptures about delighting in God many times, but what exactly happens when I say "I am going to delight in You, God, for the next hour"? I wasn't sure. It dawned on me that I had been a worship leader for ten years, and really did not know. I had asked people to delight in God in worship for years, but I had no conception what that actually meant in my own personal devotion.

Needless to say, there were some awkward moments at first. At first I tried to think of things to say to God, but I kept finding myself saying "I need" or "I want," so I would stop talking again. After a time, I just fell silent. I began to feel comfortable just sitting. I began to be aware of His presence. The tumult of my own heart started slowly to subside. Then I began finding a voice to thank Him. I would thank Him for simple things, things all around me in His creation, and then began finding unusual creativity to thank Him for things I would never have thought to mention. My heart acknowledged the gift, and in so doing, slowly turned towards the Giver. Then I noticed that praise for simply who He is began pouring out of my heart and mouth. My heart was overflowing and I could hardly find all the words to praise Him. It did not require effort on my part, and I did not have to work up the emotions or the gratitude. It was sweet and pure, and I realized what the psalmist meant when he said "taste and see that the Lord is good." I could not praise enough. I became aware of His presence, and could not leave. I found myself, after all that, delighting in God.

I narrate this long passage in order to describe a surprise that is difficult to explain or intellectually comprehend without experiencing it. *Delighting in God is a choice that draws upon our intellect, but is expressed in our emotions and our actions.* It is the heart of worship. When we submit ourselves to the enormity of God's pleasure in reverence, humility and obedience, then the entirety of our constitution is brought into the experience through the work of the Spirit. There will be no division between intellect, emotions and volition in our worship, because God communicates through the entirety of our receptors, and we respond in thanksgiving.

CHAPTER 10: THE STRENGTHS OF EXPERIENCE

There is a genuine sense of abandon in this approach. As we abandon ourselves to the simple joy of basking in God's presence, then we adopt an entirely new posture of praise. We find ourselves content simply to bow before Him, without placing expectations on the interaction. We have no sort of agenda, no conditions or restrictions that we use to limit or enhance God's activity. Rather, our spirits become placid in the hands of our mighty Maker, because we are content for Him to engage us in the manner that He desires. Delighting in God truly brings the freedom of surrender, because we no longer require that He communicate or behave in a particular way. Rather, we lay ourselves upon the altar with joy in a simple celebration of who He is, and the magnitude of His person overwhelms us.

Having said that, I suppose that it is theoretically possible to worship without ever really delighting in God. I suppose that it is possible to truly and thoughtfully praise God for His character and works without ever being deeply engaged by them. There are some who would insist that this does not constitute "true worship." While I am inclined to agree, I resist the tantalizing trap of adding the adjective "true" to an experience simply because it has reached a certain level of intensity, or because it is congruent with what I have experienced. Perhaps in worship, like love, one can swim on the surface or dive down deep, and still actually be swimming in the same pool. If worship can have levels of intimacy and still be considered authentic, then I suppose that it is conceivable to offer an intellectual sacrifice of praise without being profoundly moved in the inner self by the incredible object of our praise. Perhaps it is possible to leave the emotions out of worship, and miss the blessing of delighting in God. After all, it is possible to give or receive a gift without ever looking deeply into the eyes of the other with adoration. Maybe it is possible to praise God in worship because He is worthy of our praise, yet never truly delight in Him.

However, there are two significant problems with this worship scenario. First, God receives only a "half-hearted" sacrifice of praise from us, an offering that does not represent the totality of our being. We use the term "half-hearted" when we describe something that is not done to the best of our ability or with only lackluster participation. But in a very real sense, a worship activity in which we participate with our intellect alone and not with our passions or emotions could also be described as "half-hearted." While some might not even class this involvement as "worship," it would probably be better to say that it is substandard—not the kind of offering that we want to bring to the Creator of the universe and our magnanimous Redeemer. Praise that is passion-less is worship that is of dubious value to anyone, because delighting in God lies at the heart of worship. Second, half-hearted worship loses out on the potential richness of the interaction. The possibility of spiritual formation is abandoned in this worship scenario, because our hearts have not been opened to the Holy Spirit. Worship that dismisses the opportunity for experience—in the fullness of its manifestations—is worship that becomes impotent for deep character development, the interaction that the Holy Spirit is regularly pursuing in our lives. Rather, an "experience-open" approach to worship, one which invigorates the whole of the human constitution, has significant advantages as a tool of spiritual formation, a number of which will be considered in this chapter.

The Wholistic Nature of Experience-Open Worship

One of the strongest features of "experience-open" worship is that it desires the entire person—intellect and emotions, cognition and sensation—to be deeply moved by the Spirit of God in worship. We are not worshiping in spite of our emotions, but truly with them and through them, as well as with our thoughts and volition. We bring our entire selves to God in worship, choosing to bow down and exalt Him with praise and thanksgiving, and He blesses us with the joy of His presence. We do not need to excite our emotions, nor do we need to re-present or rehearse correct theologies for ourselves every week. As we simply submit ourselves to His innate truth and majesty, we are affected by His presence. Mercy and truth come together in a banquet of praise. The critical point here is that the initiative is on God's part, for He inspires our worship and He gives whatever emotional response He desires us to experience. Foster calls this a "holy dependency," remarking "you are utterly and completely dependent upon God for anything significant to hap-

CHAPTER 10: THE STRENGTHS OF EXPERIENCE

pen."[1] We delight in God, because He is delightful, and He delights in us as we draw near to Him with everything we are. Truly, delighting in God becomes the "heart of worship" in this experience-open approach.

As we open our hearts to God's presence, the presence that has already indwelt us in the Holy Spirit, God makes His presence known. I believe that God frequently allows us truly to experience Him through the receptors of our sensations. As Psalm 16:11 intimates "in Your presence is fullness of joy; at Your right hand are pleasures forevermore." This does not mean that the experience of worship is always warm feelings and nice emotions. Delighting in God also involves an element of obedience, and so there is often a purifying work that God does through the spiritual disciplines. However, delighting in God means choosing to find joy and satisfaction in the revealed truth of who He is and what He has done, and waiting on Him to bless us with consolation as He so desires. Piper remarks "it is not man-centered because the emotions of our worship are centered on God! We look away from ourselves to him, and only then do the manifold emotions of our heart erupt in worship."[2] It is a choice to drink deeply from the well of God's majesty and wonder, as He has revealed Himself in His Word and in all of creation. This profound amazement and awe is demonstrated in Psalm 8, when David exclaims "oh Lord, our Lord, how excellent is Your name in all the earth!" God responds by amazing us with the wonder of Himself, causing us to feel joy and delight as we seek Him in praise.

I define this as "experience-open" worship, not "experience-oriented," because I believe that a person who is truly seeking God in worship should be open to and desire an experience of God, but should not have set parameters on what that must be. Perhaps this approach retains more faithfully the aspect of worship as a spiritual *discipline*, as opposed to a technique that one employs to generate an emotional experience. Moreover, I am not claiming that this approach to worship is exclusively the domain of the neo-romantic paradigm. Both worship paradigms can fall to either side of this "experience-open" dynamic, a result of the various excesses that they emphasize. The neo-romantic paradigm tends to make experience the criterion of worship, evaluating all worship in terms of affect; whereas the modern paradigm, which tends towards a Kantian view of morality, struggles with what kind of experiential expectations the worshiper ought to bring to worship. Piper writes "the person who has the vague notion that it is virtue to overcome self-interest, and that it is vice to seek pleasure, will scarcely be able to worship."[3] David agrees when he writes in Psalm 36:8 that the "children of men" are "abundantly satisfied with the fullness of Your house, and You give them drink from the river of Your pleasures."

Therefore, the category of delighting in God can be especially challenging for some modern worshipers, because it implies having affective expectations in regards to the worship activity. As a result, they sometimes find it difficult to bring their whole selves to worship. Indeed, I have witnessed first-hand how this modern approach can often train people to separate their intellect and emotions when they come to worship, and so their hearts—which are the conjunction of intellect and emotions—are only partially engaged. Often the level of vulnerability alone can make the exposure of their emotions to God in a large-group setting a frightening prospect for them. Unfortunately, if the emotions are excluded from the worship activity, then the worshiper will be unaware of this spiritual exchange, unaware of the immense gift that the Holy Spirit will give, unaware of what it means to delight in God in worship. "In praise we see how totally the emotions need to be brought into the act of worship. Worship that is solely cerebral is an aberration."[4] While the neo-romantic paradigm has its own issues—many of which we discussed in the previous chapter—it definitely leans more toward an open-ness to experience in worship.

Delighting in God as the Heart of Worship

As I mentioned, the concept of delighting in God in Scripture is actually broader than simply the inner experiential or emotional component of worship. In truth, delighting in God unites the two aspects of *experience* and *obedience* in a unique way. One does not have to look far in the Psalms to find the experiential dynamic expressed. David's psalms, among others, are replete with references to a desire for worship, and to the satisfaction that

CHAPTER 10: THE STRENGTHS OF EXPERIENCE

comes from experiencing God's presence in the sanctuary. In Psalm 63, David exclaims how his very soul longs and thirsts for God, desiring to see His power and glory manifested in worship, and going on to proclaim that his soul is satisfied in the sanctuary as with "marrow and fatness." He writes this psalm during his sojourn in the wilderness of Judah, separated from the experience of God's manifest presence in the tabernacle. Thus, he finds himself eager to return to worship before God's face. In Psalm 42, the sons of Korah express a similar sentiment while in exile, remembering the sweetness of temple worship.[5]

The idea is that worshiping God, coming into His presence in the temple, was something that brought joy and delight to the heart of the worshiper. Bringing offerings was not drudgery for them, nor was it a cerebral or intellectualized sacrifice of praise. Given that the process of animal sacrifice was far from a warm and fuzzy aesthetic, it is surprising that it is described in these terms. However, the Old Testament worshiper found the process of worship to be something that invigorated their emotions, and something that their souls craved when they were removed from it for too long. The presence of God brought life to their souls, resulting in joy and gladness when He lifted His countenance upon them (Ps 4:7). Delighting in God drew upon the fullness of one's emotions.

However, there is also an obedience/lifestyle aspect to delighting in God. God is the object of praise, and His desires are found in His Word. The experience of delight in the Psalms is overwhelmingly connected with a delight in God's Word, particularly in a desire and commitment to follow His commands. The whole of Psalm 119 is focused on this dynamic, as the psalmist cries out "Your word is a lamp to my feet and a light to my path." (119:105) David also reflects this heart attitude of delighting in obedience when he exclaims in Psalm 40:8 "I delight to do Your will, O my God, and Your law is within my heart." Perhaps this passion for obedience is why he is described in I Samuel 13 as a man after God's own heart, as the immediate context has just described a king who did not delight in following God's commands. This dynamic is also behind Jesus' stinging rebuke of the Pharisees in Matthew 15:8-9, when he remarks "these people draw near to me with their mouth, and honor me with their lips, but their heart is far from me. And in vain they worship me, teaching as doctrines the commandments of men." Delighting in God not only involved an emotional bond in one's heart, but it expected deep delight in the commands of the One who received praise and adoration. Thus, there was an interlocking relationship between the experience of God and obedience to His Word.

Furthermore, God responds by delighting in those who fear Him and keep His Word. Psalm 147:10-11 states "He does not delight in the strength of the horse; He takes no pleasure in the legs of a man. The Lord takes pleasure in those who fear Him, in those who hope in His mercy." Also, Psalm 51:16-17 affirms "for You do not desire sacrifice, or else I would give it; You do not delight in burnt offering. The sacrifices of God are a broken spirit, a broken and a contrite heart—these, O God, You will not despise." The obedience of the one who delights in keeping God's Word inspires a response of joy on God's part, as He delights in his or her faithfulness. In essence, God delights in us as we delight in Him.

Thus, when Psalm 37:4 asserts "delight yourself also in the Lord, and He shall give you the desires of your heart," it is within a context of engaging with God's works and character throughout the daily grind of life, in the crucible of one's experiences.

> Trust in the LORD, and do good;
> Dwell in the land, and feed on His faithfulness.
> Delight yourself also in the LORD,
> And He shall give you the desires of your heart.
> Commit your way to the LORD,
> Trust also in Him, and He shall bring it to pass.
> He shall bring forth your righteousness as the light,
> And your justice as the noonday. (Ps 37:3-6)

Delighting in God provides a different focus for one's experiences, relating the truth of God's character with His love and delight of obedience. Delighting in God through one's lifestyle actually rejoices God's heart, and it is not surprising that this blessing is poured out upon the worshiper. Jesus claims the same exchange, that He will manifest His love to those who keep His commandments. (John 14:21) Delighting in God brings one's life into the

CHAPTER 10: THE STRENGTHS OF EXPERIENCE

worship experience, creating a deeper desire to obey as He amazes us with His grace and glory. It is truly an integrated experience of God through one's intellect, emotions and will, as we are awed by His character and wooed by His incredible love. As we delight in Him in all of life, including the worship activity, He delights in us.

Coming to God with everything He made us to be affirms that we are able to experience God and interact with Him on a variety of levels. We experience Him in our intellect as well as in our emotions, and this approach anticipates that all these receptors will be invigorated. If the Spirit desires to give us consolation or desolation, we are ready and open to receive that experience, and we validate its occurrence against the revealed truth of the Word. The experience-open approach allows this spiritual exchange to take place, because it wholeheartedly affirms that experience has a place in worship, and does not suggest that receiving a blessing is somehow inimical to the offering of praise. It is a wholistic approach, as it recognizes the whole beings that God created us to be.

Spiritual Growth through Experience-Open Worship

The experience-open paradigm also recognizes that spiritual growth happens in the heart, which is the nexus of the will, intellect and emotions,[6] and affirms that the worship activity is a legitimate and desirable place for this kind of spiritual growth to occur. Not only is the worship experience a wonderful venue in which to lift a sacrifice of praise, it provides a potent and poignant opportunity for God to respond by deepening the faith and character of the worshiper. As the worshiper bows before God, he or she is changed by his or her decision to worship as well as by the spiritual exchange with God. Worship possesses, through the indwelling Spirit, an incredible potential to change us, because God has determined that it should.

Throughout Scripture, the heart is described and understood as the absolute core of the human personality, the spiritual center of all intellectual and emotional activity that emanates from, and is intrinsic to the essence of character. In the biblical authors' use of the term "heart," there is an obvious/yet unspoken, nebulous/yet concrete relationship between cognition, affect and volition. Proverbs 23:7-8 reflects that as a person "thinks in his heart, so is he," loosely identifying the rational component.[7] Deuteronomy 6:5 exposes something of the affective component, instructing Israel to "love the Lord your God with all your heart, with all your soul, and with all your strength." Although this passage truly reflects the broader understanding of "heart," the heart is also described as experiencing other emotions, like being terrified (Ps 22:14), rejoicing (Ps 33:21), being haughty (Ps 131:2) and being broken and contrite (Ps 51:17). Third, the heart is also credited with actions of the will, like trust (Ps 28:17) and obedience (Ps 44:18). These three elements of "heart" are found throughout Scripture.

Scripture is not really interested in attempting to break down the distinctions between these processes, choosing rather to represent them as a whole unit—the self of the person—and connecting them with the movements of volition. The psalmist in Psalm 26:2 requests that God examine his mind and heart, using the two words interchangeably to "refer to the innermost person."[8] They are described as working in cooperation, and the primary connection that the Scripture desires to make is how these capacities of the heart are drawn together in the actions of the will. A central text in this regard, Proverbs 4:23 urges the reader to "keep your heart with all diligence, for out of it spring the issues of life,"[9] and continues by connecting this pursuit with the choices of life. "Ponder the path of your feet and let all your ways be established." From a biblical perspective, the heart is the essence of character and the source of all actions. Jesus reflects this dynamic in Matthew 15:19, when he remarks "out of the heart proceed evil thoughts, murders, adulteries, fornications, thefts, false witness, blasphemies."

Spiritual growth, which the Holy Spirit produces, begins in the heart with characterological change, and so *worship as an activity of the heart precedes worship as a lifestyle.* This is the pattern of spiritual growth throughout the Christian life, that heart change precedes external change. Spiritual growth must begin in the domain of the heart, which is the nexus of the intellect, emotions and will, and one's actions simply reveal the heart. It is the workshop of the Spirit where transformation is initiated, and that change in-

CHAPTER 10: THE STRENGTHS OF EXPERIENCE

volves the complementary workings of intellect and emotion in accordance with volition. The choice to worship God with one's external choices flows from an internal dynamic, an inner submission, from the worship of the heart, with the result that the one is naturally prior to the other. Therefore, it makes sense that worship as a heart activity would precede worship as a lifestyle. Foster notes "if worship does not propel us into greater obedience, it has not been worship. To stand before the Holy One of eternity is to change."[10] Worship that is transformational must begin in the inner person and proceed outward to the limits of one's actions, because that is the direction of spiritual growth. Worship of the heart proceeds worship as a lifestyle.

The experience-open approach affirms that the spiritual disciplines, particularly worship, are significant windows of opportunity for the Spirit to catalyze spiritual growth in the believer's life. Worship is highlighted as the most important spiritual discipline in this pursuit, as the worshiper intentionally focuses his or her eyes on Christ as the object of worship, and is transformed into the same image through the work of the Holy Spirit. As Paul recognizes in 2 Cor 3:18, "we all, with unveiled face, beholding as in a mirror the glory of the Lord, are being transformed into the same image from glory to glory, just as by the Spirit of the Lord." The Spirit focuses on worship of the heart to facilitate these external readjustments.

In order for worship as a lifestyle to occur, it is critical that the fullness of the heart be submitted to the Spirit whenever the activity of worship takes place. If worship is to be transformational, it must invigorate the whole heart, including the emotions, the intellect and the will. Worship that does not receive an open connection with the heart will never penetrate the actions, and will never transform the individual. The Spirit will certainly find other means to expose and transform the heart, but the experience-open approach understands that the spiritual discipline of worship will be effectively lost as a transformational activity.

While the modern paradigm clearly would assert some of these principles, the neo-romantic paradigm understands this as a primarily internal process that occurs on a personal level between the worshiper and God *during the public activity of worship.* Here is where the two paradigms clearly diverge, and where the neo-romantic approach is often accused of being individualistic. In this paradigm, worship is treated more as a spiritual discipline, private in nature, an intimate conversation with God, whereas the modern paradigm highlights the more external, corporate aspect of mutual edification.[†] Worship becomes a time of private devotion for the neo-romantic worshiper, with music and liturgy that catalyzes this dynamic. The transformation of the heart happens through meditative and celebrative reflection, an internal conversation with the Spirit that is facilitated by the worship liturgy and/or repertoire. Indeed, the authentic exposure of the heart to the Spirit truly requires this kind of personal, intimate dynamic.

Thus, the worshiper is changed by a profound exposure to the presence of God, both in the revealed truth of His Word and in the inner reality of His indwelling presence. Morgenthaler writes "very simply, to experience God's presence is to be transformed from the inside out."[11] While edification might occur from the contributions of the other worshipers, the focus of this activity is far less an external conversation between pastor and congregant, and more an internal conversation with God. The experience-open approach celebrates and facilitates this interaction.

As the worshiper gazes on Christ as the embodiment of grace and truth, the Holy Spirit draws attention to items in the worshiper's life that need adjustment. The truth of God's character, as it is faithfully exposed by the worship meditations and repertoire, is juxtaposed against the weaknesses of the believer's life. "The Spirit invites the believer to fellowship with Him in the weaknesses of our heart that the power of Christ may be real."[12] Coe notes that in this process, the dynamic of Romans 8:26-27 is reenacted:

> Likewise the Spirit also helps in our weaknesses. For we do not know what we should pray for as we ought, but the Spirit Himself makes intercession for us with groanings which cannot be uttered. Now He who searches the hearts knows what the mind of the Spirit

---

[†] There are certainly examples of modern services that would highlight worship as a place where private, spiritual communion takes place. However, these are not normative. The neo-romantic approach tends to highlight transformation as a private process in the service, whereas the modern paradigm tends to highlight the aspects of edification that can be shared by all present.

CHAPTER 10: THE STRENGTHS OF EXPERIENCE

is, because He makes intercession for the saints according to the will of God.

Through the Spirit exposing our hearts, divinity becomes a foil for creatureliness. God's holiness revealing sinfulness causes a reaction of repentance and compliance in the heart of the worshiper. "The pervasive sinfulness of human beings becomes evident when contrasted with the radiant holiness of God. Our fickleness becomes apparent once we see God's faithfulness."[13] The worshiper is both awed and humbled by the magnificence of God's glory and grace—His transcendence and immanence—in stark contrast to his or her own life. The worshiper draws near to God in wonder and is met by Him on an internal plane with conviction, consolation and transformation.

Moreover, the base passions and desires of the worshiper's heart are gradually changed, not by sublimation or repression, but by replacement with a greater passion, a delight in God. Hearts are not changed by denying their true desires or by attempting to cover them over with layers of piety. Passions are not eliminated by pushing them down, or by trying to convince oneself that they no longer exist. The twelve-step program has long ago realized this dynamic, but Christian formation is far behind. Hearts are changed by the development of a new passion, a greater passion,[14] replacing the old. The intent of the worship activity is to facilitate this very dynamic. By focusing on the splendors of God in His transcendence, and the graciousness of God in His immanence, the worshiper is drawn into a deeper love for the Lord.

Delighting in God reveals a satisfaction and fulfillment that far outweighs what little the old desires provided, and actually creates more desire for God in the process. As worshipers begin to drink from the river of God's pleasures, they become thirstier for His fulfillment alone, and are even less satisfied by what the world provides. The Holy Spirit affects this transformation by causing the worshiper to experience an even greater desire for God, and the worship activity which touches the whole of the worshiper's being allows this change to take place.

This transformation of the whole being is facilitated by the opening of the entire heart to the Spirit in the process of worship. Worship becomes a window in which the whole self is exposed to the purifying splendor of God's holiness. However, it requires that the whole heart be submitted to God, and that the worship activity promotes this kind of wholistic approach. If worship is to be transformational, it is an absolute necessity that the whole heart be involved. The lifestyle of worship must begin with this supernatural exchange, and the venue of worship is an incredibly powerful opportunity for it to occur. The experience-open approach exults in this activity, highlighting the experience of God's presence in worship as a critical element in the heart's transformation.

The Value of the "Numinous" Experience

Third, the experience-open approach affirms that aspects of God's presence are experienced through non-rational means, that is, through sensual perception which flies "under the radar" of the rational receptors; it does not require that the apprehension of God's presence conform itself to purely cognitive forms. The idea of "numinous," which was explored by the likes of Rudolf Otto and C.S. Lewis, was described in chapter six as a special perception of God's presence that is manifested through one's sensations and/or emotions. It is a mystical interaction with the presence of God in which the worshiper is allowed a brief, mitigated or shielded glimpse into God's glory. It is a metaphysical brush with His incomprehensible attributes, like holiness or transcendence that produces a reaction outside the parameters of cognition.[15] This perception is manifested in several typical emotional reactions, including fear, awe or fascination, mystery, desire or longing, a sense of creatureliness and deep consolation. Otto has referred to it as the "mysterium tremendum," describing it as follows:

> The feeling of it may at times comes sweeping like a gentle tide, pervading the mind with a tranquil mood of deepest worship. It may pass over into a more set and lasting attitude of the soul, continuing, as it were, thrillingly vibrant and resonant, until at last it dies away and the soul resumes its "profane", non-religious mood of everyday experience. It may burst in sudden eruption up from the depths of the soul with spasms and convulsions, or lead to the strangest excitements, to intoxicated frenzy, to transport, and to ecstasy....It may become the hushed, trembling, and speechless

CHAPTER 10: THE STRENGTHS OF EXPERIENCE

humility of the creature in the presence of—whom or what? In the presence of that which is a mystery inexpressible and above all creatures.[16]

The basic principle behind the concept of "numinous" is that God is much greater than the ability of our cognition to apprehend, and so His presence is sometimes allowed to be experienced primarily through our innate sensations.[17] Calvin explains this in part as "accommodation," and Dowey summarizes his position by remarking that it is "the process by which God reduces or adjusts to human capacities what he wills to reveal of the infinite mysteries of his being, which by their very nature are beyond the powers of the mind of man to grasp."[18] Either our cognition is too limited or it is inappropriate to experience God's presence, and so His "non-rational" attributes overwhelm and overflow our puny, intellectual receptors. Thus, we experience a variety of emotional responses and sensations that reveal His presence, not because He has moved closer in proximity, but because He has allowed us to experience Him in a more immanent manner. Peter Kreeft discusses this presence in the following manner:

> It is the sense that the world we see is haunted by something we do not see, an unseen presence. It often inspires awe and fear because it is not humanly predictable and controllable, not definable and tameable. It seems to come from another dimension, another kind of reality, than the world it haunts. It is the primitive wonder that is the source of fairy tales and myths and also of the instinct to worship.[19]

Interestingly, the experience of numinous is most often produced by reflection on other objects, particularly natural wonders or incredible, aesthetic works of art or music. The sensation is not produced by these objects, but instead comes alongside one's sense of aesthetic appreciation. However, it is not simple aesthetic wonder, for it is sudden and enormous, and completely out of proportion with the object of contemplation. In these aesthetic settings, numinous or "sehnsucht" (a German word for desire) is experienced as a spontaneous feeling of immense wonder, bottomless desire and unquenchable longing that overwhelms and transcends the natural experience.[20] It is by definition an ecstatic, transcendental experience, as the etymological meaning of "ecstasy" actually means to stand outside of oneself.[21] Corbin Scott Carnell remarks "such moments are rare; they may come with a mounting sense of grandeur in the presence of natural beauty or with piercing sweetness on hearing a certain strain of music. It may be a dance, a painting, or a chorale which awakens this feeling of aesthetic exaltation."[22] Lewis describes the same sensation in his autobiography <u>Surprised by Joy</u>, which is largely a treatise on the subject.

> Only when your whole attention and desire are fixed on something else…does the "thrill" arise. It is a byproduct. Its very existence presupposes that you desire not it but something other and outer…All images and sensations, if idolatrously mistaken for Joy itself, soon honestly confessed themselves inadequate. All said, in the last resort, "It is not I. I am only a reminder. Look! Look! What do I remind you of?"[23]

As the above quote indicates, this sense of numinous is credited as a window to God, a divine pointer that is intended to inflame desire and reinforce the source of that desire.[24] It is a brief moment of sensual insight, catalyzed by a natural wonder, which is positioned by God in order to lead the worshiper to Himself. God invigorates the desire of worshipers with a glimpse of His glory, drawing their attention unto the true and life-giving object of worship. He utilizes an aesthetic object, something as astounding as the Grand Canyon or as simple as a flower to open a window unto the divine, and the quick and fleeting flash of incomparable exaltation is believed to be a brush with His majesty. Lewis stumbled upon his own experience of sehnsucht primarily in literature, particularly in the Norse mythology found in Longfellow.[25] I myself have experienced it on several occasions, once listening to Beethoven's Ninth Symphony, and another time simply gazing abstractly on the wonder of a human face. These objects, which are natural in origin, take on a supernatural luminescence as God uses them as vessels to briefly overwhelm us with His glory.

Unfortunately, the fascination sometimes turns into idolatry, as the worshiper comes to believe that the object actually caused the fascination, and so turns what was a beautiful gift into an idolatrous pursuit.[26] Perhaps this was the source of pagan worship, particularly the worship of natural wonders like the sun or stars, or human experiences like sex or fertility. This idolatry can also occur when worshipers become too enamored with the experience of worship itself, as was earlier illustrated in chapter eight. Regardless, the numinous is believed—by those who accept its reality—to be a wonderful gift of divine perception into the fountain of desire, to which the worshiper will return again and again. It is a unique opportunity for God to reveal Himself to the worshiper's sensations through the wonder of aesthetic experience.

At heart, the experience-open approach affirms that God's presence is not exclusively experienced in rational forms, through the written and spoken word, but that He also can be experienced on a more visceral and sensual level, and that the activity of worship enables this exchange. It suggests that there are alternate ways of knowing to the purely cognitive, and that the experience of God in worship draws upon these resources. What this conviction signifies for its adherents is a basic open-ness to the spiritual realm, not requiring that the apprehension of God be condensed to our rational receptors. They affirm that experience is also a valid instrument to obtain knowledge, and do not attempt to lock God within the rational box of a modern worldview. While this kind of approach must certainly be balanced with discernment, it entails cognitive humility before God and an open-ness to His movement that certainly must be accepted as a very positive position. God is much broader than the creatures He created, and an open-ness to His revelation is an incredible asset to the experience of worship, as well as the Christian life. More will be said on this subject in the last chapter.

Experiencing God in Worship

In the experience-open approach, desire and delighting in God become a wonderful and welcomed result of truly worshiping with the entirety of one's being. Worshiping God begins to be connected with desire for Him on every level. Gone is the notion, however implicit, that worship is an intellectual enactment of praise. The joyful access of the worshiper to the throne room becomes the focus of the worship activity, and the resulting conversation with God is an intimate and deeply experienced delight in the wonder and majesty of His works and character. God is experienced with the intellect as well as with the sensations and emotions, in the fullness of one's heart, and this desire for God begins to permeate all aspects of the worshiper's life. Indeed, the experience of worship as a heart activity becomes a precursor to delighting in God with acts of obedience. Worshipers seek to open their hearts to God's indwelling presence, and their entire lives are changed as they approach the throne of grace in worship.

The last two chapters have demonstrated both the drawbacks and strengths of the neo-romantic approach to worship as an experience of God's presence, and have hinted how the experience-open approach is perhaps an ideal middle road between the various paradigms. Regardless, the neo-romantic approach simply represents one manner in which experience, as a belief-forming structure, is brought into in the worship setting. While it contains certain self-evident advantages, it is by no means the only way, nor is it the only "right" way. However, it is one culturally relevant example, as has been shown, because it draws upon a variety of elements from postmodern culture in its unique integration of faith and culture.

There is a broader question to be answered, however, one that is both idealistic and practical. How should the intellect and experience, cognition and sensation ideally come together in the worship setting? Regardless of how these two paradigms have answered the question, how *should* the revealed truth of the Word be weighed against the internal experiences of the worshiper? How should the truth of one's own personal narrative and the narrative of Scripture be encouraged to interpenetrate one another in the sacrifice of praise? What should the postmodern worshiper legitimately be able to expect by way of cooperation between intellect and emotion in the worship setting? These questions will be the subject of the final chapter.

---

[1] Foster, Celebration of Discipline, 171.
[2] Piper, Desiring God, 84.
[3] Ibid., 87.
[4] Foster, Celebration of Discipline, 168.
[5] Earl Radmacher, Ronald B. Allen, and H. Wayne House, eds., Nelson's New Illustrated Bible Commentary, 676.

CHAPTER 10: THE STRENGTHS OF EXPERIENCE   195

[6] John Coe, "Healing the Heart's Deep Beliefs in the Spirit: Intentionalizing Spiritual Formation through Soul Work."

[7] Ibid.

[8] Earl Radmacher, Ronald B. Allen, and H. Wayne House, eds., <u>Nelson's New Illustrated Bible Commentary</u>, 666.

[9] Coe, "Healing the Heart's Deep Beliefs in the Spirit: Intentionalizing Spiritual Formation through Soul Work."

[10] Foster, <u>Celebration of Discipline</u>, 173.

[11] Morgenthaler, <u>Worship Evangelism</u>, 52.

[12] Coe, "Healing the Heart's Deep Beliefs in the Spirit: Intentionalizing Spiritual Formation through Soul Work."

[13] Foster, <u>Celebration of Discipline</u>, 160.

[14] Tim Keller, "Enduring Grace" (sermon preached at Redeemer Presbyterian Church, New York, 10 March 2002).

[15] Otto, <u>The Idea of the Holy</u>, 58.

[16] Ibid., 12-13.

[17] Ibid., 28.

[18] Edward A. Dowey, Jr., <u>The Knowledge of God in Calvin's Theology</u> (Columbia University Press, 1952; reprint, Grand Rapids: William B. Eerdman's Publishing Company, 1994), 3 (page citations are to the reprint edition).

[19] Kreeft, <u>Heaven: The Heart's Deepest Longing</u>, 97-98.

[20] Otto, <u>The Idea of the Holy</u>, 151.

[21] Corbin Scott Carnell, <u>Bright Shadow of Reality: C.S. Lewis and the Feeling Intellect</u> (Grand Rapids: William B. Eerdmans Publishing Company, 1974), 19.

[22] Ibid.

[23] C.S. Lewis, <u>Surprised by Joy</u>, 168ff.; quoted in Kreeft, <u>Heaven: The Heart's Deepest Longing</u>, 155.

[24] Carnell, <u>Bright Shadow of Reality: C.S. Lewis and the Feeling Intellect</u>, 162.

[25] Lewis, <u>Surprised by Joy</u>, 17-18.

[26] Kreeft, <u>Heaven: The Heart's Deepest Longing</u>, 21.

CHAPTER 11

REVEALED AND EXPERIENCED TRUTH

The Critical Complement of Experience

You may have noticed that I have begun almost every chapter with some kind of personal or observed experience. Many authors have utilized this strategy, and so there is certainly nothing original about my borrowing the same approach. Indeed, I have found in reading other authors that these little stories they insert into their manuscripts are often the most powerful points of learning, the moments in which the truth they are conveying comes through in the most poignant and profound manner. Hence, I have employed this technique in order to demonstrate a point that I will now rationally discuss. I have tried to allow you, the reader, to "experience" the truth that now I will explicate.

In our belief-forming and maintaining pursuit, *experience is a most critical complement to the coupling of rational thought and revealed truth.* By "experience," I intend the broadest fabric of internal perceptions and sensations as well as external events and occurrences that compose lived reality. I mean truth that is apprehended not through propositions or disembodied statements about reality, but through the sensual experience of living and interacting with the world. Indeed, the revealed truth of Scripture is largely human experience that has been divinely endowed through human authors with a rational, interpretational framework. While experiences without some kind of cognitive structure would be meaningless, abstract principles without the accompaniment of experience are rarely *meaningful*. Knowing that God is love is wholly different from experiencing His love in one's life, and sometimes experiencing it in the depths of one's sensations is the most profound and meaningful way to know it. In essence, meaning follows experience in the framing of truth. Thus, experience and revealed truth must go together in our approach to knowledge, as well as in our approach to worship.

As human beings, we are created with special receptors of knowledge that are both rational and sensual. While these receptors can be artificially divided into regions representing intellect and emotion, the human body contains both elements in an unique, interpenetrating structure. To deny one is to assert that it is superfluous to our essential being. To massively exalt one over the other is to effectively deny the other. To make this our approach to a relationship with God is even more damaging, as it is suggesting that the way God made us is not appropriate for our relationship with Him. God communicates with us through both our intellectual and emotional capacities, which come together in the "heart," and the interpenetration of these instruments provides an epistemological framework that is both trustworthy and meaningful. Rational thought can evaluate and control experiences, and experiences can enrich rational thought. We were created with this complementary structure, so it makes sense that our whole beings are required in order to hear and understand God's voice. God is known to us and evident in both spheres, and we apprehend Him with both cognition and sensation.

Clearly, cognition has precedence over sensation, because rationality is required in order to interpret experience, but the two structures must still be allowed to cooperate in the pursuit of spiritual growth. However, the exaltation of reason and rational thought by the modern dynamic has actually devalued experience, characterizing it as unreliable, misleading, and only superficially important to knowledge. Conversely, the exaltation of the deep interior in the romantic dynamic leaves the worshiper wildly grasping at inner experiences for truth. At the end of the day, there must be a meaningful interpenetration of intellect and emotion, cognition and sensation, reason and intuition.

Furthermore, this interpenetration must permeate our approach to God in worship, or we have sacrificed a very critical aspect of our communion with God. The presence of God is everywhere, and He has decisively drawn near the believer through His Spirit that is already indwelling our hearts.

However, is it not possible that God might manifest His presence to us in several different ways, through cognition that appreciates His Word, and through emotions and sensations that truly experience the consolation or conviction of the Spirit? Would not an experience of worship that was vitally open to these various receptors represent an incredibly important posture in which to meet with God? Piper agrees: "It follows that forms of worship should provide two things: channels for the mind to apprehend the truth of God's reality, and channels for the heart to respond to the beauty of that truth—that is, forms to ignite the affections with biblical truth, and forms to express the affections with biblical passion."[1] Is it really such a stretch to suggest that an honest open-ness to both forms, particularly in worship, is warranted?

I have sat in a Quaker meeting, an "unprogrammed service" in which I waited upon the "Inner Light" of the Spirit to give me a sense of the presence of God. A deep, inner communion with God was the primary purpose of the meeting, and this pursuit was punctuated by comments of edification from other members in the meeting. I waited as God revealed things in my life that needed attention, and discovered that we were able to have a meaningful conversation about those experiences. I "experienced" God in a deep, inner capacity as He brought these things to my mind, and we conversed after a fashion. After a time, however, I found my mind going back to Scripture. God seemed to say to me "how do you think you are going to change these things in your life? Do you think you are going to wrestle them to the ground in your own strength? Do you think that you can remake yourself in My image? Do you think that you can sanctify yourself, making yourself holy as I am holy? 'Be still, and know that I am God.'"

Ultimately, my experience of God in that service could not fully substitute for His revealed truth. In the solitude, my mind was irresistibly drawn back to the revealed Word of God in Scripture verses that had been memorized. As truth about God began to fill my mind, I began prayerfully to praise Him for His works and His attributes. My soul began to magnify the Lord, and it was at that moment of worship that I started to "feel" most aware of His presence. He did not enter the room in a metaphysical sense, but it was at that moment that my sensations or emotions began to pick up on His activity. I began to experience exultation in the wonder of who He is, and in His graciousness to me. It was in that act of worship, which was catalyzed by Scripture, that I experienced God. The revealed truth of God opened my heart to Him and allowed me to worship, and I began to experience clarity in my inner self, emotions and life experiences when His biblical truth came to my mind. Experience needed to combine with revealed truth in order for the worship of God to occur, and for it to be deeply meaningful and transformational.

What happened in that meeting was that I was able to make the choice to worship God out of the labyrinth of my inner struggles, but the meeting itself had little to do with it. In truth, the meeting did not hinder me from worshiping God, nor did it greatly help me in that pursuit. At the very least, worship services must seek to "do no harm," but it would seem that they should also be willing and able to assist in a more meaningful sense than I can do on my own. Is that not an appropriate and valuable service they should render to the worshiper? I have sat in liturgical services in which I wept because of the intensity and poignancy of the liturgy, but the service itself did nothing to help me make that connection between the truth of God and the truth of my experiences. Therefore, I chose to make the connection. I have stood in charismatic services in which I exulted in the grandeur and majesty of the Lord, regardless of the fact that the praise repertoire was almost exclusively focused on my experiences alone, and not on the truth of who God is and what He has done. In both cases, I chose to worship, and so I had an incredibly meaningful and transformational time of praising God.

Neither service really hindered me from worshiping, but neither helped me as much as it could or should have, because both fell down in one aspect or another. One missed out on my need to connect "truth" with my experiences, and the other disregarded the fact that I need truth in order for my experiences to be meaningful. Doing no harm in a worship service is not good enough, however. A service should not simply *allow* me to worship, but it should prompt that activity, catalyzing both receptors of cognition and sensation. There must be a meaningful interpenetration of experience and biblical truth. Otherwise, we are fundamentally missing out on who God created us to be as humans.

The Importance of Narrative in Worship

Worship services must provide an actual opportunity for worshipers to bring the narratives of their lives into a real juxtaposition with both the revealed and experienced truth of God's presence. It is critical that personal narratives be invited into our worship services, because it is by this vivid juxtaposition that worship is most deeply offered and spiritual growth most lastingly experienced. The revealed truth of Scripture must be allowed to stand as a foil or background against the deep experiences of the worshiper's life, in order for him or her to experience vital transformation. However, the experienced truth of God's presence must also be allowed to speak into the worshiper's narrative. In this regard, the sensation and cognition of the worshiper are both addressed and neither given tacit preference. The worshiper should be given a real chance to wait and listen for the Spirit, sensing the truth and blessing of God's presence on an internal, experiential level. Both revealed and experienced truth must be legitimately opened as avenues through which God might speak into our narratives.

Those who condemn the inclusion of personal experience in the worship service miss out on the critical fact that true worship and spiritual growth thrive on this kind of interpenetration. For worship to be transformational, it must accurately reveal the God of the universe, of course, but it also must illumine His all-powerful, yet gentle hands in the details of the individual worshiper's life. Mercy and truth come together as the worshiper is able to comprehend the eternal works and character of God, and then witness how that shadow has actually played out in his or her own life. The whole setting of Psalm 85 is this kind of deliberate intermixture of God's graciousness with human experiences, and the result is a wonderful hymn of praise:

> LORD, You have been favorable to Your land;
> You have brought back the captivity of Jacob.
> You have forgiven the iniquity of Your people;

> You have covered all their sin.
> Mercy and truth have met together;
> Righteousness and peace have kissed.
> (Ps 85:1-2, 10)

It is this intentional intermingling that induces the most authentic praise and worship, because it is has tapped into one's deepest thoughts and emotions at the crossroads of experience.

The key is the narrative, and the necessity is for worship services to provide real, existential windows where the Spirit can speak directly into these narratives, not just in an abstract sense, but in a meaningful life penetration. The structure and repertoire of the service must provide an authentic opportunity for the worshiper to bring his or her story into the meta-narrative of God's overarching story in Scripture. Perhaps this inclusion happens in a time of silent and open confession, or maybe through a song that juxtaposes the truth of God's character against the struggles of the individual. Perhaps the element of communion becomes the threshold upon which God's presence is welcomed into the personal life of the worshiper. Instead of continually filling the ears of the worshipers with information, windows of actually listening for God must be opened wide for their benefit. Indeed, these are the dual responsibilities of the worship service: *proclaiming truth about God and helping the ears and hearts of worshipers to be opened to the voice of the Spirit.* If worship is truly a conversation, then there must be moments when we speak and moments when we listen. There must be times when we present our narratives before the Lord, as well as times when we ponder the illuminating light of His truth bursting into our darkness.

In this interpenetration of experience and truth, the worshiper finds the context of revealed truth as a safe, epistemological haven where their experiences become endowed with meaning. This emphasis is fully in keeping with postmodern culture, which tends to formulate truth in terms of a narrative structure, and base beliefs upon experience. In this sense, it is culturally relevant in a very critical manner. Within Christ's redemptive story, the worshiper finds a meta-narrative where his or her struggles can be interpreted and can make sense. Christ's narrative should be allowed to intermingle with the reality of the individual's story, highlighting how He has redeemed the painful circumstances of his or her life. The rejection of a painful divorce is displayed next to the Savior who was "despised and rejected of men." Choices that were made in rebellion to God are backlit by the work of the great Redeemer, who loved us while we were His enemies. Meaning is connected with the context of God's narrative, so the worshiper endows his or her narrative with meaning that is drawn from a trustworthy and eternally reliable source. The worship service facilitates this deep spiritual interaction.

When the worship service allows the worshipers to bring their personal narratives into God's story, then it is providing a venue in which an objective standard of truth can be introduced into the narrative structure. The postmodern worshiper will still assemble reality from his or her experiences, but into that structure is introduced a narrative that is not only meaningful, but objectively true. This admixture is exactly what occurred when the Jesus movement latched onto the truth of God's narrative, and began to bring their experiences together with God's truth in the context of worship. They found One Way that stabilized the rest of their narrative structure. When worshipers are allowed to bring their own experiences into the activity of worship, they are enabled to connect the truth of their lives with the revealed truth of Scripture. The worship conversation provides this legitimate context of truth, and one's experiences can finally begin to make sense.

As revealed truth brushes against the experiences of the worshiper's life, worship happens. God's kind magnificence and gentle sovereignty in creation make us aware of our creatureliness, and we worship His holiness. God's incomprehensible transcendence and holiness are revealed in the need for atonement, and the worshiper comes to know his or her sinfulness and need for propitiation. God's goodness and graciousness are evident in the climactic event of Christ's sacrifice, and therefore we bow in humble adoration and gratitude. The truth of God that is revealed in the liturgy and worship repertoire provides a context for one's own experiences, and the fitting response is worship. It produces this reaction when it is juxtaposed with the experiences of the worshiper, because worship is at heart a response or reaction to who God is and what He has done. This interchange of experience and truth produces the heart response that we call worship.

One of the greatest opportunities for this existential intersection to take place is in the practice of thanksgiving. Thanksgiving is truly the door to experiencing the presence of God, for it turns the eyes of the worshiper to the gift and then to the Giver. It provides the most real and organic context in which the personal experiences are compared against the truth of God's works and character. Moreover, thanksgiving starts within the story of the worshiper, and so actually can catalyze worship of the heart, for it turns blessings into praise.[†] It does not require a lot of abstract, propositional truth about God in order to get worship started. Rather, it is a very practical, introductory act of worship because by its very nature, thanksgiving starts with the worshiper's experiences and then moves to God as the object of worship. Perhaps this is why David instructed the worshiper to enter His gates with thanksgiving and His courts with praise. (Ps 100:4)

As the worshiper begins to thank God for specific points of intersection and providence in his or her own life, he or she becomes aware of God's qualities and the natural result of the human heart is praise. That is the essential difference between praise and thanksgiving: thanksgiving is a response to what someone has done, but praise is a statement about the character of that person in general. Thanksgiving can thus provide the bridge to praise. Thanking God for the food He has provided causes the worshiper to praise God for the fact that He is gracious. Thanking God for forgiveness of specific sins causes one to praise God for the fact that He is merciful. Thanking God for His creation of the world with the capacity to sustain human life causes the worshiper to praise Him for the fact that He is love. Thanksgiving allows the worshiper to bring his or her own personal experiences into the worship setting, and transforms them into praise.

I have experienced this dynamic on countless occasions. When I would come to God in my private devotions and find that my heart was distracted, thanksgiving would change that attitude. As I focused on thanking God, my disinterested heart would turn and begin to delight in God. As I

[†] Songwriter Matt Redman has introduced the concept of turning blessings into praise. Matt Redman, <u>Blessed Be Your Name</u> 2002 Thankyou Music (Admin. by EMI Christian Music Publishing).

made a list of specific points of thanksgiving, my heart became grateful. I would find that praise for God's character came much easier, and I no longer had to struggle to find a voice to praise. The intersection of my experiences with revealed truth about the kind of God I serve made praise possible. Thanksgiving was exactly that intersection of experience and truth.

Worship as a Tripartite Concept

Worship that draws the experiences or lifestyle of the individual into the heart activity is worship that is wholistic and biblical. As was argued earlier, a biblical concept of worship is one that involves the three components of heart/attitude, obedience/lifestyle and activity/sacrifice. When Scripture discusses worship in general, these three elements are understood and intertwined in its basic definition. Conversely, when one of the three elements was missing, Scripture understood it as an abomination to the Lord. For the act of worship to be considered biblical, it had to begin with a heart attitude of submission and be manifested in a lifestyle of obedience to God's commands. Thus, God condemns their fasting in Isaiah 58, not because they did not delight in approaching Him (58:2), but because the fast or activity of worship that pleases Him is the one that involves obedience to His commands. (58:6, 13-14) Worship involves life experiences.

Moreover, this tripartite concept follows the general direction of spiritual growth. It has been argued in previous chapters that worship as a heart activity precedes worship as a lifestyle. Inner change precedes external actions, and so transformation of the heart results in actions of obedience, and not vice versa. And yet, it seems from the above that worship as an activity also flows from worship as a lifestyle. In truth, both flow from delight in God, and that heart condition transforms all of life. Obedience flows from a heart that is submitted to the Lord in humility, and the activity of worship should ideally flow from a heart that delights in His goodness. Given that transformation permeates the individual from the inside out, it makes sense that the heart activity of worship should be organically connected with the rest of one's life in order for transformation to begin. The Holy Spirit affects lasting change through the spiritual disciplines by bringing a submitted heart into contact with life experiences that have yet to be transformed. Worship that draws one's experiences into its process is worship that fundamentally reconnects the heart activity with the lifestyle of worship.

When the activity of worship does not draw the narratives of the worshipers into the service, then it becomes that much easier to compartmentalize worship as an activity alone, and lose the lifestyle of obedience. Conversely, if the service provides windows in which the worshiper's life experiences are brought into the illumination of the Spirit, then the delight in God's presence in worship begins to permeate his or her narrative. One of the most powerful windows in which this interpenetration occurs is through the liturgical element of confession. Interestingly, confession has fallen into disuse in the Evangelical churches, probably due to the tendency to discard liturgical and seemingly ritualistic elements of worship. Confession can be a powerful window in which the Spirit is given freedom to speak into the narrative of the worshiper, but it must be planned and executed in a fresh manner. It must be catalyzed by the revealed truth of Scripture, but must also involve open spaces of listening for the worshiper to actually ascertain the voice of the Spirit. Experience and truth must come together in this meaningful interpenetration.

I believe that this dynamic of experience and truth is the essence of what I have called the "spirit and truth connection" from John 4. John Piper has convincingly argued that the "water" that Jesus gives in this passage and elsewhere is the Holy Spirit, and that the presence of the Spirit in the life of the believer allows him or her to worship God in a way that pleases Him.[2] The Spirit satisfies the thirst of the worshiper (John 7:37-39), but He also develops a real connection between the worshiper and God, who is Spirit. (John 4:24) He allows us to experience God in a manner that is life-giving and thirst-quenching. The Spirit is the voice of God in the believer's life, interpreting and applying Scripture for the inner person, and manifesting His presence in an essentially experiential manner.

But the spirit and truth connection also requires the element of revealed truth. The context of Jesus' discussion with the Samaritan woman was the correct location of worship, and Jesus made it clear that the Samaritans worshiped out of ignorance. (John 4:22) They had legitimized a system of worship that was completely outside of Scripture, setting up a place of worship on Mount Gerizim and rejecting all of the Old Testament except for their own version of the Pentateuch.[3] When Jesus said "you worship what you do not know," He was saying that the worship experience alone, unaccompanied by the truth of God, is not legitimate worship. He alerts her to the fact that a new era is coming, the era of the New Covenant, in which the Spirit will be poured out upon the hearts of true worshipers. (Ezek 36:27)

Jesus was introducing her to a new connection of worship, in which the worshiper would find God through revealed truth as well as through an indwelling of the Spirit. He also emphasizes the truth that worship is no longer centered in a place but in a person—Himself—and He pours out His Spirit into the hearts of those who seek to worship God.[4] Revealed truth and experience would come together in this unique interpenetration, and it would become the way in which true worshipers would now approach God.

Worship as a Countercultural Activity

Whether we like it or not, the pendulum of culture will swing to extremes, and what is popular one moment will be rejected and scorned the next. Due to the dynamics of human culture, it is probably impossible to stop time and stay the merciless swing of this unrelenting pendulum. Some churches have attempted to accomplish this very feat, staying locked in a culture of the past, hoping to preserve something of what they have perceived to be truth. Instead of making the complicated effort to translate truth into a culturally relevant form, they have sought to deny change. In so doing, they have themselves become culturally irrelevant.

Somehow, their pursuit seems antithetical to the desire of Jesus that His disciples be in the world, but not of the world. (John 17:15-16) Certainly this emphasis is used to justify cultural entrenchment, as if the vessel of one culture inherently contained truth and another could not. But there is an essential misunderstanding of this concept throughout Christianity. The phrase "in the world, but not of the world" has become a colloquialism for the rejection of cultural contamination, with no distinction made regarding what kind of cultural penetration is in view. Interestingly, the phrase itself is not even in the Bible, but is rather a popular reconstruction of several verses that describe Jesus' desires for His disciples.

Human beings are never called out of culture. Indeed, culture is the existential fabric in which we live our lives. It is a human creation, but is no more or less fallen than humans themselves. Culture is simply a vessel in which to hold our apprehensions of truth, and the sanctity of its contents in no way sanctifies the vessel itself. This is not to say that culture is neutral, but that the task of being in the world, but not of the world is the project of evaluating culture.

Indeed, a distinction must be made between cultural *values* and cultural *forms*. Jesus left His disciples in the world, inhabiting cultural forms, but called them not to be of the world, which primarily involved cultural values. He was calling for new kingdom values to be incarnated into existing cultural forms. This distinction was the essence of his discussion of new wine and wineskins in Matthew 9:17. However, many Christians misunderstand this distinction, and so confuse the countercultural nature of Christianity. Cultural forms are an essential part of living life as a human being, in a human family, working a human job and having pastimes that are human. That is being "in the world." However, cultural values are a completely different proposition. Christianity carries a radical message that dramatically reverses our cultural values. To follow Christ as Lord is to turn one's cultural values upside down, rejecting the world's values and receiving God's priorities as a blueprint for one's life. Living as a Christian means experiencing life clothed in forms that are cultural, but with values that are transcendent. It means to take on human clothing and serve God in culture, without being penetrated by its values.

Certainly some cultural forms are penetrated by cultural values, and so the very tricky and sticky project of human existence is evaluating cultural forms, and if possible, redeeming them for the use of Christian values. Christians are never called to develop a kind of secretive sub-culture, with specific forms that are safe and in no way intermingle with the world. Indeed, that is the opposite of the Great Commission. I have always said that we err in using the word "Christian" as an adjective to describe things, for things are not Christian, but people are. Rather, Christians are to be redeeming agents in the world, reforming culture and becoming instruments that give all glory to God once again. We are called to make disciples, and that involves taking people, who are vessels of human culture, and implanting them with God's values by the transformation of the Holy Spirit. Cultural forms must be thoroughly scrutinized for their penetration by the world's values, and then redeemed for the service of the gospel.

As this work has sought to demonstrate, many facets of our faith and practice have been penetrated by the cultural values of postmodernism. Understanding these values is not so difficult, but ascertaining their invasion of our cultural forms is much more so. However, our purpose in understanding this dynamic is *not* so that we can then reject postmodernism and become culturally irrelevant. Whether we like it or not, we are all postmodern to some degree who live in this day and age, and to reject it completely would be to seek to eviscerate ourselves. We cannot extract postmodernism from culture any more than we can from ourselves, but we can discover the manner in which it has invaded both our values and forms. We can reject whatever postmodern *values* are found to be antithetical to historic Christianity, but we can redeem those *forms* that can be vitally transformed into instruments for the glory of God.

Years ago, I was involved as the worship leader on a team that sought to plant a new, alternative service in a large, downtown church. The team was formed of several very intelligent and well-informed individuals, far more than myself, and so we spent a good deal of time reading up on postmodernism and current cultural movements. As we would discuss these features, however, I became confused. We would identify how the trends and facets of postmodernism had invaded cultural forms, and then would decide how we would not accommodate that negative development. I began to wonder, are we discovering these features of culture so that we can do the exact opposite, or so that we can redeem them from culture? Is the church interested in making the gospel culturally irrelevant by denying these forms, or in transforming culture so that it is an appropriate vessel to advance the message of the gospel? The church should be in the business of learning the language of culture so that it can translate the gospel into that language, a cultural language, without compromising the values and message of the kingdom.

In what sense, then, is worship a countercultural activity? The values of the worship activity should be essentially foreign to our surrounding culture, but the basic forms need not be. In fact, holding onto cultural forms that are foreign to the surrounding culture would be like a foreign missionary requiring would-be converts to learn English in order to receive the gospel. It is complete nonsense. However, the cultural values of worship should certainly be a different category for those outside of the church.

Before I went into worship ministry, I worked in the secular, record industry. Although we were a secular company, we were one of the first record labels to begin signing Christian artists to cross over into the secular market. As a result, we would all receive free tickets and attend some of these "Christian" shows. One well-known band would include within their set a "worship" time, in which they would read Scripture and play standard, worship repertoire. People all over the audience would stand up and start raising their hands, singing along and praising God. I remember watching the faces of my fellow labelmates to see their various reactions. It was a fascinating juxtaposition, a true oxymoron of culture. The music, the cultural form, was definitely comprehensible to them, and in no way countercultural. However, the cultural values of worship that were expressed in that activity were completely foreign to them. In essence, these outsiders to Christianity understand the form, but not the value.

There is no valid reason to suggest that our forms of worship be completely countercultural to our society. Doing so would create a cultural language barrier that would make it impossible to communicate the gospel. However, the values of worship and the activity that they inspire—coming before the truth of the eternal God in order to celebrate His greatness and experience His presence—should be alien to those who are not Christ's followers. The values of the kingdom are absolutely countercultural to our world, for we are in the world, but not of the world.

CHAPTER 11: REVEALED AND EXPERIENCED TRUTH

Thus, the postmodern gravitation towards experience should not be something that we reject out of hand, and consider inappropriate for the worship service. Some reactionary groups go to these extremes, but especially enthusiastic, cultural movements often react with more extreme energy in the opposite direction. Experience is a critical necessity in order for a truly transformational activity of worship to occur, but it must be coupled with revealed truth. Indeed, the truth of Scripture can provide an anchor for the wayward and misguided spiritual attempts of the postmodern worshiper, if it is presented in a manner that is not exclusive of personal experience. If the postmodern is encouraged to bring his or her experiences into the sanctifying context of biblical truth, then objective truth can be reintroduced into his or her narrative structure.

Worship can become a force that will actually redeem culture, just as it did for the Jesus movement. The countercultural values of worship can be safely stored in culturally relevant vessels, and worship as an experience of the power and presence of God can be a form that draws true worshipers to Him. The stabilizing force of biblical truth can instead bring freedom to experience worship in all of its facets, because it provides an accurate and reliable filter through which the worshiper can evaluate cultural forms.

Experience need not be feared or stamped out of the worship activity, nor must worship be dominated by its pursuit. These two scenarios occur as a result of truth and experience becoming out of balance with one another. Neither one can become either an idol or a slave in the worship activity. However, when a complementary relationship exists, the kind of relationship that the Creator built into the human constitution, the two features of cognition and sensation can begin to interact and interpenetrate in a healthy and positive manner. Experiencing worship need not mean worshiping experience, nor must the worship experience mean propositional truth devoid of personal interaction. If the church takes seriously the task of redeeming cultural forms with the countercultural values of Christianity, then worship can become about experiencing the power and presence of God with everything we were created to be.

[1] Piper, <u>Desiring God</u>, 92.
[2] Piper, <u>Desiring God</u>, 74.
[3] Ibid., 73-74.
[4] McKelvey, <u>The New Temple</u>, 80.

BIBLIOGRAPHY

Allen, Ronald B. The Wonder of Worship. Nashville: Thomas Nelson Publishers, 2001.

Avery, Tom. "Music of the Heart: The Power of Indigenous Worship In Reaching Unreached Peoples with the Gospel." Mission Frontiers Bulletin 18, no. 5-8 (1996): 13-14.

Babbitt, Irving. Rousseau and Romanticism. Cleveland: World Publishing Company, 1919.

Barna, George, et al. Experience God in Worship. Loveland, CO: Group Publishing, Inc., 2000.

Beasley-Murray, George R. Word Biblical Commentary. Vol. 36, John. [CD-Rom] Dallas: Word Books, Publisher, 1998.

Borgmann, Albert. Crossing the Postmodern Divide. Chicago: The University of Chicago Press, 1992.

Carnell, Corbin Scott. Bright Shadow of Reality: C.S. Lewis and the Feeling Intellect. Grand Rapids: William B. Eerdmans Publishing Company, 1974.

Carson, D. A., ed. Worship by the Book. Grand Rapids: Zondervan, 2002.

Clark, Walter Houston, H. Newton Malony, James Daane, and Alan R. Tippett. Religious Experience: Its Nature and Function in the Human Psyche. Springfield, IL: Charles C. Thomas Publisher, 1973.

Clements, Ronald E. Old Testament Theology. Atlanta: John Knox Press, 1978.

Clinton, President William Jefferson Clinton. Speech delivered at Georgetown University, Washington D.C., 7 November 2001. Available from http://www.georgetown.edu/admin/publicaffairs/protocol_events/events/clinton_glf110701.htm. Internet. Accessed 5 January 2004.

Coe, John. "Drawing Near to God When God Seems Far Away: Practicing the Presence of God Despite Feelings." Lecture presented at the Talbot One-Day Spiritual Retreat. La Mirada, California, 26 September 2003.

_____. "Healing the Heart's Deep Beliefs in the Spirit: Intentionalizing Spiritual Formation through Soul Work." Lecture presented at the Talbot One-Day Spiritual Retreat. La Mirada, California, 26 September 2003.

_____. Interview by author, 18 September 2003, La Mirada, CA. Biola University, La Mirada, California.

_____. "Musings on the Dark Night of the Soul: Insights from St. John of the Cross on a Developmental Spirituality." Journal of Psychology and Theology 28, no. 4 (2000): 293-307.

Dawn, Marva. Reaching Out Without Dumbing Down. Grand Rapids: William B. Eerdmans Publishing Company, 1995.

Dowey, Jr., Edward A. The Knowledge of God in Calvin's Theology. Columbia University Press, 1952. Reprint, Grand Rapids: William B. Eerdman's Publishing Company, 1994.

Dubay, Thomas. Seeking Spiritual Direction: How to Grow the Divine Life Within. Ann Arbor, Michigan: Servant Publications, 1993.

Dunn, James D.G. Word Biblical Commentary. Vol. 38a, Romans 1-8. [CD-Rom] Dallas: Word Books, Publisher, 1998.

Durham, John I. <u>Word Biblical Commentary</u>. Vol. 3, <u>Exodus</u>. [CD-Rom] Dallas: Word Books, Publisher, 1998.

Duriez, Colin. <u>The J.R.R. Tolkien Handbook</u>. Grand Rapids: Baker Books, 1992.

Edwards, Jonathan. <u>The Religious Affections</u>. Reprint, Edinburgh: The Banner of Truth Trust, 2001.

Eichrodt, Walter. <u>Theology of the Old Testament</u>. Vol.1. Translated by J.A. Baker. Philadelphia: The Westminster Press, 1961.

Ellwood, Robert S. Jr. <u>One Way: The Jesus Movement and its Meaning</u>. Englewood Cliffs, NJ: Prentice-Hall, Inc., 1973.

Enroth, Ronald M., Edward E. Ericson, Jr., and C. Breckinridge Peters. <u>The Jesus People: Old-time Religion in the Age of Aquarius</u>. Grand Rapids: William B. Eerdmans Publishing Company, 1972.

Erdman, David V., ed. <u>The Poetry and Prose of William Blake</u>. Garden City, NY: Doubleday & Company, Inc., 1970.

Foster, Richard. <u>Celebration of Discipline</u>. San Francisco: Harper Collins Publishers, 1978.

Frame, John M. <u>Worship in Spirit and Truth</u>. Phillipsburg, NJ: P&R Publishing, 1996.

Frye, Northrop, ed. <u>Romanticism Reconsidered: Selected Papers from the English Institute</u>. New York: Columbia University Press, 1963.

Furst, Lillian R. <u>Romanticism</u>. London: Methuen & Co Ltd, 1969.

Furst, Lillian R. <u>Romanticism in Perspective</u>. New York: Humanities Press, 1970.

Geivett, R. Douglas. Interview by author, 12 June 2003, La Mirada, California.

Gergen, Kenneth J. <u>The Saturated Self</u>, 2d ed. New York: Basic Books, 2000.

Gomes, Alan. <u>Reformation & Modern Theology Course Syllabus</u>. La Mirada, CA: Biola University, 1998.

Grout, Donald Jay. <u>A History of Western Music</u>, 3d ed. with Claude V. Palisca. New York: W.W. Norton & Company, 1980.

Hayter, Alethea. <u>Opium and the Romantic Imagination</u>. Berkeley, CA: University of California Press, 1968.

James, William. <u>The Varieties of Religious Experience</u>. New York: The Modern Library, 2002.

Kaiser, Kurt. <u>Pass It On</u> 1969 Bud John Songs, Inc. (admin. by EMI Christian Music Publishing).

Keats, John. <u>The Selected Letters of John Keats</u>. Selected and with an introduction by Lionel Trilling. Garden City, NY: Doubleday & Company, Inc., 1956.

Keller, Tim, "Enduring Grace." Sermon presented at Redeemer Presbyterian Church, New York, 10 March 2002.

Kendrick, Graham. <u>Learning to Worship as a Way of Life</u>. Minneapolis: Bethany House Publishers, 1984.

Kilman, Brad. <u>We Are Hungry</u> 1999 Brad Kilman Publishing (admin. by The Loving Company)/(admin. by The Loving Company)

Kimball, Dan. <u>The Emerging Church</u>. Grand Rapids: Zondervan, 2003.

Kreeft, Peter. <u>Heaven: The Heart's Deepest Longing</u>. San Francisco: Ignatius Press, 1980.

Lafferty, Karen. <u>Seek Ye First</u> 1972 Maranatha! Music (admin. by The Copyright Company) & CCCM (admin. by Maranatha! Music).

Lennon/McCartney. "Tomorrow Never Knows." 1966 EMI Records Ltd.

BIBLIOGRAPHY

Lewis, C.S. <u>The Pilgrim's Regress</u>. Grand Rapids: Wm B. Eerdmans Publishing Company, 1933. Reprint, 1977.

Lewis, C.S. <u>Surprised by Joy</u>. San Diego: Harcourt Brace Jovanovich, Publishers, 1955.

Lyotard, Jean-François. <u>The Postmodern Condition: A Report on Knowledge</u>. Translated by Geoff Bennington and Brian Massumi. Minneapolis: The University of Minnesota Press, 1984.

McKelvey, R.J. <u>The New Temple</u>. London: Oxford University Press, 1969.

McLaren, Brian. <u>A New Kind of Christian</u>. San Francisco: Jossey-Bass, 2001.

MacDonald, George. "The Imagination: Its Function and its Culture." In <u>A Dish of Orts</u> [book on-line]. Available from http://www.er90481.dial.pipex.com/imagination.htm. Internet. Accessed 23 March 2004.

Martin, Ralph P. <u>The Worship of God</u>. Grand Rapids: William B. Eerdmans Publishing Company, 1982.

Maslow, Abraham H. <u>Toward a Psychology of Being</u>, 2d ed. New York: D. Van Nostrand Company, 1968.

Merton, Thomas. <u>The Ascent to Truth</u>. New York: Harcourt, Brace and Company, 1951.

Middleton, Richard J. and Brian J. Walsh. <u>Truth is Stranger Than It Used to Be</u>. Downers Grove, IL: InterVarsity Press, 1995.

Morgenthaler, Sally. Phone interview by author, 22 September 2003, Los Angeles, California.

_____. <u>Worship Evangelism</u>. Grand Rapids: Zondervan Publishing House, 1995.

Niebuhr, H. Richard. Christ and Culture. New York: Harper Torchbooks, 1951.

Noll, Mark A. The Scandal of the Evangelical Mind. Grand Rapids: William B. Eerdmans Publishing Company, 1994.

Nystrom, Martin. As the Deer 1984 Maranatha Praise, Inc. (admin. by The Copyright Company).

Otto, Rudolf. The Idea of the Holy. Translated by John W. Harvey. Oxford: Oxford University Press, 1923.

Park, Andy. To Know You More: Cultivating the Heart of the Worship Leader. Downers Grove, IL: InterVarsity Press, 2002.

Peterson, David. Engaging with God: A Biblical Theology of Worship. Downers Grove, IL: InterVarsity Press, 1992.

Peyre, Henri. What is Romanticism? Translated by Roda Roberts. University, Alabama: The University of Alabama Press, 1977.

Piper, John. Desiring God: Meditations of a Christian Hedonist. Sisters, Oregon: Multnomah Publishers, Inc., 1986.

_____. Brothers We Are Not Professionals: A Plea to Pastors for Radical Ministry. Nashville: Broadman & Holman Publishers, 2003.

Radmacher, Earl, Ronald B. Allen and H. Wayne House, eds. Nelson's New Illustrated Bible Commentary. Nashville: Thomas Nelson Publishers, 1999.

Redman, Matt. Blessed Be Your Name 2002 Thankyou Music (Admin. By EMI Christian Music Publishing).

Redman, Robb. The Great Worship Awakening. San Francisco: Jossey-Bass, 2002.

The Religious Society of Friends Website. Available from www.quaker.org. Internet. Accessed 5 January 2004.

Riley, Tim. Tell Me Why. New York: Alfred A. Knopf, 1988.

Schenk, H. G. The Mind of the European Romantics. Oxford: Oxford University Press, 1979.

Selections from the Book of Psalms. With an introduction by Bono. New York: Grove Press, 1999.

Schaeffer, Francis A. The God Who is There. L'Abri Fellowship, 1968. Reprint, Downers Grove, IL: InterVarsity Press, 1982.

St. John of the Cross. Dark Night of the Soul. Translated by Mirabai Starr. New York: Riverhead Books, 2002.

Sting, "Russians." Published by Magnetic Publishing Ltd. (PRS), represented by Regatta Music, administered by Irving Music, Inc. (BMI) in the U.S. and Canada.

Sweet, Leonard. Soul Tsunami. Grand Rapids: Zondervan, 1999.

Tomlinson, Dave. The Post-Evangelical. El Cajon, CA: emergentYS Books and Grand Rapids: Zondervan, 2003.

Tozer, A.W. Whatever Happened to Worship? Compiled & edited by Gerald B. Smith. Camp Hill, PA: Christian Publications, 1985.

Webber, Robert E. Ancient-Future Faith: Rethinking Evangelicalism for a Postmodern World. Grand Rapids: Baker Books, 1999.

_____. Signs of Wonder: The Phenomenon of Convergence in Modern Liturgical and Charismatic Churches. Nashville: Abbott Martyn, 1992.

_____. Worship is a Verb. Peabody, Mass: Hendrickson Publishers, 1992.

Zschech, Darlene. Extravagant Worship. Minneapolis: Bethany House, 2001.